MOVING
MOUNTAINS

CLAIRE BERTSCHINGER

with Fanny Blake

BANTAM BOOKS

LONDON • TORONTO • SYDNEY • AUCKLAND • JOHANNESBURG

MOVING MOUNTAINS
A BANTAM BOOK: 055381723X
9780553817232

Originally published in Great Britain by Doubleday,
a division of Transworld Publishers

PRINTING HISTORY
Doubleday edition published 2005
Bantam edition published 2006

1 3 5 7 9 10 8 6 4 2

Set in 12/16pt Granjon by
Falcon Oast Graphic Art Ltd.

Bantam Books are published by Transworld Publishers,
61–63 Uxbridge Road, London W5 5SA,
a division of The Random House Group Ltd,
in Australia by Random House Australia (Pty) Ltd,
20 Alfred Street, Milsons Point, Sydney, NSW 2061, Australia,
in New Zealand by Random House New Zealand Ltd,
18 Poland Road, Glenfield, Auckland 10, New Zealand
and in South Africa by Random House (Pty) Ltd,
Isle of Houghton, Corner of Boundary Road & Carse O'Gowrie,
Houghton 2198, South Africa.

Printed and bound in Great Britain by
Cox & Wyman Ltd, Reading, Berkshire.

Papers used by Transworld Publishers are natural, recyclable products made from
wood grown in sustainable forests. The manufacturing processes conform to the
environmental regulations of the country of origin.

CONTENTS

THANKS

There are many people to thank for the support and encouragement they gave me.

First my parents for their continuous love and belief in me throughout my hardships. Special thanks are due to my father, who meticulously kept my letters and diaries in chronological order, stowing them in old shoeboxes in the garden shed. They have been invaluable in prompting my memories of events.

Fanny Blake for her patience and enthusiasm. It was thanks to her that the documents saw daylight, the cobwebs, mouse droppings and dust were brushed away, and I knew what to do.

Brenda Goldblatt for standing by me during and after my return to Ethiopia in 2003 and for introducing me to my wonderful agent Catherine Clark of the Felicity Bryan agency. Also my editor at Doubleday, Marianne Velmans. They saw my potential and steered and supported me all the way.

Michael Buerk for making the world take notice and giving me the chance to return to Ethiopia.

Janine and Dominique Kohli, Carolyn Fujii, Howard and Jan Jones, Kazuo Fujii, Tony Bedford and Sandie Powell, who have nurtured and guided me in recent life.

Maggie Burgess and her husband Patrick for their encouragement and guidance on the technicalities of writing a book.

Anna Shepherd for being human and helping to show me how to overcome the obstacles of modern society.

Mike Christy and Colonel John Blashford-Snell for helping to show me that I could survive.

The St John Ambulance Association for providing me with the necessary knowledge to begin my dream.

Last but not least, my Canadian friend John Scott for giving me fresh adventures and helping me to laugh again.

Because of the International Committee of the Red Cross's role as a neutral intermediary in conflict situations, I have restricted myself to mentioning only political events that were publicly reported. At times I have changed some names and the chronology of events to protect the privacy of certain individuals.

1

FAMINE

OUTSIDE THE SUPPLEMENTARY FEEDING CENTRE ON THE edge of Mekele, the local Ethiopian staff had organized the starving men, women and children into orderly lines. The hundred or so who had been waiting, huddled together outside the compound, when we arrived first thing in the morning, had quickly swelled to well over a thousand. I tried to count them, reaching twelve rows with over a hundred in each. They sat on the flat, parched earth, their once-white tunics worn into rags – literally just a few rags that hung from their skeletons, usually not enough to give them any modesty. These clothes were thick with dust, and their skin and hair was covered with it, so that they blended into the almost colourless landscape which was relieved only by the flashes of silvery green from the eucalyptus trees growing close by.

Children were screaming and adults begged for help, while others sat silently, some crying, others looking utterly lost and bewildered. The smell of wood smoke drifted across from the hole in the kitchen roof to mingle with the stink of vomit and shit, and the odour of human sweat, unwashed bodies and the donkeys that had brought in the firewood we'd bought. At first the morning had been cold and the mist rising, but by midday the people were sitting under the beating sun protected only by their tatters of clothes. Flies buzzed everywhere. Brushing them away provided only a moment's respite before they were back, spreading infection, crawling persistently over us all.

It was the first day of our new selection procedure. Before I came to work in Mekele, the children chosen for intensive feeding had been the most needy ones who just happened to be near the gate when others were discharged and spaces at the centre became available. I had felt that this was unfair on all the other starving children in the camps outside town who were just as deserving. I had agreed with the local staff that instead we would put the word out among the displaced people, letting them know which day we would be having a new intake so that any of them could bring their children in the hope they might be chosen: that way they would all at least have a chance. But the numbers that had come were overwhelming.

At first I had suggested the local staff chose them, but they refused: 'They're our brothers, our sisters, our cousins. How can we? You must do it, Claire. We can't.' The pressure was unbearable. As I walked up and down between the rows, I was careful never to stop in case someone thrust a baby into my arms, but even so parents tugged at my clothes, calling, 'Mama, mama. Come, come, come,' pleading with me to take their child. If I had taken one, I would have had to take them all, and that wasn't possible. I couldn't take just the children of those who were the strongest and could shout out. That wouldn't have been fair. To be fair, I would have to pick the right ones. And the right ones weren't necessarily the most malnourished or closest to death, because we knew that those ones would be dead within twenty-four to forty-eight hours anyway. We didn't have sufficient food for more than a fraction of the sick children, let alone the starving adults. We had to do the best we could with the little we had. This meant that I had to select those I knew would have the best chance of survival if they were helped now but who would die without emergency feeding.

But how do you select only fifty or sixty from over 1,200 children who are starving and sick in one way or another? All of them either screaming or lying too still, their flesh hanging off their bones with pus pouring from infected scabies lesions. Flies crawled over infected eyes that were gummed shut. Many of the children were permanently blind from vitamin A deficiency, their bellies grotesquely swollen from malnutrition. Often their heads were shaved, with just a tuft of hair left. I was told that, according to local belief, if they died, God could grab it and pull them up to heaven.

The selection procedure took a long couple of hours under the baking sun. By putting my hand around each child's arm, I could feel how malnourished they were. Not difficult when they were all so dreadfully thin, their dry papery skin covering just bone – no muscle to speak of, no fat. With a nod of my head, they were either in or out. I picked the ones who I estimated fell between the 60 per cent and 75 per cent weight-for-height ratio, those who I could see still had a spark of life in them, who would have the best chance of responding to our feeding. I inked a cross on arms or foreheads to show which ones I'd selected. I knew that if I simply touched them, parents desperate for their child's life to be saved would try to swap their own child with the chosen few as they walked into the centre. We'd seen it happen before. I had to force myself to turn away from the despair of the parents and children I passed over. This selection process was the fairest we could achieve, but hell – what a job, what a decision.

I couldn't understand how everyone remained so orderly. Although people tugged at me, no one really got out of line. Perhaps what I took for a sense of dignity was simply resignation and hopelessness. It was terrible to see people brought so low. I felt they expected so much of me. And what did I have to give? To most of them, nothing. They must have thought I was playing God, but I certainly didn't feel like a god. I felt guilty and ashamed that I could save so few and was sending most of them to certain death. I felt like a Nazi condemning innocent people to the death camps. I've lived with that ever since.

It was July 1984, I was one of two nurses who had been posted by the International Committee of the Red Cross (ICRC) to the remote town of Mekele in the Tigray province of northern Ethiopia. Our job was to run a supplementary feeding station for children under the age of five, chosen from among the tens of thousands of displaced people who had descended on the town. The conflict between the Marxist government troops and the rebels in Tigray and Eritrea had driven countless civilians from their homes, forcing them to trek for miles to towns rumoured to have feeding centres, in the hope of finding food and shelter. In addition, overgrazing, deforestation and poor agricultural practices had combined with three years of drought to parch the land, and many more starving families had had no choice but to leave their homes in search of food. It was a disaster of epic proportions.

Those who arrived in Mekele found a town virtually cut off from the outside world by the war, able to offer neither food nor shelter. They were herded into a holding area outside town. There were literally thousands of them, at one point as many as 85,000, dehydrated, malnourished and covered in grey dust. They huddled in dips in the land or by low piles of stones to ward off the cold night wind. Some had a little food; most didn't. Those who did tried to cook what they had on open wood fires. Wood was hard to come by and people would walk miles to find enough for cooking. Water was scarce, the only source available to them being an almost dried-up river bed. When I went there, I found the muddied trickle of a stream being used by both animals and humans for drinking and washing in, and as a toilet. The situation was deteriorating fast and the people were dying in droves.

The scale of the disaster was of such magnitude that I was completely unprepared for what I would see. I had received three days of briefing at the ICRC headquarters in Geneva and spent hours studying past reports of famine and nutritional emergencies; but once I was actually on the spot, the task seemed overwhelming. However were we to help this mass of human misery? The feeding centre – the only supplementary feeding centre in town – had been up and running for a few months under Ruth, the Swiss nurse I had come to help. The two of us worked with local volunteers from the Ethiopian Red Cross. The ICRC delegate responsible for coordinating ICRC operations in the area was based in Asmara, an hour's flight away in Eritrea province, and his responsibility extended to a vast area of the country, so he was able to visit us only every week or two. He worked with a local Ethiopian Red Cross worker who ran an ICRC warehouse for distributing dry rations to the starving in a different part of Mekele.

Emergency rations of flour, beans, butter oil and sugar were flown in every four to six weeks on a C-130 Hercules chartered by the ICRC from Air Botswana. We never knew when it would arrive or how much it would bring. The only other way for supplies to reach us was by armed convoy, but such deliveries were erratic and could be months apart. We were cut off from the rest of the world.

As time went on, the rations became more and more inadequate, as the number of displaced people kept growing and supplies dwindled. The idea was that each family should receive a general ration, but in practice they didn't. There wasn't enough. Some of the worst off were the old people with no family of their own, who therefore didn't qualify for rations from any of the official sources. I found it profoundly upsetting to see these men and women suffering. I've always considered old age as deserving respect and consideration. These people had once been the pillars of their society and now they had nothing. However Ruth and I were kept so busy with the children that we had no time to help anyone else. The authorities prevented us from leaving the town for security reasons, so we had no idea exactly how many men, women and children were camped outside. All we knew was that we were seeing just the tip of the iceberg.

Sometimes, when we were selecting children, parents left their babies on the ground outside the centre and then tried to run away. But our local Red Cross workers would call them back and persuade them to pick up their children and look after them. With such limited resources we couldn't take total responsibility for any one child and, against insurmountable odds, we were trying to help these people help themselves. I particularly remember an old man who was with his grandson. He could barely look after himself, let alone a three-year-old. I hadn't picked the boy for the feeding programme because there were others worse off than him. An hour or so later, we found him toddling alone by the gate, crying. Realizing that he'd been abandoned, we asked if anyone had seen his grandfather. One of the guards thought he'd seen him sleeping rough somewhere. We sent one of the local workers to find him – an almost impossible task. He did not find the grandfather but he found another displaced family with only one child, who were willing to take on this toddler and look after him. As far as I know, that's where he stayed.

Every morning, I'd wake as dawn broke to the distant sound of horns, which were accompanying the bodies of those who had died in the night as they were being taken for burial. In the camp, the people were beginning to move stiffly after a night spent in the cold. Columns of men and women followed the corpses, which were wrapped in old flour sacks and being carried as far from the town as possible. The men, mostly silent in their grief, carried the bodies, while the women wailed, hurling themselves around, waving their arms, tearing their hair, trying to throw themselves on to the corpses. They were restrained by their female relatives and friends, who held their arms tightly in support. The grave areas were already full and the bodies had to be taken further and further away. Gravediggers were already at work as the bodies were laid side by side on the ground. Many mothers were shrouded with their children and children were wrapped together to be placed in double graves to save space. The graves were covered with stones to prevent the hyenas from digging the bodies up at night.

I'd get to the feeding centre early to check that the cooks had managed to light the fires and that the water was boiling before they began to mix in dried skimmed milk, butter oil and sugar to make the high-energy milk drink that we gave to the starving children. In an ideal world, each child would have been given its own individual regime, depending on its condition; and we would have given them as many as five or six small meals a day. But this was far from an ideal world. At that point we didn't have the time, the food supplies or enough trained personnel to give more than three supplementary feeds a day to two sittings of up to 250 children each. We divided each sitting into groups of about twenty-five children, each accompanied by their mother or a member of their family, with a local Red Cross worker in charge of them, helping to coax the children into taking a little milk.

The first group was fed at 08.00, 11.00 and 14.00 and the

second at 09.30, 12.30 and 15.30. Each sitting took at least an hour, and we had to allow time to prepare the high-energy milk drink and wash the spoons and cups, as well as examine children who were ill or not responding to feeding. A curfew prevented us staying in that part of town after dark, so we had to have the centre cleaned and closed before sunset. Each child we admitted to the feeding programme was given an identifying wristband. If they lost it, they weren't allowed back into the centre, even if we were told that other parents had stolen the band from them to put on their own child. At first, this seemed cruel to me, but I soon realized that if we weren't strict, everyone would claim they'd lost one and we'd be overwhelmed. I was aware that the wristbands of several children were conveniently loose and that they shared them around their families. How could I blame them? In a similar situation, I'd have done the same myself.

Given the number of starving children with which we were faced, this was the most effective supplementary feeding programme we could manage. We were dealing with about four to five hundred each day. Hundreds more were left outside to die. Every week we'd weigh and measure each child and recalculate their weight-for-height ratio to see their rate of improvement, carefully recording the statistics in ledgers. We simply couldn't cope with doing this more often: it took all day for the team to get through all the children. We all knew that our way was inefficient, because the graphs used were based on Western children whose body size was very different from those in the areas in which we were working, but at the time they were all we had. We sat each child in the weighing pants, suspending them from the scales, then laid them flat on a board to measure their height. If the ratio was less than 75 per cent of the norm, the child was considered malnourished. It wasn't until the late 1980s that body mass index (BMI) plotted on gender-specific growth charts was recognized as being a more effective measurement. Generally, it took the children about six to eight weeks to recover sufficiently to reach the 80 per cent weight-for-height ratio, at which point they were well enough to return to their families. To begin with, we found that we were releasing the children too early. When we realized that they were soon returning to the centre as malnourished as when we had first seen them, we made sure that their weight remained stable for two weeks before letting them go. Every week or so, we'd discharge around ten or twenty children. Then came the awful task of selecting those who were to take their place.

Every day we dealt with the same problems, in ever-increasing numbers. It was a nightmare from which there was no relief. The only time the centre closed during the entire six months I was in Mekele was on 12 September, Revolution Day, the day that marked the 1974 coup when Emperor Haile Selassie was ousted by the Marxist dictator Colonel Mengistu. Ironically, Haile Selassie's fall had been precipitated by his being filmed eating a big birthday cake during a previous famine. On the anniversary in 1984 suddenly Mekele became a ghost town. Those who were sleeping in the streets on the outskirts of town were removed at gunpoint in the middle of the night and taken to a 'camp' five kilometres away so that they didn't litter the place. Everyone else had to go to the stadium and rejoice. Preparations had been going on for weeks. Armed police were posted all over town. Everywhere houses had been freshly painted and signs removed or freshened up at the government's command. In Addis, thousands of dollars had been spent on the houses lining the main roads to impress visiting dignitaries. Enormous commemorative statues, pictures and slogans found their way on to every empty wall and street corner. We heard that millions of dollars were spent on the celebrations. And all the while thousands of people were starving to death. I felt such anger at the injustice of it all.

As the weeks went by, the strain on the feeding centre at Mekele grew as more and more people arrived at the town from further away, all in terrible condition and begging to be let in. But our supplies didn't increase with the greater demand. Occasionally we took in brothers or sisters of the children we were feeding, but most we had to turn away. If we were feeding a child, we also provided their family with basic dried rations, limited though they were. The desperation of the displaced people was pitiful to see. One day we had some food left over after the feeding so we mashed it together and gave it to those sitting patiently at the gates of the compound. When some of it spilled on the ground, there was a rush of people who bent down and licked it up, dust and all. I was shocked. It was humiliating for any human to have to stoop so low to live. I felt I'd provoked the situation by providing the slops. What should I do? Part of me wanted to stop them from eating filthy food off the ground, but at the same time I realized that this was all they had. I had to force myself to look away and try to make sense of the situation. As numbers increased we were forced to stop giving out leftovers, worried that we'd cause a riot. After we had given out dry rations, we would see people following the departing trucks, just to pick up one or two stray grains. I wanted to give all those people more. I wanted to give them decent food and was in despair that we didn't have it to give.

There simply wasn't enough food to go round. We were told we'd get more, but it never came. I fought against despair by concentrating on the positive and on our successes. Sometimes grateful mothers would ululate with a high-pitched cry to express their thanks or happiness. There were also memorable individual cases.

One was that of Kiros, a lanky young boy who was a skeleton when he came in, a pathetic-looking bundle of bones. His legs were like twigs, too long for his body and too weak to support his swollen belly. His eyes were infected, swollen and gummed shut with pus, and his mother had no water with which to wash them. His body was covered in sores. The first time I really noticed him was when I saw his mother beating him as he fell to the ground, crying. I pulled her off him. Asmara, my field worker, said he was asking his mother why she was hitting him. Through Asmara, I repeated his question to his mother. She said that she couldn't cope with him any more. He had constant diarrhoea and was so weak that he couldn't walk and kept falling down. She was trying to keep him going but she didn't know what more she could do. Her despair tore me apart. It was the first time that I understood such desperation and exhaustion. She was beating him to make him get up and keep moving because she didn't know what else to do.

That evening I wrote home for my father's birthday. I had planned to draw him a picture of the mountains but the memory of Kiros' face kept appearing in my mind. I wrote this instead, with a note to Papa apologizing for its grimness.

'The Why of a Four-year-old'

Why do you beat me, Mummy?
What have I done to make you so mad?
I have a pain in my tummy. Why do you want to give
*   me some more?*

Is it my fault I am so sick, that I am too weak to walk,
  and have no strength to stand?
Why can't I see you any more, Mummy?
I don't want to eat; I'm no longer hungry.
Why should I eat?
It passes straight through me, and only makes you mad.
Why do you hate me, Mummy?
What makes you always so sad?
Why do you beat me, Mummy?
Why?

I'm glad to say that after a programme of emergency feeding Kiros filled out. His eyes opened and we managed to stop his sight deteriorating any further. Then one day at the centre, I noticed that he was proudly wearing a bracelet of grass. He told me that his mother had made it for him. When I looked over to her I saw that she was watching him with love in her eyes. Her attitude towards him had changed completely.

Another day I noticed a group of three children in the lines. The baby was severely malnourished and had been brought to the centre by his two young brothers. I never found out what had happened to their parents; we certainly never saw them. It seemed that these three children were alone in the world. After I selected the baby for the re-nourishment programme, the two boys brought him every day, carrying him even though they were not much bigger than him themselves. They'd find a spot where they'd sit together with the baby on one of their laps, one of them spooning liquid into his mouth while the other held his hands so that he wouldn't knock away the spoon. Their care for their brother was extraordinary to see, as was their pleasure as he gradually became stronger.

It was small but significant incidents like these that kept me going.

I was asked to develop the medical and sanitation side of the feeding centre. Under a small shelter about four feet by four in the corner of the compound, I set up a small clinic where we could address the medical problems of the children. Trying to keep the sanitation arrangements in a controlled area, we dug latrines just outside the centre. Mark you, I had my work cut out to persuade anyone to use them. These people's concept of hygiene was different from ours. Until then, they had peed or shitted anywhere inside or outside the centre, sometimes kicking a bit of dirt to cover it up, and wiping the babies' bums with the hem of their dress. They preferred not to use the stinking, fly-blown latrines along with everyone else.

If one of the children had contracted a serious illness that needed medical treatment, such as pneumonia, convulsions, respiratory tract or eye infections, high fevers or complaints that didn't respond to courses of antibiotics, I'd take them to the Mekele hospital. I'd often have to fight to get them admitted because the local medical establishment knew that they wouldn't get paid for treating them. I had to be just as persuasive when I needed extra supplies from the Ethiopian Red Cross stores. The local townsfolk resented the displaced people taking what they saw as theirs. Inevitably I sometimes made myself unpopular because I had no choice but to put people's backs up to try to get what was needed.

But it was impossible to give the displaced people what they needed. There was never enough of anything for them. More and more of them were dying.

What made the difference in the end was the arrival, some months after I'd begun working there, of the BBC reporter Michael Buerk. Until then, most people in the outside world had no idea of the scale of what was happening in Ethiopia; or, if they did, they turned their backs. I could never have imagined the powerful effect Buerk's four or five minutes of film would have. It was his reporting that brought this desperate situation to the world's attention in such a way that it couldn't be ignored any longer. Thanks to him, the much-needed aid began to flow into the country at last; and in the UK, Bob Geldof was spurred to mastermind the Band Aid record and Live Aid concert, which raised millions of pounds towards the relief effort.

I had gone to Ethiopia for six months but eventually stayed for a year. At that time a year was usually the longest time the ICRC would keep their delegates in any one disaster area. When they pulled me out, I was exhausted, both physically and emotionally. I wondered what was the point of a world where people were made to suffer so horribly. The burning question I had was, 'Why?' How could such a disaster happen in the twentieth century, costing so many thousands of lives? My feelings of guilt about my own role in the famine were so strong that I couldn't face them for twenty years. I forgot those I had helped and remembered only those who had died because of the cruel selection process. To send children to a certain death was not the reason I had gone into nursing. I hid myself away as far as I could, preferring never to answer questions about my experiences in Ethiopia. I didn't want to hear the praise of people who didn't understand what it had been like and who didn't know the true story. Instead I focused on the present, throwing myself into other work with the ICRC, which took me to the war zones of Uganda, Kenya, Afghanistan, West Africa – places where my training could be put to good use and where I could be useful to people who were in need.

It wasn't until 2003, when a BBC researcher tracked me down and asked whether I would go back to Ethiopia with Michael Buerk for a programme the BBC was making about the state of the country twenty years on, that I was forced to make a decision: was I prepared to face my demons and try to make sense of what had happened there? I wondered how I would be received by the people I felt I had let down so badly. I remembered the feelings that accompanied having to choose who should live and who should be turned away. I remembered those who had suffered so dreadfully and those who had died – all for the lack of a handful of beans, some butter oil and some flour. My own life had never been on the line. I had been able to leave that place and make myself useful elsewhere. Finally, though, I was persuaded to return to confront my feelings and meet some of the people I had known there in 1984. On that visit, I saw my time in Ethiopia through new eyes and I was finally able to reconcile myself to the part I had played in that human tragedy.

Looking back over my years of nursing in war zones with the ICRC, I feel I have been on an extraordinarily fulfilling journey, physically, emotionally and spiritually. It has been sometimes dangerous and often harrowing, but in return I've had the privilege of experiencing the warmth, friendship and generosity of exceptional people, many of whom were suffering as a consequence of war. From my experiences, I have learned that war is not the answer to any problem: it comes at far too great a cost to human life. We must look for valid and peaceful alternatives.

I'll always remember, when I was working in Afghanistan, sitting round a fire in the Hindu Kush and talking to a group of mujahidin warlords, explaining how, as a representative of the ICRC, I was trying to help people in their country divided by civil war.

Through my translator, one of them asked, 'How can

you, a gentle woman, make any difference to this situation, Miss Claire?'

My reply was simple. 'There's nothing sweeter, gentler or softer than water,' I said. 'But water has the power to move mountains.'

2

WAR

'YOU GO IN THERE, YOU WON'T COME OUT ALIVE.'

Never in my life had I felt so intimidated. The voice belonged to a massive brawny Israeli soldier on the Lebanon border. His legs were like tree trunks, his gun was within easy reach.

'You won't be allowed out,' he threatened.

It was September 1983, the year before I went to Ethiopia and, as I embarked on my first mission for the ICRC, this was my first official brush with international security.

'Yes, yes. That's fine. Thank you.' Jens, a Norwegian doctor who was my travelling companion, was completely unfazed. I looked at him, with a dawning realization that this was how travelling in a war zone was done. Remain calm and don't argue. 'That's fine. We won't need to come out.' It worked. So into the Lebanon we went.

After a long drive, we arrived in Saida (Sidon) in the late afternoon to be told that I was to join the relief convoy that left at 07.00 the next morning. I barely had time to get my bearings and a restless night's sleep before I was down at the ICRC warehouse as the sun dawned. Six supply lorries, four ambulances and two staff cars, all white with giant red crosses on their sides and roofs, and large Red Cross flags flying from the sides, were lined up ready to make their way to the besieged town of Deir El Kamar in the Chouf Mountains. We were taking relief supplies to as many as 25,000 displaced people (reports of the actual number constantly contradicted one another) who had converged on the town. Some were Lebanese forces on the run after losing a war with the Druze militia in the mountains; others were villagers who had escaped from their homes in the combat zone. They were all trapped in the town and surrounded by hostile forces. The ICRC convoy had tried four times to reach them the previous week but the vehicles had been fired at *en route*, and on one occasion all the stores and equipment had been looted.

As every vehicle was searched the waiting seemed interminable. And the whole procedure was to be repeated at each checkpoint we crossed. Soldiers were everywhere, rifles at the ready, poking them into anything that looked suspicious. Being in a real war zone at last, I was on tenterhooks, simultaneously excited, frightened and overawed.

Eventually the convoy set off on its six-hour journey through the mountains, slowly negotiating narrow roads that wound around hairpin bends, up the mountainsides and then steeply down into the valleys. We crawled along at a snail's pace. I found it impossible to get my head around the number of fighting factions, checkpoints and front lines that we had to cross. Once we reached the fighting area, at that time just past Jezzine village, I saw that the mountains had been cleared of trees and heavy shrub. Once they had been covered in majestic Lebanese cedars, the trees so inextricably bound to the country's identity; now these ancient legions had been cut down so as to remove any potential hiding places for troops and artillery. I could imagine how beautiful it must once have been and was saddened by this destruction.

Gritty red dust blew up over the vehicles, clouding into our eyes and hair. The landscape we travelled through was rough and rocky; olive trees were rooted in the man-made terraces, and occasional villages sprawled higgledy-piggledy across the lower slopes. In many places the side of the road fell away in a sheer drop down the mountain to the valley below. Bridges were pock-marked by bullets and often partially destroyed or shored up with rough stone supports.

I was travelling with Béatrice, the nurse I was replacing, who was to show me the ropes. As we drove, she explained a little of what to expect in Deir El Kamar, expanding on what I'd been told at the ICRC headquarters in Geneva. She told me how, in the days to come, we'd be visiting health centres all over the region, assessing their needs and resupplying them. At the various checkpoints, we sat for two or three hours, waiting to be allowed through. We amused ourselves by listening to music, and sometimes Béatrice pointed out where the soldiers were, which of the fighting parties they belonged to and who the commanders were. Apart from feeling excited at working in disaster relief at last, which I'd always wanted to do, all that really concerned me was the length of the journey and when I'd next be able to have a pee. I later learned to drink little during the day because the opportunities for peeing were few – there were no trees to hide behind, no possibility of going 'off-road', as the verges were often mined. Nor was there time when we arrived at our destinations; we usually had to work incredibly quickly and leap back into the vehicle to get out of the area before the ceasefire that had allowed us into the town ended.

As we approached Deir El Kamar, a few shells exploded above the town, their smoke drifting across an otherwise cloudless sky. The tension in the convoy was palpable. Eventually we pulled safely into the main square. It was full of people, who crowded round us, some of them standing on the surrounding rooftops to get a better look. Some simply stood with tears rolling down their cheeks; others stared in disbelief, while others were still, smiling with relief. It's impossible to describe the shock I felt seeing them. I didn't know which way to turn or to whom to offer help first. Displaced people of all ages had been packed into the schools, churches, mosque and synagogue for shelter, leaving no room for the few who lay in the streets, bewildered and exhausted. Many of the women wore slippers, having fled their villages in too much of a hurry to pick up any of their belongings. Béatrice hurried me through them, reiterating that our job was to work directly with the Lebanese Red Cross and the doctors in the local hospital. As the ICRC, we were there to support them and, where necessary, to provide protection and transport, and to treat the war-wounded, evacuating the worst to specialized hospitals outside the area under the protection of the ICRC. Vitally, we also had to evaluate the supplies they had and provide what was needed.

These people had come from brick-built houses in often luxurious surroundings and were frequently highly educated and well travelled. All of them were in despair over their future, many having lost relatives in the fighting, all of them possibly having seen their homes and belongings for the last time. Lack of drinking water was a real problem. The water mains had been cut off for six months and the town's underground source provided barely enough water to go round. All the trees lining the road into town had been cut down for firewood.

The head of our delegation, Françoise, visited the local mayor with a gift of newspapers, the first information from the outside world that the people of the town had had for days. The mayor explained that the local Red Cross had arranged a group of villagers to organize the distribution of food, medicines and blankets that we had brought. He provided volunteers, who took only about an hour to unload our lorries.

Some of the delegates set about making a list of all those stranded in the town and distributed Red Cross message forms so that the displaced people could get in touch with their relatives elsewhere in the world. These lists would be handed in at one of the checkpoints surrounding the town and then picked up the following week once they had been read and censored to ensure that no military intelligence was being sent out from behind the front line. While we were collecting last week's forms, I noticed an English name on one of them. Angela turned out to be a young nun from the Home Counties who was working as a teacher in the local convent school. Because of the ICRC's declared impartiality, I couldn't contact her family directly. We had to do our job according to the Geneva Convention, always going through the official channels and remaining strictly neutral. Any direct contact with someone's family would have breached those rules. However, on my return visits to the town over the next weeks, we'd occasionally meet and chat, reminiscing about the weather and the food we missed at home.

Béatrice and I saw to the medical supplies, and set up a dispensary in the hospital under a local Lebanese Red Cross nurse who was remaining in the town. Perhaps the most distressing thing there was the sight of the ward for mentally ill and handicapped children, who were kept in appalling conditions by Western standards, although I was assured that these were good for the area. Some children were tied to their beds for their own safety so that they couldn't wander away. There weren't enough staff to monitor and care for them. There was no electricity, so their clothes and sheets couldn't be washed regularly. The noise was awful: relentless screeching, banging, rattling, crying. In one corner, I remember, there was a little girl with her legs in callipers clutching a ragged teddy and quietly singing, 'Alouette, gentille Alouette,' to herself.

We couldn't stay too long because we had to be out of the combat area before nightfall. Leaving was unbearable. We were unable to evacuate any of the wounded because the town's authorities thought it would be too dangerous. Many others came up to us, crying, and begging us to take them out. We had to refuse. They would never have been allowed through the checkpoints on the road back to Saida. A woman desperately pleaded with one of our drivers to hide her two little girls in his truck, lifting them up to him, all three of them sobbing. I saw the sadness in his eyes as he explained why it was impossible. I found it deeply upsetting to see the desperation of these people without being able to do anything more to help them. I wanted to scoop the children up and take them out. But Béatrice reminded me once again what we were there for. The diplomats and delegates in the ICRC headquarters had the responsibility of negotiating the displaced people's safe passage out of the town. If we grabbed one or two of them and ran, it would be dangerous for everyone. It was safer to leave them where they were, however upset we might feel.

This was my introduction to working in a war zone. It was a dramatic change from the nursing I knew. The concept of caring for the multitude not the individual was completely new to me, not like the one-to-one nursing I was used to at all.

Before I was sent to the Lebanon, I had been working in Leeds General Infirmary as an accident and emergency (A&E) sister for two years. Getting itchy feet, I contacted someone I'd heard about who'd worked for Christian Outreach in a refugee camp on the Thai/Cambodian border, and arranged to join them. I had given in my notice at the infirmary and was ready to leave when at the last minute the project was called off because of the dangerous security situation in the area. Feeling fed up, I went off on holiday with a nursing friend. On the spur of the moment we decided to get a rail pass and go camping in Europe, starting in the south of France. On the way home we stopped off in Switzerland, where I stayed on with my aunt

Ruth while my friend went back to England. At that point I really didn't know what I was going to do with the rest of my life. I talked endlessly with Ruth, telling her all about my long-held dreams of nursing abroad and having a role to play in disaster relief. She suggested I join the Swiss-based International Committee of the Red Cross. 'I think you should be eligible because you're a Swiss national. You'd be ideal with your casualty work and your experience of tropical nursing.'

I'd never thought of it, but it was true that although I had been born in Essex, my Swiss-born father had made sure that I had dual nationality, which meant I was eligible to apply. A few years earlier I had nursed on expeditions to Panama, Papua New Guinea and Sulawesi with Operation Drake, so I had some knowledge of nursing in remote places with only limited medical supplies. Ruth arranged for me to see a cousin who had worked as a nurse for the ICRC. That was it. As soon as she started describing their work, I knew I'd found at last what I wanted to do.

The ICRC's main purpose is to bring protection and assistance to victims of war, whoever they are, whether through providing emergency medical help and relief supplies, visiting political detainees or prisoners, or evacuating and caring for the wounded. As a neutral non-political organization whose role is to be guardian of the Geneva Convention and international humanitarian law, it upholds minimum standards for living and reunites families via the Red Cross message system. My cousin had been working for the ICRC in the Lebanon, a country torn apart by civil war, since 1975. She arranged for me to have a meeting with the ICRC a week later. During that week, I borrowed some respectable clothes to replace my old jeans and, with the help of my cousin, learned by heart some French phrases that might be useful. I still remember '*Je donne le meilleur de moi-même quand je fais face à une défi*' (I give the best of myself when faced with a challenge). One month later I was *en route* for Lebanon myself.

I had been given a minimal briefing by various individual departments within the ICRC. The delegate from the Middle East desk explained the complex political situation. The population of Lebanon was a mosaic of different religious communities within the broader definitions of Christian, Muslim and Druze. In June 1982, the Israelis had mounted Operation Peace for Galilee from south Lebanon into Beirut and the Bekaa Valley, aimed at wiping out the presence of the Palestine Liberation Organization (PLO) there. As a result the PLO had agreed to leave Beirut under the supervision of a multi-national force of American, French and Italian troops while the Israeli troops withdrew to south Lebanon, just north of Saida, where I would be based. As they pulled out of the nearby Chouf Mountains, civil war had erupted between the various Druze and Christian militias. I was asked to sign a confidentiality agreement that still binds me today, so

I'm unable to identify the individual fighting factions I encountered.

One of the doctors in the medical division briefed me about the job I'd be doing, supporting the medical infrastructure in a war zone. The pharmacy explained the first-aid sets that were used and how I had to make sure that I got a receipt for everything I dispensed so that the supplies could be properly audited. I was given a routine medical to make sure that I was fit to undertake the work and had had the necessary injections. Every interview I went to seemed as surreal as the last. Half of them were conducted in French, so I listened hard, trying to say '*oui*' and '*non*' in the right places, but not much of it really went in until I saw the personnel officer, who told me I had to make a will. For the first time, I understood the seriousness of what I was about to do.

When I told my parents what I was planning, they were nothing but encouraging. If they were worried about their daughter going to a war zone, they certainly didn't show it. I think Papa thought it was a fine thing for me to do with my life. To him, challenges were what life was about, and helping people less fortunate than oneself was even more important. They concentrated on the practical side of things, making sure I was properly equipped with light, loose-fitting clothes, sandals, a radio and writing paper. Once I was prepared, it was only a question of waiting until there was a ceasefire long enough for me to get into the area safely.

It was as well that as representatives of the ICRC, our brief was to remain strictly neutral, since I found the intricate politics of the different fighting factions extremely confusing. I listened to people in the field and the news reports, and read the literature. The more I learned, the more complicated it became and the less I seemed to know, so I decided it was better not to have an opinion. I just got on with my job.

There were over a hundred thousand displaced people in central Lebanon, the Bekaa Valley and in the Chouf Mountains. Soon I was travelling throughout the area, often only with my field officer, who acted as my translator too. Evacuating any wounded or delivering relief supplies needed careful planning. We had to make special contacts with all the local commanders, arranging ceasefires that would let the convoys through. The security precautions were paramount and we might spend days checking and double-checking arrangements before we could cross a front line or enter a combat zone.

Getting through the checkpoints on the front lines was a recurring problem. Life for the locals had to go on, and they tried to get to the market or visit friends, creating long queues of traffic. The problem was that no one knew when the road blocks would open and sometimes whole families would be camped out in their cars for days. Even when the road blocks opened, often only a few would be let through at a time.

I frequently had to walk to the front of the queue with soldiers peering out from sandbagged and reinforced look-out posts or trenches behind the checkpoint, training their guns on me as I made my way through the rolled barbed wire marking the 'sterile area' to speak to them and explain who I was. I put my confidence in the hope that they were less likely to shoot a woman. Sure, I knew that people got shot – I'd read about it and seen it on news reports. But why would they want to shoot me? I was no threat, just an innocent party out to help. I assumed that because I thought that, so would they.

Once I drove up to a checkpoint, where I was signalled to stop. I knew the soldiers there, so when we weren't waved on as usual, I jumped out of the car to investigate. I was walking confidently towards them when I heard a gun being cocked. I froze. The staff on the checkpoint had changed. Closer to them, I couldn't see a familiar face. Moving very slowly, I half raised my hands in the air, showing that I wasn't carrying anything.

'Can I come and talk to you?' I yelled, hoping the soldiers would see the red cross on our vehicle but not daring to move a muscle until I got permission.

They waved me forward. Slowly I walked towards their raised guns, forcing myself to keep going until I was near enough to talk to them. I explained who we were and that we needed to get to a village beyond the checkpoint because we were carrying vital medical supplies. There was a long silence as one of them went back to talk to whoever was in charge. When he returned I was beckoned forward again. My heart was thumping as one of them, his gun levelled at my chest, asked me again what I wanted.

This time my reply prompted him to speak to someone on his walkie-talkie. Then he looked at me, 'Right. You can go.'

The walk back to the car seemed the longest I had ever taken. I was only too aware that the guns remained trained steadily on me. I climbed back in, the barrier was raised and we drove slowly through into the relative peace of no-man's-land. I had been rudely awoken to the tension and insecurity of life on the front line.

Usually, once the soldiers had agreed to let us through, we'd have to drive the ambulance or car past the waiting vehicles, often with the tyres precariously close to the edge of a steep drop. It was here that I learned to manoeuvre a car so well. Driving in the Lebanon was the best road assault course you could design. I remember an occasion when we had urgently to evacuate a pregnant woman with a suspected placenta praevia to a specialized maternity unit in Beirut, and the road had been blocked for days. Finally we got permission to take a muddy, potholed tank track that ran almost vertically up a mountainside. I was driving a Peugeot 504 with rear-wheel drive, so the only way to get enough traction was to reverse up the slope. It was a hair-raising journey for all of us.

All the ICRC vehicles were constantly submitted to thorough searches. One day some hidden cigarettes and coffee were discovered in our vehicle at the last checkpoint before Deir El Kamar. We didn't know that the nuns in Saida had packed them for their sisters in the hospital. This nearly got us shot, and certainly set back our relations with the soldiers which it had taken us weeks of diplomacy to build up. A worse disaster was averted when we discovered detonators hidden in cans of baby milk powder in our warehouse, fortunately before loading the lorries. That opened my eyes to the danger of infiltration, and after that I became hypervigilant about everything I transported. In fact, I earned myself a reputation for insisting that all packages were opened and searched before I took them with me. If people were travelling with me, I always made them open their bags. It made me unpopular occasionally but I felt safer and more likely to be trusted by the soldiers *en route*.

The field officer I travelled with was always a local man who, as well as translating for me, shared the driving, acted as my chaperone, and had to act as my ears and understand the sometimes very hot situations we could find ourselves in. One day we were working at a small dispensary and he began to hurry me up. I knew that the ceasefire would be over at four o'clock, but I was reluctant to leave as I wanted to finish what I was doing, and telling the villagers when our time was up would compromise our neutrality because we would be giving them classified information. Thanks to my field officer's insistence, we just got through in time: the firing started up behind us as we crossed the last check-point. As we travelled, we would play I Spy the snipers' hidey-holes. I soon learned not to point at the snipers if I didn't want to get shot, only to nod my head in the right direction. We never knew what danger might arise between one checkpoint and the next, but I felt tremendously privileged to be able to go into the fighting zone and carry out my work.

My days in A&E when I dealt with drunks and down-and-outs stood me in good stead with the soldiers. Some of my fellow delegates dismissed them as animals without ever trying to get to know the people they were. Yet I would often look at a person they had dismissed so unfairly and remember how we'd spoken together about his family and home. I empathized with these men over their living conditions on the front line, especially during the winter when they were cold, often wet and hungry, and had limited contact with the outside world and their families. Many of them were there against their will and didn't want to fight. Often I quietly talked to them about alternative methods of peace-making. I was intrigued how these were ordinary people, not the mass murderers of media reports, whichever fighting faction they were from. Maybe I was naïve, but I believed that if I were honest and straight-forward with them I would be accepted.

It was during my first encounters with the Druze militia in the Chouf Mountains that I was taught the appropriate way of greeting them: right hand on heart and no body contact. Nasib, the spokesman through whom I co-ordinated my visits in that area, had been educated and brought up in America, and nine times out of ten I'd forget what he had told me and go to shake his hand on greeting him. I never saw any of the Druze women but I couldn't help but notice how handsome the Druze troops were – dark-skinned with big bushy black beards, their eyes dark in faces full of character. They seemed able to talk without words; a single nod or a raised eyebrow said more than a whole sentence. Nasib told me, 'While the Druze are not regarded as Muslims by other Muslims, they regard themselves as Muslims.' They were always smartly dressed with big pistols down the back of their trousers.

Once on my way back from Chehim with a woman in labour and her three kids in the back, some Druze militia stopped us and suggested we might like to hand our vehicle over to them. Fortunately, I'd met one of the soldiers before – I remembered him because he always winked at me – and he came to the rescue and explained to his friends who we were, so they let us through.

Another time, we were invited to eat at the home of one of the captains. He was extremely good-looking and always 'turned up' to see me when I was in the area (radio link contact told him where I was). I refused, because we knew we had a busy day ahead. However, hours later as we were leaving the area and driving home, we heard shouts from a little house on the left of the road. Who should it be but Captain M with his family and some of his colleagues. They were sitting under the almond blossom, having a grand picnic in the garden. We were greeted by pistol shots and then invited to join them for something to eat and drink. The men were drunk and kept pressing me to try the local spirit, arak, with them but I stuck strictly to orange juice. The captain was very friendly but I didn't like the look of his pistol glinting in the sun beside him. Although the party was fun, I was quite relieved to leave after twenty minutes with the excuse that we had to be home by dark.

The job itself gave me enormous satisfaction. I had imagined I'd be working with the wounded but in fact I did very little hands-on nursing. I didn't mind one bit. My knowledge and qualifications gave me the ability to advise on what was and wasn't needed. I'd look at a list of supplies drawn up by a dispensary, asking the staff to clarify anything I didn't understand or thought they didn't need, and then was able to provide what was required. I wrote home to my parents: 'I am doing the job I like and have always wanted to do, so live it with me – up to my death, if that happens. But I'm here because I must be here. I am more scared of the dogs that chase me in the villages than the soldiers' guns.'

I had never been comfortable with dogs since one chased

me on my bike when I was a girl and I had fallen off. Here, the flea-ridden village dogs always chased the vehicles, barking fiercely. Once I was about to get out to buy a kebab at a roadside stall in the mountains when a dog ran up, growling. I sat in the vehicle, petrified and unable to move, while all the local men laughed at me. Eventually my field officer had to buy the kebab for me.

Apart from doing convoy duty, I regularly visited local hospitals, dispensaries and first-aid posts in the Chouf Mountains. The direct route from Saida via the coast road took no more than an hour, but because it was always closed by the shelling and mines of the hostilities, my field officer and I would travel for up to six hours along mountain roads and tracks to avoid the minefields. When we finally reached a village, there would often be a patient who needed to be transferred to hospital in Beirut or Saida in my car or ambulance.

One I remember was a woman in her thirties whom a local doctor had asked us to evacuate from her village of Kfarhim as she had suspected appendicitis. I radioed the medical coordinator in Beirut to ask his opinion. He agreed with the doctor and told me that he'd contact me once he'd spoken to the head of the delegation there. I went to the woman's home, which was perched on the side of a mountain with stunning views over the valley. She lay on a sofa in the living room, the floor covered with colourful local rugs. Her husband and mother were concerned that she was in such pain and let me put up a drip and give her antibiotics. Her young children peeped in at me through the windows. A slight breeze fluttered the curtains while I wiped the sick woman's face with a damp cloth, refusing her requests for water in case she had to have an operation as soon as she reached the hospital. The grandmother gave me some fresh figs from the garden, and was horrified when she saw me eat them skin and all, instead of prising them open and sucking out the inside. After forty minutes, the medical coordinator radioed to say he had arranged for the sick woman to be admitted to the American hospital in Beirut and I was to bring her out.

As we drove there we were stopped at every checkpoint, asked for our names, and grilled about what was the matter with the patient, where had we come from and where were we going. Soldiers stuck their head in the car window to inspect her, some concerned for her, others totally disinterested, while she moaned in pain. The security and safety of the patient were entirely in my hands and I was anxious to get her treated as quickly as possible. When we arrived at the Beirut hospital, true to form the emergency room claimed they hadn't been told of our imminent arrival. I got back to the ICRC medical coordinator to find out who he'd spoken to. Eventually I managed to contact the consultant who had reserved a bed for her. He came rushing down to us and admitted her immediately. Two weeks later, I returned to Kfarhim and found her back at home recovering after an appendectomy. I left with another bowl of fresh figs given in gratitude.

The local first-aid posts or clinics for different areas were frequently in the basements of houses that were sand-bagged up, often without electricity and water. Conditions were usually very primitive, but the staff still managed to care for the injured there, setting up intravenous infusions and dressing wounds. Many of these places hadn't received any medical supplies for at least six months. I'd assess what they needed and make arrangements to supply what I could from the basic drugs and kits that we had available. The kits came in boxes marked 'Paediatric', 'Dispensary', 'Dressing sets', 'Infusion sets' and 'Front A' or 'Front B' boxes. It took me some weeks to understand what a 'front set' meant until another nurse said, 'Claire. You're English. You must know what it means.' Shame-faced, I confessed I didn't. She explained that these sets were meant for the heavily wounded on the front line. They included traction equipment, splints, heavy wound dressings and bandages. We also carried things like blankets, stretchers, blood taking/giving sets, strong analgesia, and other odds and ends. Labels could be printed in anything from Greek to Finnish, and so they were often useless unless a translation came with them.

It was amazing how even near the front line of the conflict, life went on much as usual during the day. Streets and shops that were bombed in the morning would be open and trading again by the afternoon. I got used to the sound of gunfire and shells dropping and the constant looking over one's shoulder to see who was standing where and what they were doing. Did they look suspicious? Were they carrying a gun? This vigilance became a natural part of my everyday life. I was never caught in a raid myself, but I knew that in Israeli-controlled Saida, the patrols were often ambushed by insurgents.

After a few weeks I was fixed up with a small apartment in a little place eight kilometres east of Saida on the road to Jezzine. The residents called the building 7 Up because it was by the soft drink manufacturer's main local depot. I had two rooms, a small kitchen area and a tiny loo/shower room. It had hot water most days, radiators that worked and enough water pressure for me to rinse my hair at night. It might sound pretty basic, but many of the more luxurious apartments in town failed to live up to its standards.

By December I had moved into a flat in the ICRC block above the bureau in central Saida, which I shared with a loud and kind Swiss-Italian, Jean-Pierre. He was one of the delegates in charge of the area, although his job meant that he spent most of his time in Beirut or in the field, where he got on well with his Chouf contacts.

Saida is a small port forty kilometres south of Beirut. During the time I was in the Lebanon, it was the front line of the Israeli Defense Forces (IDF). Much of the town was built several centuries ago and although pock-marked by bullets and dramatically destroyed in places, it still preserved a medieval charm. Vehicles crowded the roads, hooting their horns and pushing through the throng of people going about their daily business. Driving in town was a nightmare. The old souk with its maze of passage-ways was always crowded, although it was very insecure, with IDF patrols frequently being attacked and ambushed by insurgents. Whenever I went there, I broke out in a sweat if I ever saw an armed patrol and would make a swift detour to keep out of their way.

After a six o'clock start, I'd be on the road all day, travelling all over the Chouf Mountains, negotiating the crossing of front lines and arranging ceasefires so that we could reach the remoter villages that needed our help. I was always dead beat by the time I got home. Other ICRC personnel lived in the same block, and we often visited one another, taking turns to cook. They were very friendly and I relaxed quickly into life there. I was so exhausted by the work that I'd usually be in bed by nine or nine thirty. There I curled up and listened to the World Service on a little portable Sony transistor radio – otherwise contact with the outside world was scarce.

Because of the heavy fighting the airport in Beirut was closed and all post had to be sent and received via a 'diplomatic bag' that went with anyone from the ICRC delegation who arrived or departed either by road via Tel

Aviv or by boat via Cyprus. Nevertheless I wrote regularly to my family and they to me. Sometimes they were able to send me a parcel of all the things I missed from home, such as Crunchies and Star bars and women's magazines so that I could keep up with the fashions. They also sent music tapes, which always cheered me and, if I played them loudly enough, drowned the sound of the gunfire that was intermittently in the background. A Christmas parcel lost when Beirut airport was attacked for the last time before it closed down had contained — so my mother told me later — some black lacy underwear. We still laugh at the thought of the look on the faces of the black marketeers on finding the 'spoils of war' in that parcel.

During my first three months, our major task was the welfare of the displaced people in Deir El Kamar and then their gradual evacuation once the fighting factions agreed to give them safe passage to spend Christmas with their relatives. We called the project Operation Lama. While I monitored the needs of nearby villages, some of my colleagues prepared the ground at Deir El Kamar, manning regular food and emergency transfer convoys, and evacuating the sick and the wounded first. Then, on 17 December, I was given just an hour's notice to leave for Deir El Kamar to help organize the evacuation of all the elderly and all the young orphans. By this time I had my own field officer, Ibrahim, who travelled everywhere with me. He was a real livewire who spoke pretty good English and was mad on Pink Floyd. When asked at the interview whether he minded working in dangerous combat areas, he replied, 'But that's why I want to join the Red Cross.' An important bonus, or so I thought at the time, was that we shared the same blood group, so if the worst came to the worst, we'd be useful to each other in an emergency. The hospitals were so short of blood that if you were wounded you had to rely on friends. The only snag was that we'd probably get shot together. I know now that the last thing I'd want if I were badly injured or wounded would be a blood transfusion, particularly in a war-torn country where the medical facilities are severely stretched and the cross-matching and blood-grouping can be haphazardly done.

It was quiet as we made our way up the twisting pot-holed roads to Deir El Kamar. Arriving just as the sun was setting, we immediately pitched in to help find and identify the evacuees. It was getting cold and very dark as at last we set off to find somewhere to sleep. No lights were allowed in case they attracted sniper fire. We had been told to stay in any of the many empty houses. Just then, firing began from the village on the other side of the valley. A bullet skimmed Ibrahim's hair. We dodged into a narrow alley-way leading off the main street, running between the houses so that the infrared rifle sights wouldn't be able to pick up our body heat. The sky was alive with bangs and flashes, so we decided to take shelter in the first deserted house we found. Inside, the objects of daily life lay strewn where they'd been abandoned in their owner's haste to leave town. As in most villages in the Chouf, neighbours and friends had become adversaries overnight, according to their religion or politics. I could hear the blasts of heavy artillery as the heavens opened and it began to pour with rain. I chose a bed for myself and looking underneath it I pulled out a Kalashnikov. I gingerly returned it to its place and lay down, my sleep interrupted by thoughts of what would happen if its owner were to return. But at least I had a bed. I remembered all those who didn't and reminded myself that I had nothing to complain about.

Next day, it was still pouring with rain and the streets were rivers. My soaking wet jeans rubbed against my skin, and my legs and shoes were drenched as we trudged, freezing cold, up the stepped streets between the old stone houses to visit the elderly and sick, assessing whether they could travel in a bus or needed an ambulance. Each person had to be registered and 'labelled', just like a parcel, and their photo taken with a Polaroid camera. After weeks of being pent up there, everybody was excited and eager to get out, longing to be reunited with their loved ones, looking forward to the luxuries of electricity and good food. Many of them expressed their hopes of eventually returning to their own villages when the situation had calmed down.

For the next week, seven convoys evacuated five hundred people at a time in buses via Jezzine or Kfarhim to Beirut. On one of our trips to the town, we helped rescue

David Lomax, a BBC reporter for *Panorama*, and Malcolm Bartrum, a sound recordist, from the outskirts of Deir El Kamar, where they had been pinned down by sniper fire. They were making a special report from the Lebanon and had obtained permission from the fighting factions to leave their car at the last checkpoint and walk across the three or four kilometres of no-man's-land into town with their equipment, following the route of the Red Cross convoy. After filming for two or three hours, they were ready to leave, but three hundred metres from town they came under fire from across the valley. They had forgotten to obtain permission to exit the town. Lying flat on the roadside, as bullets whistled over their heads, they were unable to move as they watched their assailants climbing the mountainside to get a better shot at them. Malcolm was shot in the leg. Jean-Pierre, the ICRC delegate, temporarily staying in Deir El Kamar to coordinate the evacuation, had driven past them three times without noticing them until, the fourth time, David threw himself in front of the car. By this time he had decided he had nothing to lose. Jean-Pierre screeched to a halt. He bundled them into his Land Cruiser and took them to the local hospital in Baakline because Malcolm was quite badly wounded. It was here I found them the next day, after Malcolm had been successfully operated on and his leg well splinted. Our return journey out of the fighting area was uneventful, although initially both men were nervous, sweating and shaky, worried about what might happen next. But they eventually relaxed and I thoroughly enjoyed the journey with them – I'd forgotten how funny English banter could be.

At last the time came for the final convoy on 22 December. This time we were to escort all those who had escaped to Deir El Kamar in their cars. There was a grand total of 485 vehicles to be accompanied to the coast road, where they would be out of the main fighting area and able to travel on to Beirut or Saida. We left Saida for Deir El Kamar at 02.30. We wanted to complete the operation before there were too many people on the roads, and planned to start the evacuation before dawn broke. The long mountain route had been made even more treacherous by the heavy rains but at least there wasn't any trouble, and we reached Deir El Kamar in good time. Those being evacuated were called up by loudspeaker and searched to make sure that they weren't carrying any arms. For security reasons, only two people were allowed in each car, without any luggage or belongings, so that nothing – a third person, maps, private notes, arms – could possibly be hidden in the cars. Then they had to wait nervously until everyone was ready. Many of the vehicles were ancient and a number of them needed a jump start.

I was in charge of the medical team, with three ambulances to carry the sick and wounded. We had delegates and members of the Lebanese Red Cross positioned every kilometre along the route to the coast so that we could be sure that no one unofficially left or joined the convoy and that nothing was passed into or out of the cars *en route*. On those remote mountain roads, we had to be prepared for anything to happen on any corner. The planning behind it all had been phenomenal. The 485 battered old boneshakers crawled down through the mountains, many without windows or lights and most scarred with great dents and scratches. The ICRC had labelled and numbered every car, supplied each one with ten litres of fuel, and instructed the drivers that on no account were they to stop. If a car in front broke down, the driver behind was to shunt it along until they reached the coast.

In the middle of it all, there was a cry over the radio that someone had been ambushed in no-man's-land. Ibrahim and I leaped into an ambulance and zoomed back up the road to find a man lying in the road in agony, having been shot in the shoulder by a sniper. His wife was crouching by the car, terrified and uncertain what to do. After staunching the bleeding, we bundled the man into the ambulance and whisked him through to Beirut, while the Lebanese Red Cross brought his wife along separately. I returned to the road to offer help with any more incidents but fortunately everything else went smoothly. After the cars reached the coast, they lined up at the first garage they came to for petrol and to collect the luggage that we'd bagged up and transported separately. The look on the displaced people's faces as they reached relative safety at last was unforgettable. Seeing their relief was a welcome reward.

One elderly man, unshaven and almost toothless, drove down in a battered Mercedes with only one working head-light. I remember him because his wife was in the car, wearing the traditional long dark billowing skirt and a headscarf. She was very emotional, in tears as they got out of the car. He put his arm round her protectively. She gave a cry as two people I took to be their son and daughter ran over and hugged them. After their happy reunion, the old man crossed over to those of us standing nearby and shook us all by the hand, tears rolling down his cheeks.

By 10.00, all the displaced people had reached the safety of the coast and, to celebrate, the Lebanese Red Cross joined us in opening two crates of champagne on the motorway to Beirut.

3

LIFE ON THE EDGE

THE ENORMOUS TANK-MOUNTED GUN PIVOTED ROUND until it was pointing directly at the front seat of the ambulance where I was sitting with Ibrahim. I recognized one or two of the soldiers manning the tank and greeted them, smiling, but for once they did not smile back.

'The convoy must follow us,' one of them ordered.

I laughed, making a joke of it, but slowly it dawned on me that they weren't being funny. Only the previous week, one of the local ICRC drivers had been forcibly removed from his vehicle and beaten up by soldiers, so our drivers were extremely nervous. A few minutes before, the ICRC delegates travelling with our convoy had gone ahead in one of the cars to the checkpoint at Chateau Moussa to meet the military commanders. They'd left Ibrahim and me behind in our ambulance at the head of the supply lorries. I urgently attempted to radio the delegates but with no joy. Neither could I raise headquarters in Beirut. We were caught in a dead area where radio signals were blocked by the surrounding mountains. The soldiers became impatient and gestured to me to get out of the ambulance.

'You stay here. The lorries come with us.' They levelled their guns at the terrified drivers and then shot into the air a few times to show that they meant business.

I stayed resolutely in the driver's seat. 'Forget it. I'm not leaving the drivers. If you're taking them, you're going to have to take me too.'

These soldiers were the boys who regularly invited us to join them in the local custom of drinking *maté* tea, a bitter green concoction. The danger didn't cross my mind. There was simply no question of my abandoning the men who worked for us. We were led down a slip road. Then as I realized the gravity of the situation fear began to kick in. Where were they taking us? What would they do to us when we got there? How the hell was I going to get us all out of this? We wound up a mountain road out of the area I knew well and at last they ordered us to park by the roadside. I kept on trying the radio, willing it to transmit to the rest of my team. To my relief, a signal finally got through. There was a tense period of waiting while my colleagues negotiated with the commanders to get us released. After an hour or so, word was sent to let us go. We were mightily relieved. But before we could turn back, the militia emptied the lorries of the relief supplies we were carrying. We never saw any of that stuff again.

There was no room for complacency in that job. You never knew when something would go wrong.

One day, a group of expats from the delegation drove up to Nabatiye, on the edge of the zone controlled by the Israelis, where Shiites were celebrating their festival of Ashura. Hundreds of men paraded through the streets, hitting themselves with rocks, sticks and knives until the blood flowed down their white robes in memory of the terrible martyrdom of Imam al Hussein, massacred when trying to claim his position as caliph in 680. Even boys hardly big enough to walk had wounds made in their hairline by their fathers so that they could be a part of it. Heads were wrapped with large bloodstained bandages and those too badly injured to walk were supported by their friends. By mid-morning, we had seen enough and it was getting crowded in the town square, so we decided to head for the coast to get something to eat.

Minutes after we left, Israeli tanks entered the town and tried to break up the crowds, who retaliated by throwing stones. A gun battle broke out, killing three and injuring many more. It was afternoon by the time we heard what had happened and we immediately headed back to Nabatiye to see if we could help. The Israelis had cordoned off the town but let us through. In the spot where hours earlier we had parked our car we found a huge crater where a bomb had exploded, surrounded by charred tanks and cars. I went to the hospital to see if any extra supplies were needed but found it well equipped and organized. In the general excitement, we'd completely forgotten to radio headquarters with our whereabouts, so a delegate had been sent up from Saida to find out what had happened to us. Unable to contact us, they had feared the worst – as it so easily could have been.

One morning the new ICRC medical coordinator and a visiting nurse left with Zadir, a local field officer, for Sibline in the Chouf Mountains to carry out a routine survey. I stayed in Saida to do a stock-take. Twenty minutes after they'd left, I was up to my eyes in paperwork and counting boxes in the warehouse, when I picked up an emergency call from them on the VHF radio. They had just left the coast road and crossed the last Lebanese forces checkpoint towards Ouadi Zain when a mine had exploded under the car and they found themselves under fire. Thomas, one of the delegates, and I immediately jumped into an ambulance each and arrived at the scene about ten minutes later.

We got close to the last checkpoint and borrowed some binoculars from the Lebanese soldiers. We could make out that the ICRC car was on its side and looked quite badly damaged. Gunfire was raining down on them from the mountain. Over the VHF radio, Zadir told us that they were all injured but were going to crawl from the car to a spot where they'd have more cover from the shooting. But if they did that, we'd lose radio contact with them.

We couldn't work out what had gone wrong until we noticed a line of six or seven rocks across the middle of the road that hadn't been there the last time I'd used the route. It seemed from the tyre tracks that instead of recognizing this as a warning and turning back to request updated permission to pass into the area, they had skirted the rocks and continued on the road. We realized that whoever was shooting probably had no idea they were firing at a Red Cross vehicle, so we hastily made contact with our head-quarters. After about an hour we managed to get a message through to a contact in the mountains, asking them to send someone to stop the shooting.

By the time things had quietened down, we'd been joined by our intrepid delegate Jean-Pierre and my nursing colleague Béatrice, who was due to leave the following week. In our haste to help, we'd forgotten our Red Cross identity tabards with large red crosses on their back and front, but we decided to risk walking towards the stranded party, carrying the metre-wide Red Cross flag from the car, a stretcher and medical supplies. Jean-Pierre held the flag high as we gingerly walked in single file along the tarmac towards the car, trying to keep calm as we cracked nervous jokes about the flag being perfect for target practice. As we got closer, we could see wires leading to what looked like an enormous net about twenty metres from the car. Jean-Pierre identified it as anti-personnel mines and the two enormous potholes by the car as explosions that must have been triggered as it went by. Our wounded colleagues had crawled out of the car and were huddled by its side. It was very scary being so close to them but unable to run over to help. The medical coordinator's leg had been badly injured by shrapnel, while the nurse travelling with him was injured in her head and arm. Zadir had escaped with superficial wounds to his head that were bleeding ferociously. Slowly, we negotiated the mass of wires and metal fragments and, more by luck than judgement I suspect, we dragged and carried our co-workers to safety, back the way we had come. We took them to Beirut for X-rays and immediate treatment before they were evacuated to Europe to recover fully.

I had made plenty of friends among the delegates. Amongst these, a special friend was Yves, a prosthetics maker, a bearded Corsican with a great sense of fun. In an area that was so heavily landmined, there was a huge need for the artificial limbs he and his colleagues made. He was always the life and soul of the party, able to make everyone relax and enjoy themselves. I'd never had such a wild time as I did with him. I think it was in part because of the uncertainty of the situation I found myself in. I first became aware of it only a few weeks after arriving. Several of us were having dinner on a balcony when what I thought was a wonderful display of fireworks was set off close by. As I was admiring it, I hardly noticed the others diving inside until Yves jumped up and dragged me down with him.

'Don't you realize those are tracer bullets? There's a shoot-out in the next street.'

A frisson of fear ran through me. I would never have imagined that anything as beautiful could be so deadly. I was shaking like a leaf, so Yves comforted me – and then my social life only got better. I'd watched people falling in love in a wartime situation in films, their emotions intensified by never knowing what the next moment would bring. In real life, I discovered, it was even better. I'd heard that war acted as an aphrodisiac and thought, What nonsense. Little did I know.

I learned a lot from Yves, also in practical ways. It was Yves who set me straight about certain essential security procedures, the unwritten but commonsensical code of working in a war zone. For example, if you had to take a vehicle across a front line, you should always take one with a diesel engine, because if your fuel tank got hit by a bullet, the diesel would simply leak out, whereas a petrol tank would instantly explode. He also taught me about land-mines, his experience born of the time he had spent in Angola and Mozambique. When he heard about our rescue of our colleagues in the Chouf Mountains, he explained what a foolhardy thing we'd done. Just because the road looked clear didn't mean that it wasn't perfectly possible for a mine to have been tunnelled underneath it from the roadside.

Soon after I met him, he told me that I'd have to drink alcohol when I went into the field, otherwise I wouldn't be accepted by the local dignitaries and commanders. Blow that for a lark, I thought; no way. So I always stuck to Fanta, Coke or tea. Invariably one or other of the officials would lean over towards me. 'It's good to see you are just like my wife and sisters,' they'd say. 'They don't drink alcohol either.' In fact, it turned out to be another way by which I earned their respect.

One of Yves' wisest pieces of advice, however, one that I was to remember often in years to come, was to trust my own instincts and never rely on anyone else's judgement. 'If it doesn't feel right to you, Claire, don't do it. Think before you dash in. We don't want any extra wounded, do we?'

By Christmas he'd been posted elsewhere and I was left feeling utterly miserable, knowing that our paths were unlikely to cross again. The highlight of my Christmas Day was to run a 'hot' bath with a plastic bag over the plughole weighed down with a gas cylinder and a tin of baked beans. There I sat in tepid water, in lonely isolation, eating an orange and a Star bar, listening to my Christmas present from home, a tape of John Lennon's 'Imagine'. But my blues soon passed as work occupied me again, and the good friends I'd made among the rest of the delegates made sure I was never at a loss for something to do in my leisure hours. We entertained one another all the time. Amazingly, we could order almost anything we wanted from Beirut and there were several wild parties with champagne flowing like water accompanied by gourmet food.

When we could, we explored the region. We saw the archaeological ruins at Baalbek. We visited the centuries-old Chateau Beaufort, perched high above the rushing Litani River, before walking down to the red-mudded valley and picking wild cyclamens and anemones which stained the earth like splashes of arterial blood. I was constantly struck by the beauty of the country and astonished to find that red anemones grew like weeds on the uncultivated stony ground. They reminded me of the poppies of the First World War.

At about that time, I was asked to move into Yves' old flat with his friend Thierry, a thin but handsome French guy with a big moustache and dark, curly hair who was another prosthetics maker. We became great friends and soon slipped into a very comfortable and familiar routine without the complication of a sexual relationship. Whoever got up first set the table for breakfast. Then we'd companionably dunk our toast in bowls of coffee and drink freshly squeezed orange to a background of classical music before going off to work. If we weren't entertaining in the evening, one of us would make soup (you can't just open a packet of soup for the French) with lashings of cream and butter if Thierry was cooking, and we'd eat it with bread,

cheese or an omelette. I soon realized that my Marks &
Spencer cookery book and WeightWatchers scales were the
best things I'd brought with me from home. By nine or
nine thirty we'd drag ourselves to our separate bedrooms.
Mine was hung with Arabic scarves and photos from home.
I'd try to read a few more pages of the history of the last
war in the region before I drifted off. I got into the habit of
covering my head with a scarf to prevent myself from being
hurt by anything falling on it should we be shelled in the
night. I don't suppose it would have protected me much but
it gave me some comfort.

The pleasure of sharing a flat with a gourmet certainly
had its moments. Once I got home to find Thierry in the
kitchen up to his elbows in blood, the washing-up bowl
overflowing with pieces of wild boar marinating in wine,
brandy, garlic, spices and herbs. As he moved to cut up the
onions, a huge smile of contentment shone on his face.
Outside on the balcony, the boar's bloody hide was drying.
Thierry had used up all our salt in his efforts to tan it. He
regaled me with stories of his wonderful day's hunting,
how his back ached having carried this huge dead beast
several kilometres to the Land-Rover. With glee, he
described the look on the Israeli soldiers' faces at the checkpoint when they saw the blood dripping out of the doors of
the Red Cross vehicle. Thierry proposed that we turned the
meat daily in its marinade until the following Sunday,
when he had invited the other hunters and their families to

come and eat it with us. The stench stayed with us long after the meat had gone.

He was equally skilled with fish, as I found out one day after delivering a Red Cross message form to someone on one of the steep terraced mountainsides outside Jezzine. After hunting through the bombed-out houses, Ibrahim and I found a dirt track that took us to a small wood, which opened out into a terraced area of several concrete pools and gushing streams. Despite being on the front line, this was still a working trout farm. I couldn't believe it. When I told Thierry, his eyes lit up. The next time I was in that direction, it was with an order for twenty fresh trout. Twenty! Ibrahim found the farmer, who showed us round the ponds and asked me what size of fish I wanted before netting them and thwacking them on the head. The kitchen back home was soon a riot of blood, guts and fish scales as Thierry prepared a trout party for all our friends with a meal fit for royalty.

After the evacuation of Deir El Kamar was finally complete, we were allowed four days' rest and recuperation, so, at the end of January 1984, Thierry and I took a four-day trip to Jerusalem. It was only when we got to the bustling normality of Jerusalem that I realized for the first time how dangerous life in the Lebanon really was. Coming out, I felt tremendous relief. I hadn't recognized the tension and fear we lived with daily, always looking over our shoulders, watching our backs. The city was so alive, vibrant with people milling about the markets and shops, going about their ordinary daily lives without the background accompaniment of gunfire or shelling that I'd become so used to. There were no checkpoints and, best of all, no curfew, so we could enjoy ourselves eating out late and wandering the streets. We spent most of our day exploring the labyrinthine Old City with its narrow twisting alleyways, negotiating our way past the shopkeepers in the souk pressing any potential customers to come inside, and finding our way to the obvious sights – the Western Wall, the Church of the Holy Sepulchre and Holy Mount. We took a day trip to Bethlehem where, in the cold and rain, we trudged round Manger Square and the Church of the Nativity, and another trip to float in the Dead Sea.

When we returned to Saida, I went straight back to my work, evaluating hospitals, dispensaries, ambulances and places where we'd be able to work underground if necessary, in preparation for the time when the Israelis pulled out of southern Lebanon and fighting between all the factions inevitably ensued. One day an Israeli patrol was attacked right next to the delegation where I was working. When we heard the machine guns outside we flung ourselves on the floor. In such closeness to combat, I found I was frightened, but at the same time I felt strangely exhilarated. It wasn't until much later, when I was nursing in Afghanistan, that I really appreciated the life-or-death threat faced by myself and my fellow members of the ICRC and other aid organizations working in war zones. In the Lebanon, I was still young enough to believe that nothing would happen to me.

In the middle of February, the Israelis bombed Ein al-Helweh, the Palestinian camp just outside Saida. We could see a big black column of smoke floating over the horizon. The action was getting closer. The next day they dive-bombed the town, flying only five hundred feet from the ground to frighten the inhabitants. Writing home to my parents, I described it as 'fantastically, mind-blowingly frightening but still not quite the real thing for me'. On many nights, the sound of machine-gun fire and explosions came from the nearby hills north of the Awahli River, but I had conditioned myself to sleep with my scarf over my face and wax earplugs when it got too noisy. I'd persuaded myself that if I could sleep in a nurses' home in Paddington during the day with roadworks outside, I could sleep anywhere. I had to have my sleep and a clear head if I was to be alert during the day.

Many of the ICRC delegation had been relocated to the safety of Tyr, while those of us left in Saida were ordered to stay inside. It was the first time since I had arrived that such orders had been given. By now, I was the only female foreign national left in the Saida delegation, along with four delegates, four prosthetics makers plus local field officers and secretaries. There was fighting on most days and nights, and several bomb ambushes were laid for the

Israelis. In spite of the curfew, we managed to distribute our special frontline packs of medical supplies. Thankfully the clash was over very quickly and the death toll was relatively low.

One evening before the curfew, I found myself alone, slap in the middle of an ambush. I was on my way home from a day in Tyr, down the coast road. I'd made the necessary radio call to our headquarters to report that I was on my way. Everything was quiet. Then suddenly I heard shooting and could see the tracer bullets against the night sky. I realized that I was surrounded by Lebanese soldiers, ambushed by shooting that seemed to be coming from all directions. I extinguished my headlights to make myself less of an obvious target. Because there hadn't been any trouble expected along this stretch of road, I didn't have the big Red Cross flag or light mounted on the outside of the car. To the soldiers, I could have been anybody. I shouted at them to let me through, but they were too nervous to pay me any attention. Jeeploads of troops brandishing automatic machine guns drove up to join them as they prepared to hurl grenades in the direction of whoever was firing at them. It was terrifyingly surreal, with everything unfolding fast. I felt as if I was on a film set but had no idea of the plot. Spotting a slip road leading away from the scene, I decided not to wait to see what would happen next and gunned my Toyota towards it through the darkness, hoping for the best. Once I'd got round a bend and away from the action, I switched on the headlights and radioed in to report the situation, before taking the back roads home, my shaking hands steadied by the wheel and my heart still thumping.

Despite the risks we ran almost every day, our morale was high and we had fun in out-of-work hours. Whenever Thierry and I cooked for others, we inevitably ended up with seven or eight for dinner. There was a masked party, where we improvised with masks moulded in the orthopaedics workshop by the prosthetics team. Thierry helped me to make mine by first covering my head in cling-film and then in plaster of Paris that took fifteen minutes to set. By cutting up the back of it and getting my head out, we had a mould, which we filled with pink plastic foam to make a bust of my head. From this we made a perfectly fitting mask. Plain white with long black eyelashes, it covered the upper part of my face with holes for my eyes and nostrils. I even had a birthday party – my first since I was about ten. I used a bed sheet as a tablecloth with red candles and serviettes and a centrepiece of anemones and daisies. We had smoked salmon, roast beef, my famous strawberry mousse and a four-layer chocolate cake brought by my good friend Hazel, an Irish nurse working at the nearby Hariri Medical Centre. Many bottles of wine were drunk and then we danced, rock'n'rolling until well into the early hours.

Throughout my time in Lebanon, I was very glad of the

self-sufficiency that my father had drummed into me. Never more so than the day I went into the Ikleam el Kharroub area without a field officer when giving the region's ICRC medical coordinator a whistlestop tour of my patch. François, the doctor, was a young outdoor type who had taught me the Swiss national card game of Jass. We made a good card team and on the long trips up into the mountains we would devise codes we could use to let each other know what was in our hand. On this particular day, as we were driving along the side of a valley, we got a puncture. The area was notorious for snipers, so not a place where you'd want to linger. To my astonishment, my card-playing companion had no idea how to begin to jack up a car, never mind loosen the nuts or change the wheel. I had to do it all myself, scrambling to get it done so that we could get moving again as soon as possible. I realized then what a great gift Papa had given me and how important it is to understand how to survive in the world without being dependent on anyone else. Changing a tyre, driving, reading a map, always carrying a needle and thread, spare water and food, or a reserve of money – he taught me all these things. To this day I always carry a small amount of extra cash and something to eat – just in case.

Finally in April 1984 the first section of the coast road between Saida and Beirut was re-opened for the ICRC. At last we were able to use the direct route instead of making the long detour through the Chouf Mountains. The ICRC made contact with the authorities and all the landmines and stones, rocks and trees thrown there by the shelling were removed. This was a tense but eventful time for the Lebanon because once the ICRC had passed through safely, it usually meant that civilians would be able to follow a week or two later. Within the first few days of the road opening, Dr François and I left Saida for Beirut for an important medical meeting. To get there, we had to cross the Green Line into the Christian sector. As we arrived at the checkpoint, there was the usual queue of vehicles, and that was when I discovered the quickest way to clear a traffic jam. A couple of bursts into the air from an automatic rifle and the cars and lorries queuing up disappeared as if by magic. François and I ducked down in our seats, but fortunately that was the end of the shooting.

Life was noticeably different in the Christian quarter of Beirut where we were to stay. The motorway was smooth, not a pothole was to be seen, the cars were flash Mercedes with curtains looped back from the windows, and the shops were full of meat, Camembert, smoked salmon and summer fashions. The buildings weren't riddled with bullet holes or the bomb damage that I was so used to seeing in and around Saida. On the way back, we stopped off in Deir El Kamar. It was now so different from the Deir El Kamar I had known before Christmas – so much quieter without the hordes of displaced people. I visited my friend Angela, the nun, who welcomed me so warmly that I couldn't resist giving her and her sisters some of the strawberries, chocolate and Camembert I'd bought in Beirut for Thierry. I thought their need was greater. Luckily Thierry agreed. I could still remember how I had felt in the Panama jungle when I laid my hands on a precious fresh orange or an apple.

My year-long contract in the Lebanon was running out. I knew I would be sorry to leave. I had lived life intensely there and had so many experiences of life and death, and of course I had made some good friends. But I knew I didn't have a choice. I'd watched how other relief workers changed during their time in the Lebanon. Everyone said it was one of the hardest missions. I'd tried my best to keep my equilibrium in the face of the tragic Lebanese situation, but I often felt despair at the thought of leaving behind all those people who had to carry on living in what seemed an irresolvable situation. I could see that the ICRC's policy of short-term contracts was essential in this kind of situation. Neutrality was difficult to maintain in the long term.

I had been visiting a first-aid post in Baaquline, a village an hour and a half's drive away in the Chouf Mountains, when I received a radio call telling me to get back to Saida urgently for a call from the medical coordinator over the HF radio. This had never happened before so, petrified that something had happened to my family, I dashed back. In fact the news was that the ICRC at Geneva was inviting me on a mission to Ethiopia, a country I knew was devastated by famine and civil war. They wanted me there as soon as possible because there was a tremendous need for qualified nurses to run feeding centres for young children. What an opportunity – but would I be able to handle it? Thierry and the medical coordinator reassured me that I was more than capable of running a centre and the coordinator knew just the book to teach me. Egged on by their enthusiasm, I accepted the post the next day and before I knew where I was I was reading *The Management of Nutritional Emergencies in Large Populations*.

By mid-May I was expecting the new nurse who was going to take over from me. At the same time I was wrestling with my very mixed feelings about leaving the job, the flat and my friends, especially Thierry. I had never shared such a comfortable apartment with someone with whom I'd really got on. It was also the first time that I'd ever lived and worked without my family next door. I had made good friends with the rest of the team too. I had enjoyed this side of my existence so much that I now felt a very strong urge to have a place of my own.

But not quite yet.

As far as I was concerned I had come only some of the way towards fulfilling the childhood ambitions that had led me to nursing abroad.

Lebanon had been my first experience of war, but five years earlier I had joined Operation Drake, memorably described by Prince Charles as offering 'the challenges of war, but in a peacetime situation'. Early in 1978, I had seen a magazine article about the explorer Colonel John Blashford-Snell, one of the founders of the Scientific Exploration Society. In 1972, he had led a scientific expedition from Alaska to Tierra del Fuego, passing through the notorious Darien Gap in Central America. This article was the tinder to my fire. What caught my imagination was the variety of accidents that had befallen the team *en route* and how they had needed nurses to keep things going. It mentioned that Blashford-Snell was soon embarking on another great expedition called Operation Drake. This was an ambitious two-year, round-the-world sailing expedition on a 150-ton brigantine, the *Eye of the Wind*, that would follow the route taken by Sir Francis Drake's *The Golden Hinde* some four hundred years earlier. Its aim was to develop self-confidence and leadership in young people by involving them in adventure, scientific exploration and community service in different parts of the world. The expedition was to be broken into nine separate three-month phases, some land-based, some at sea, with groups of experienced explorers, scientists, geographers and engineers from all over the world accompanied by members of the armed forces and about fifty young civilian volunteers or 'Young Explorers'. Of the fifty thousand young people who had applied from all over the world, the shortlisted applicants were subjected to rigorous selection weekends. I thought, 'That's what I want to do. I could do that.' I immediately wrote to John Blashford-Snell asking if I could join as a nurse.

My interview was in the basement of the old war offices in Whitehall, where the interviewers did their best to put me off. 'On this trip, you won't get proper food. There'll be 100 per cent humidity. You'll be drenched in sweat, muddy, plagued by flies and there won't be decent washing facilities. You won't be able to communicate with home.' They painted an incredibly bleak picture but all I could think was, 'Yes. Yes. That's what I want.'

My undampened enthusiasm must have made an impression on them because I was invited to join them on the first leg of the trip to Panama. From then on my sights were entirely focused on getting the £2,000 sponsorship money I needed to be taken on as one of the directing staff. I worked as a nurse in various private London clinics to earn as much as I could. The rest of the money had to be raised by finding some sponsors. This was the chance I had been dreaming of.

4

UP THE JUNGLE

ON 13 DECEMBER 1978, CAROLINE ASH, AN ENTOMOLOGIST, and I arrived with several others at Colon, the port at the northern end of the Panama Canal. We were on our way to Caledonia Bay on Panama's Atlantic coast. We were excited, dying to get down to the real business of the expedition at last. We arrived at Colon at night, marching past the armed guards, who shone their torches into our faces. Our new jungle boots creaked as we passed fishing boats containing families lying in hammocks, smoking quietly.

'Americanos?' they asked.

'No, British!'

We made out the dim outline of the 65-foot Panamanian gunboat we were to travel in silhouetted against the night sky in front of us. Stumbling up the gangway in the pitch dark, we found ourselves on a greasy deck guarded by a flimsy safety rail, some of which had collapsed. We perched ourselves on a shelf near the one and only, very small, lifeboat, which I nervously noted was equipped with only two life jackets and two lifebelts. Neither of us had any idea that we'd be spending fourteen hours on board and that there were no loos.

The engine chugged into action and we were off. A cool breeze blew in our faces, sweeping away the stale smell of sweat and grime and the toxic fumes of the engine. We watched the lights of Colon disappear as we made our way towards the open sea. I ate the sandwich I had brought and took a precautionary seasickness pill. As we approached the mouth of the channel, I could see the waves breaking over the rocks, so I put on my anorak. Once we were in the open, the wind was much stronger and the waves smashed over the boat as we bobbed like a plastic duck on the heaving sea. As some of the guard rail posts collapsed we clung onto anything that didn't move. Somehow I made my way to the back of the boat, where I sat on deck with my legs over the hold twisted around some iron pipes. I got drenched there so I wedged myself into the shallow luggage hold using a bag of soggy sandwiches as a pillow. Higher up on deck, I could see people being sick, the wind spraying their vomit back over them. I felt awful, so I popped another seasickness tablet – kill or cure – and tried to settle. As the boat lurched suddenly, I went sprawling. It was either join the others on deck or retreat to the cabin-cum-engine room below. I chose the latter, where I crawled into the arms of a friendly warrant officer, Paul, a member of the expedition. We clung together as the boat pitched and tossed, and despite being wet and cold, I slipped into oblivion. When I awoke, the sun was shining and the sea was calmer. Paul and I rushed up on deck. We could see land, a jetty, other boats – Caledonia Bay, at last? No. We'd returned to Colon because of engine trouble.

Second time lucky, we arrived at Caledonia Bay.

Caledonia Bay was in the middle of nowhere, close to where a small Scottish trading colony had been established in 1698 at Punta Escocés on the Atlantic coast. Within nine months, maladministration, disease and starvation had forced the early pioneers to abandon the place. On Operation Drake, an archaeological team was dispatched to investigate and excavate this slice of Scottish history.

About twelve of us made up the advance party. Our first job was to make camp, collect fresh water and dig latrines. There was no such thing as Ladies and Gents, and there was no privacy at all. We didn't have the alternative of disappearing discreetly into the jungle because of the danger of getting lost, so Caroline and I would go together to shield one another from prying eyes, although nobody took the least bit of notice of us. I later learned that this was all part of the levelling process calculated to put us all on the

same footing. Nine small marquees were enough for sleeping and stores, all fitted with mosquito nets that kept the
mosquitoes out all right but not the sandflies. Any exposed
parts of the body were viciously bitten until we all looked
as if we had measles.

Once the camp was established, work was started on
clearing an airstrip. Our days quickly took on a regular
routine. To our disappointment, Caroline and I were
immediately assigned to cooking and washing-up duties
while the guys cleared the jungle with flame-throwers and
chainsaws, burning off the rough grass and then chopping
off and levelling the hummocks. We hadn't come all this
way to be stuck in the kitchen, so we hatched a plot to produce only the most basic dishes from our tinned 'compo'
rations. We refused to spice up such gastronomic delights
as beans and pork luncheon meat with a bit of garlic or
curry powder as the men tactfully suggested. Instead we
stuck to simply heating up the tins. Within a couple of
weeks of this a rota system was agreed that shared all the
duties equally between all of us.

The only water we had to wash in was the sea; we were
always sticky and fishy smelling. Imagine the relief when
there was a tropical rainstorm. We rushed to collect the
rainwater off the tents. A bucket each was enough – first
the body, then the hair and lastly the clothes. What luxury!
We took turns to go on the water run every couple of days,
taking a small inflatable four miles up the coast to a water

hole where we'd fill twenty-seven jerry cans with precious fresh water to take back to the camp for drinking and cooking. In high seas, the trip got pretty treacherous as we dodged the coral reefs in a boat swamped with water. We came close to capsizing and being torn to shreds on the coral many times.

Caroline and I quickly became close friends with Mike Christy, a Royal Engineer, and Desmond Duggan, a forester from Scotland. My memories of that Christmas sum up the fun we had together. We were woken with tea and whisky, then we had the morning off, so we took an inflatable to the site of Fort St Andrew, an old Scottish settlement, to look for ruins in the thick jungle. Bathing in a small waterhole was a girl's best present that year. On the way back the engine broke down, so we paddled the rest of the way singing carols. In the afternoon we played volley-ball and had stretcher races until we were ready for a slap-up Christmas dinner made from compo rations in the evening. Although the party went on well into the night, I went to bed early, unable to stop myself thinking of home. I lay looking up at the sky, thinking how my family in England would be looking at the stars too. It made me feel much closer to home.

The Young Explorers started arriving the next day. Some came on the *Eye of the Wind*, while others flew in a few days later with the rest of the equipment in four planes and a helicopter – so our new runway was put to good use.

The camp soon looked more like a scene from *M.A.S.H.*, with boxes and equipment piled along the edge of the run-way and plenty of activity. Several of Panama's Guardia Nacional were permanently attached to us. Clarke, one of the trackers with the Guardia Nacional, would bring me presents of coconuts and once a red-capped woodpecker (dead, of course). The Panamanian soldiers couldn't get over the fact that I, a mere woman, was the one in charge of the health and medical requirements of the expedition. During my evening surgeries, they'd stand and watch while I gave injections and treated minor injuries such as infected sandfly bites, cuts, sea-urchin spines embedded in a foot or scorpion bites. My medical centre soon became very popular, as it was the only place where anyone could legitimately lie down and relax. Needless to say, during the first few weeks, I had many patients who'd keeled over with heatstroke and exhaustion. I was also promoted to camp hairdresser, as I was the only one with a decent pair of scissors and wouldn't let them out of my sight.

Various projects got under way. A few days after New Year, Caroline, Des and Mike trekked inland with the engineers, scientists and two Gurkhas on adventure train-ing, for the jungle location where work was to begin on a series of canopy walkways at least 100 feet above the jungle floor. Tropical rainforest is not a renewable resource so it was hoped detailed studies of the forest canopy would help to demonstrate its benefits to the world as a whole. I was impatient to join them. Then the message came that one of the Gurkhas had injured himself, catching his fingers between the ropes of the block and tackle. Our leader, George Thurston, instructed me to go up with the next supply train so that I could dress the injured hand daily, and remain on site to deal with any other casualties.

We found the jungle campsite on the bank of a wide bend in the River Turdi. To my relief, most of the snakes and scorpions seemed to have been frightened away, but there were plenty of exotic-coloured frogs, lizards, beetles and giant grasshoppers in their place. There were fewer sandflies than at Caledonia Bay but instead there were giant ants whose sting was awful. It was vital never to stand still for too long in one place or else they'd be up your legs biting. Our twelve hammocks were strung up fairly close together between the trees with a mackintosh or ground-sheet rigged up over each one to keep off the rain – very cosy. Above us, the thick primeval forest rose to 150 feet, letting very little sunshine through to the forest floor. The jungle was every bit as beautiful as I'd anticipated. There were small rushing torrents with lots of little waterfalls, with orchids hanging from the trees on the river banks; and enormous butterflies with wings that were black underneath, brilliant turquoise blue on top and flashed as they fluttered by. If you wore red and stood perfectly still, you'd hear a whirring sound getting louder and louder, and then, slowly turning, you'd see a tiny hummingbird hovering beside you, its wings a blur.

Every morning Clarke, our tracker and guide from the Guardia Nacional, woke us up at six, playing the reveille by blowing down the barrel of his rifle. I held a clinic first thing in the morning and last thing at night. But I wasn't the kind of person to sit idly round in camp waiting for someone to be sick or injured, so I volunteered to help build the canopy walkway. The platform was 100 feet above the forest floor while the walkway itself stretched about 150 feet between trees, suspended on ropes. The walkway floor was sixteen inches wide, made of metal strips with razor-sharp edges, so there were plenty of lacerations as well as torn clothing. Everything was taken up on a rope pulley system. Initially I worked as the 'gofer', sending the stuff up and then watching my head as nuts, bolts and screwdrivers crashed their way down eighty feet and more, burying themselves deep in the earth round me.

When work began on the second walkway, I was allowed up at last. People who visited us quaked at the thought of going up the hoist, let alone walking along the contraption, the whole thing swaying gently in the breeze. It needed quite a nerve to hang out over the side clipped on to a safety line and fix the nuts and bolts underneath, but I quickly got used to it, working eight hours a day up there, week after week, bolt by bolt. My hands were ruined, full of calluses, with fingers that were stiff and aching every evening. But all this was nothing compared to the exhilaration I felt at being part of the whole experience.

Like the Royal Engineer, Mike, and Des, the forester, I learned to understand the canopy walkway's every movement. Of course the work had its scary moments. Once I was about 110 feet up a new tree on my own with no platform. I had to climb the last 10 feet by clinging on to creepers. The view up there was marvellous. I could even catch a glimpse of our campsite. But as I worked my way down, I slipped and fell about 12 feet before being caught by the safety line. I managed to scramble the rest of the way down, supporting most of my weight on my arms, to shouts from below as bits of dead wood hailed down on them.

I often helped Caroline set up her insect traps at different heights along the walkway. With a fellow entomologist, she was researching the vertical zonation of insects. At night, the insect traps shone with an ultraviolet light to attract the insects. It looked like fairyland up there.

The can-do mentality drummed into me by my father stood me in good stead for all this and I loved every second. When the time came to build the third walkway, I was the only helper available, so Mike asked me if I'd be prepared to help him fix the block for the main rope about 120 feet up.

'It's difficult and not too safe because you've got to balance on the branches up there. But of course you don't have to do it if you're scared.'

That did it. I agreed to help immediately.

The tree was pitoned up – in other words, steel pegs had been inserted up the trunk to act as a ladder, and a hoist system put in place. Mike went up the rope first, pulling up his own weight. When he reached the top I clipped on and he started hoisting me up. Up and up I went, through branches full of leaves, past the hornets' nest, up among the dangling vines. I wedged myself into the angle of a large branch, clipped on to the flimsy safety line, and prepared to take the strain of the block and the rope and other tools with which Mike was working well above my head. It took about an hour and a half to finish that part of the job before Mike sailed down to the ground on the hoist, while I clung to the tree. Then it was my turn. I clipped myself on to the hoist and descended slowly. Suddenly, about 25 feet from the ground, the rope jammed and I was left dangling – a knot must have formed and stuck in the block above. There was nothing for it but to climb back up. At the top, I got my weight off the rope to half kneel and half sit on the bough. As I grabbed for a stray line, my hold on the hoist relaxed and the rope whistled through my hand out of control. It jammed and jumped out of the block ten feet above my head. Below me, there were furious shouts.

My eyes filled with tears, my vision blurred and I began to shake with fear. I was 120 feet up, perched on a slippery branch, with no means of getting down. What's more, ants were crawling over me, flies and spiders too, but I couldn't scratch myself in case I fell. The air below me was still blue from Mike's angry yells but I knew he would do something to help me. So for the third time that morning he climbed the tree, courageously pulling himself up on a rope that had jammed and could slip at any moment. Finally he reached the hoist and set about freeing it. I didn't dare look and made myself concentrate on the view: I could see the river far down below, blue and orange birds flying near by, woodpeckers, hummingbirds – and crawling along the branch next to mine a snake! At 120 feet up I tried to shift my position. My feet had gone to sleep. I kept a wary eye open for other creepy crawlies. In the distance a tree crashed down as mine swayed gently in the breeze. My mouth was dry and I was dripping with sweat. At last Mike was on his way down again, but 15 feet from the ground, he missed his grip and fell, the rope tearing through his hands, burning them. My heart stopped, but he shouted that he wasn't badly hurt and then that he was ready. I clipped on to the hoist and launched myself into space. I free fell for several feet before I felt the rope and harness taking the strain. Then I spiralled down to the ground. It had never felt so good. My legs were shaking.

That afternoon I was back up in the treetops, starting work on the bridge proper. It's amazing what you can do when you have to; the extent of human endurance is limit-less. That's what I learned that day in Panama. Besides, there was much work to be done if the bridge was to be finished before I went on the planned Membrillo River

Project, in which the entomologists were to study the dreaded buffalo gnat, an insect so vicious that it had driven the local Indians from the area. When I could, I'd been in training with Mike. Once we had walked up the river for a solid two and a half hours, negotiating our way round rocks and boulders and through enormous pools, swimming with our packs above our heads. Only afterwards did the Guardia tell us that they'd caught four alligators in there that week. However my training was for nothing. Only a few hours before we were to go, I collapsed into my hammock with a raging fever, becoming delirious during the night. It was decided that I should be evacuated to hospital. Mike, Peter Hudson, the ornithologist, and the two Gurkhas carried me out, strapped tightly to the stretcher. They carried me for three hours across rough terrain through the dripping rainforest, over rivers, gullies, and tree trunks, and up and down slippery steep hills until finally we reached the coast. There I was put in an in-flatable boat for Caledonia Bay, where a plane was waiting to fly me to Panama City hospital. I was diagnosed a month later with leptospirosis, caught, they thought, from contact with rat's urine. Lying in my hospital bed, I had time to reflect on what I'd been doing for the last two months. I watched the trees outside my window and yearned to get back to my friends and the jungle. I remembered the bliss of falling into a hammock after a hard day's work, wet clothes and all, or sitting round the campfire brewing tea, watching bats swooping up and down the river, catching a glimpse through the trees of the stars, listening to Andrew, one of the botanists, play his guitar. Eventually I was passed fit and returned to the camp where I learned that the walkway had been named after me in my absence – Bertschinger Way. I was very touched.

The walkway completed, it was time to return home to England. I had at last lived the adventure that I'd been looking for. I had pushed myself to the limits. It had been wonderful to be accepted as a member of the team. What's more, once I'd shown my true colours, I had been invited to join the phase of the operation in Papua New Guinea. As I sat on the plane planning how I would raise the funds to join Operation Drake on the next leg of its journey, I remembered the words of a poem by an RAF pilot that my parents had framed and given to me for my birthday:

> *Oh! I have slipped the surly bonds of earth*
> *And danced the skies on laughter-silvered wings;*
> *Sunward I've climbed, and joined the tumbling mirth*
> *Of sun-split clouds – and done a hundred things*
> *You have not dreamed of . . .*

5

MAGGOTS AND MANGOES

BY THE TIME I GOT HOME, A LUMP HAD APPEARED ON THE side of my cheek that I assumed was some tropical infection. During an operation to biopsy it, my salivary gland was accidentally cauterized. I was left with a fistula in the side of my face – basically a hole from the salivary gland to the outside of my cheek that dripped saliva. I hated having to hold a plate under my chin to catch the drips while I was eating. After several months of unsuccessful treatment, the consultant decided to remove the salivary gland. This was a major operation from which it took me some time to recover. However, it was great to be home, to see my family again, to smell the air and to taste fruit and vegetables from the garden – all things I'd missed while away. Nonetheless I was consumed with impatience to rejoin Operation Drake.

Finally, in October 1979, I flew to Papua New Guinea. A two-hour boat journey south from Lae along the coast took me to Buso, where the main scientific camp had been set up. Close by, three aerial walkways had again been constructed by the Royal Engineers to enable comparative studies of the rainforest's complex ecosystem, with collections of plant samples, light traps for insects and mist traps to catch bats for ringing. My job was to run the medical centre.

Every evening I held a surgery for the expedition members and the villagers. Within the first four days, I treated four cases of malaria. Otherwise the ailments were mostly unspecific fevers and septic ulcers. One day I was upriver helping collect wood with which to build a pier when we met a dug-out canoe carrying a local boy who'd badly cut his foot with a machete. The vines tied round his thigh and ankle made inefficient tourniquets and had been on for four hours. We took him in our inflatable to the village, where I gave him a jab of penicillin and sutured his wound, with the whole village straining to watch through the open doorway of the medical centre hut. Without us, his injury would have been bound in a dressing of mud and leaves and left to fortune. As it was, his wound soon healed well. When the village children were brought to me with malarial fever, I'd give them chloroquine crushed into a spoonful of jam, followed by a sweet to cover the disgusting taste. There was a lot of diarrhoea and vomiting around

– hardly surprising given the flies that got everywhere. We regularly ate the writhing white maggots that we found in our oats, cooking them up in our porridge. We even had maggots in the latrines – and this despite our rigorous cleaning ritual. Every day we took it in turns to clean the latrines with disinfectant and water. Then we'd pour in lime and dribble a line of petrol like a fuse, light it and run back and watch it explode – boom! It was pretty impressive. Particularly when someone put in too much petrol one day and burnt the whole thing down – shelter and all.

I derived enormous pleasure from the community health work that I did with the villagers. I tried to teach them little points of hygiene, like washing hands and keeping sores clean. It got a bit frustrating when *tubuna* (Grandma) would insist on blowing her nose with her fingers and wiping them on the floor of the medical centre. Because I knew we'd be leaving soon, I found a local girl keen to learn the basics of home nursing, St John Ambulance style. I gave her a few basics to use when I'd gone – soap, antiseptic solution and cream, gauze, bandages, plaster, aspirin and so on. Because she couldn't read, I taught her to distinguish the different creams and lotions by smell. I drew her little pictures – for example, for how to use aspirin I drew a picture of an adult beside a whole tablet, a child beside a half tablet and an infant beside a quarter.

I also learned the ins and outs of being a radio operator, quickly striking up a down-the-wire acquaintance with the

Lae operator, 'Pronto', who promised to take me out to dinner when I got back to civilization. He'd regale me with descriptions of mouthwatering menus at the local restaurants while I sat drooling before going off to eat my tinned pilchards and dried eggs.

Thanks to my operation, I had only six weeks in Papua New Guinea instead of the planned six months. But then I was asked to join the Indonesian phase of the expedition, initially as part of the advance party there. Kolonodale in central Sulawesi, where we were to establish base camp, turned out to be a large village of about four thousand people, half of them children, who lived in shacks or 'boogie' boats about twenty feet long and six feet wide. They were very poor and dressed in rags, but they were a happy people who were unfailingly friendly and welcoming.

I had been asked to bring a parcel for the English teacher, Maria, and was told that I'd find her at the church. So on our first full day there, 30 December, the quartermaster Ted Carradus and I set off to find her. I had decided to 'go native' and wore a beautiful batik sarong that I'd bought in the local market. The small wooden building had a high-pitched roof with a simple wooden cross on top. Inside, it was absolutely packed with worshippers. Half an hour late, Ted and I crept in quietly at the back, but as we arrived the priest stopped the service. Foreigners were a rarity in this remote part of Sulawesi, and we were

Claire wins her wings

CLAIRE Bertschinger, 21, of Little Acre, Sheering, is a high flyer.

With sights set at becoming a "flying sister" she's just won her private pilot's

to use St John trol cent Hospital training.

Student nurse aims to become a flying sister

Flying Claire—at the controls. (505)

ABOVE: From a local paper
FAR LEFT: My parents on their engagement in 1943
LEFT: Andrew, me, Richard and Anne-Marie

ABOVE: Learning to fly
LEFT: Student nurse

Panama walkway:
one hundred feet
up without a
parachute

OPERATION DRAKE

RIGHT:
Phil, Kelvin
and I on Mt
Tambusisi

BELOW, CENTRE:
The python
that ended
up as dinner

BELOW, RIGHT:
Building
the walkway
with Mike

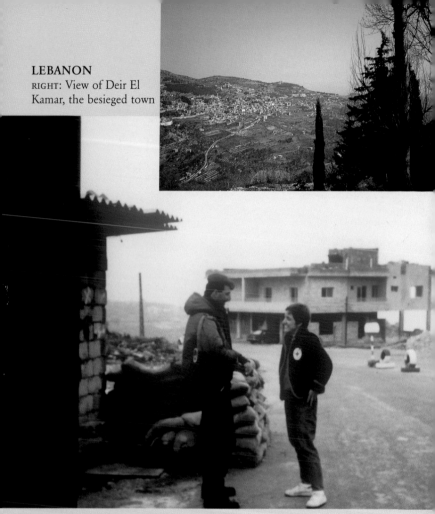

LEBANON
RIGHT: View of Deir El Kamar, the besieged town

ABOVE: Negotiating safe passage at a checkpoint in the Chouf mountains
LEFT: Convoy waiting at Israeli checkpoint

ETHIOPIA

BELOW: The selection procedure

LEFT: Afar baby suffering from malnutrition
RIGHT: Abuhanna and her father

LEFT: The two village children who adopted us in Maichew

ABOVE: The cholera outbreak
ABOVE, RIGHT: Cheeky Hagos with my stethoscope
BELOW: Outside the feeding centre in Mekele

ABOVE, LEFT: Measuring the children's height
ABOVE, RIGHT: The kitchen in Maichew
RIGHT: Me with some of my children

The unwanted flowers

welcomed and shown to the best seats in the front row. Afterwards we found Maria, who spoke good English and seemed to know everyone. Her husband was an economist but as there was no call for economists in Kolonodale, he relied on occasional casual work to supplement her teacher's salary of less than £20 a month. She explained to me that in her country women talked only to other women and never to a man outside their family. I noticed that she was uncomfortable with Ted there, even though she was so friendly to me. She also asked me why I was wearing a sarong. 'For us, this is peasant clothes,' she explained. 'We put on Western clothes for best, to go to church.' The locals found it highly amusing. I was mortified.

I went back to church with Maria several times after that. On New Year's Day, the service was dedicated to 'the English visitors', and I was the only one of our party there. I was very moved as Maria explained the service to me. When a prayer was said in English for all those far away from home, my eyes filled with tears. When they saw how touched I was, all the congregation started weeping with me, which of course only made me sob harder. I couldn't help feeling homesick, thinking of my parents, crisp frosty mornings and spicy Swiss Christmas biscuits.

The contacts I made through my friendship with Maria and the people at the church enabled our team to forge ahead quickly. I loved every minute. The base camp we were establishing was about three kilometres up the Ranu

River from the village and needed boats and helpers to get stores and equipment there. Every evening after a hard day's work, Maria would come with me to visit useful contacts in their homes. We were always offered tea and cake, which we couldn't refuse without causing offence. Children followed us everywhere, calling out 'Hello, Mister' in English. I taught them to say 'Hello, Miss Claire' as well. One evening someone brought a guitar to Maria's house. We played and sang, and then they asked me to dance Western style. People gathered round the windows, craning to see what was going on inside. The only dancing they knew was to local music played on bamboo flutes. We were the first Europeans most of them had seen. They couldn't get over me doing 'man's work' such as lifting and carrying heavy loads or chopping bamboo: in Sulawesi, women didn't do that sort of thing. They were astonished when I volunteered to be lowered head first down the local well to retrieve the bucket that I'd dropped down there. The same day, we were loading two dug-out canoes with outriggers. To reach them, we had to walk a precarious plank. I overbalanced and fell into the filthy polluted water, to great laughter from the crowd.

I'd never been to such a remote place as this, completely cut off from the modern world with no television, no cinema, no phones, no bank and only a few shops of sorts. Our only means of communication with the outside world was via our own HF radio by voice or Morse code. One day

I watched the local doctor, a lovely chap, perform an appendectomy by torchlight with only a rusty scalpel and local anaesthetic. The patient felt no pain and afterwards hopped off the table and walked back to bed. Doc Martin claimed to have carried out forty such operations over the past eighteen months and that all had been successful. I found it hard to believe, especially since I'd been given the job of swatting the flies that buzzed in through the broken window, but accepted that that was the way things were done.

I fell victim to local medical practice myself when I trod on a rusty nail sticking out of a piece of wood. I managed to pull it out, but all the watching villagers became tremendously excited, screaming, 'Infection, infection.' Our boat boy grabbed the large piece of wood with the nail and began hitting my wounded foot with it. I could just about bear the pain and I decided to see what he would do next. After about a minute, he stopped and began to squeeze the wound with his dirty nails to make it bleed. After alternating the bashing and squeezing, he rubbed some spit into the wound, at which point I said enough, thank you. As soon as I was out of their sight, I washed it in the sea and dabbed it vigorously with antiseptic.

Gradually base camp took shape. With the help of locals, we built a group of huts on stilts. We slung our hammocks inside and I made my corner home by knocking up a few shelves and pinning my Christmas cards on the rattan sides.

I made a pillow from corrugated cardboard stuffed with straw and covered with a towel – much more comfortable than the medical book I'd been using before. In the evenings I'd often join the locals round their camp fire. We'd drink weak tea, I'd practise my Indonesian and in return I'd amuse them by playing the spoons – a handy skill learned from my mother. During the day, we cleared the land and built other huts, a *runah makun* (dining room) and a *runah sakit* (medical hut) that I was allowed to design, although my leg was constantly pulled about my ideas. It turned into a five-by-four-metre room with windows covered in palm screens that could be raised or lowered by a wooden counterweight. It had a bed, shelves, a washing area and a working surface that slid back under the bed on a runner. One of the engineers surprised me by making a carved wooden 'Wendy House' sign, while, not to be outdone, another surrounded the hut with a two-bar fence so that I could at last have my own garden and plant seeds I had brought from home. I was kept busy tending machete wounds and even operating to extract a large wooden splinter from someone's foot.

Finally we were ready for the arrival of the rest of the party of scientists and the Young Explorers at the end of January.

3 February 1980. Official radio signal. Camp Ranu to HQ Operation Drake in London

Mt Tambusisi climbed by Operation team. The 7946ft. mountain was scaled yesterday by a joint British Indonesian team led by Sgt Phil Maye, 26, a Royal Engineer Surveyor from Army Apprentices School, Chepstow. With him were two Indonesian Young Explorers, Claire Bertschinger SRN, from Bishop's Stortford, together with Cpl. Kelvin Cunningham, Royal Signals. The original party included two Indonesian guides and a British ornithologist who dropped out through exhaustion. The guides also dropped out through malaria and reaching limits of the jungle unknown to them. Tambusisi rises with alpine steepness from sea level and outrivals many a European climb. For the last 2100ft. the climbers had to hack their way almost vertically through thick montane rainforest ironically short of water due to the steepness of gradient and lack of streams. The mountain is believed to have been climbed only once before in the 1920s by a Dutch surveyor. The climb was important to the expedition in order to establish a control point for the mapping of 2000sq. kilometres of the Morowali Area of Sulawesi Central Province. Here the Operation Drake Team in co-operation with the Indonesian Institute of Science and the World Wildlife Fund are all carrying out a multi-discipline Scientific Survey which it is hoped will lead to the establishment of a National Park. Major Derek Jackson, the Operation expedition leader, said, 'I am delighted that not only Tambusisi has been climbed, enabling us to produce a first-class map, but the climbing team represented every facet of the expedition.'

The reality behind that signal was the most gruelling adventure I had experienced yet.

To begin with, things went well. We crossed the grassy plain towards Mount Tambusisi and then began our climb. It was tough going, especially in the sweltering heat, and we needed many stops. At midday we came to a clearing with a fast-running mountain stream. We had a lunch of dried compo rations, biscuits and tinned cheese, and a refreshing dip, before crossing to a clearing on the other side, where the grass grew lush and green to well above my waist. Suddenly, some way in front of us, we saw someone running. It was a woman of the Wana tribe holding two long blowpipes which were used with poison darts for hunting. Hama, the older of our two local guides, called to her in Wana and went to talk to her. He came back, telling us that the Wana dislike white people, especially those in green jungle fatigues like ours. In the 1950s they had been attacked by similarly dressed Dutch soldiers and many people had been killed. He said it was dangerous to go through Wana country to Tambusisi: there was every like-lihood that they'd shoot at us with poisoned darts. He was very scared and thought we should offer them cigarettes.

Our only smoker immediately got out his precious stash, but by the time he found them, the Wana woman had vanished.

The sun was blazing down on us as we reached the next ridge. We saw a Wana woman and two children running away from a small hut, and Hama went over to talk to them. After a while they cautiously returned and we went over to meet them. One of the children had a large infected area on the back of his neck as well as some nasty scarring. It looked as though he'd been attacked and bitten by something, though they couldn't tell us what. The woman told me, through Hama, that it had been like that for two years, although they'd tried to heal the wound by covering it with mud and palm leaves. The boy let me clean it with antiseptic and I advised the mother to wash it every day with soap that I gave her and water. I wished I could do more.

As evening fell we made camp at another stream, replenishing our water supply, as the guides told us we wouldn't find more until the following evening. We slung up our hammocks, made a fire, cooked our dehydrated goulash and went to bed early. So far it had been very hard going but I was glad that no one was making any allowances for me. As the first woman to have tackled the climb, I was determined not to let down the other members of the team or myself. Like the others, I carried my own 30lb pack which included my rations, the medical pack, part of the radio equipment, a cotton sleeping bag and a spare cotton tracksuit.

The next morning we set off early. Bill, the ornithologist, was having a lot of trouble with cramp in one leg and by ten o'clock he had decided that he couldn't continue and would return with Wustum, the Indonesian soldier, to last night's campsite to await our return. Now we were only seven. We continued down a slight incline and then behind me Kelvin, the Royal Signaller, exclaimed, 'Oh no! Are we supposed to go up there?' I looked up and saw practically vertical, forest-covered mountainside in front of me. There was nothing for it but to follow a narrow trail through rattan thorns that tore at our clothes, drawing blood. Higher and higher we went, our hearts pumping, climbing for an hour and then resting for ten minutes. We were soaked in sweat, gasping for breath, our mouths dry. At a rest stop I took our pulses. Mine was thumping at 138 beats a minute; the others' were even higher. We carried on up a slightly gentler incline until we broke camp for the night. We washed in the mountain stream, removing leeches with a lighted cigarette, and washed our shirts and trousers. They wouldn't be dry by morning but at least they'd be fresher.

The next day, we left as much kit behind as we could, taking only the bare necessities including our water bottles. Blazing our own trail, and hauling ourselves over fallen tree trunks and huge rocks, we climbed upwards and upwards into the montane rainforest, which was hot and humid with everything covered in moss, and where we clambered over huge tree roots that twisted and inter-twined above the ground. With our machetes, we cut down vines and drained and drank their water, so as to preserve our own supply a bit longer.

Then Hama developed a fever and decided he'd return to the last camp to wait for our return. Mindan, the other guide, decided to join him. Now we were five. We clambered on up through this weird, eerie landscape. Every time we reached a summit, there was another one beyond. My mind was saying, 'Go! Go! Go!' but my legs screamed back, 'No! No! No!' At 16.30 we collapsed, exhausted, with only 2 pints of fresh water left in our water bottles even though we had supplemented it with the bitter water trapped in the giant fly-catching pitcher plants. It was only afterwards that we learned that these plants used enzymes to break down the flies and moths that got trapped inside them – oh well, they added protein. The sky was beginning to cloud over, so we set up a rain trap, stringing a poncho between trees with a dip on one side so water would collect and run down into a strategically placed tin. Then we downed a quick meal of dehydrated stew and prayed for rain as we crawled into the shelter we'd made. The wind got up, the temperature dropped and it suddenly started to rain – our prayers had been answered. We tried to huddle together to keep warm but by 03.00 I was frozen and shivering. Kelvin told me to buddy up in his sleeping bag – a survival technique that I was only too pleased to adopt. Not that I fancied him: I was just bloody cold.

I woke just before sunrise to discover that we'd collected enough water to fill three bottles. We all felt refreshed and set off again to reach our goal. After one and a half hours' climbing, we reached the summit. The view was breath-taking: it was as if we were standing on top of the world. Had I known at the start what I was in for, I don't think I could have faced it, but having done it I had proved to myself that where there's a will there surely is a way. And now I was the first woman ever to have climbed Mount Tambusisi.

We checked the altimeter and set up the survey flag on the summit's trigonometry point. There were two old wine bottles there with messages inside them – no doubt left by the Dutch surveying party many years before. The paper had disintegrated, so we couldn't read them, but we put our own messages inside for the next expedition that made it up there. Our mission accomplished, we slipped, slid and jumped from boulder to tree as we made our way down the mountain, elated by our success and eager to get to good food and fresh water before nightfall.

Back at Ranu Camp, life went on much as expected. An aerial walkway was erected nearby and work was carried out there by scientists with the help of the Young Explorers, while various groups ventured out to survey and map a huge area of forest to aid the Indonesian government in establishing the Morowali Nature Reserve. The next big drama was when Kelvin, my Royal Signaller buddy, came down with a dreadful earache.

He thought he must have picked up an infection from swimming in the river, which was polluted by the locals using it both for washing and as a toilet. That night he was in great pain. I radioed the doctor on the *Eye of the Wind*, explaining Kelvin's symptoms. He thought it sounded like mastoiditis, an infection of the bone behind the ear, and that we should get a specialist's opinion. Kelvin was extremely anxious that if it permanently damaged his ear he would be forced to give up his role in the army parachute team. We decided to evacuate him to Soarko, about 150 kilometres to the south, where the International Nickel Company (INCO) was based in a large community with a fully equipped American health centre, far more sophisticated than the health clinic at Kolonodale. We set off downriver in the inflatable, with Kelvin on a stretcher on its floor with a poncho rigged up as a sunscreen. When we reached Kolonodale, there was the usual crowd to greet us, this time with 'Oh! Mr Kelvin sakit [sick].' We had arranged to borrow a helicopter and I went to discuss the flight with the pilot and ask him to fly at as low an altitude as possible, which was essential to prevent Kelvin's eardrum from perforating. I clambered aboard, propping Kelvin against the door and supporting his head with life jackets when we found that the cabin was too small for the stretcher.

It was an alarming but exhilarating forty-minute flight through thundering rain that made its way in through the gaps in the fuselage, as the pilot flew low along the valleys and round the mountains, finding his way through almost nil visibility to our destination. Suddenly the rain stopped, visibility returned and we saw an enormous lake with Soarko on the far side. As we circled, looking for a helicopter pad, we could see what an incredibly neat township it was: serried ranks of houses, cars, buses, a church and a school. It could have been somewhere in the United States, not a clearing bang in the middle of the Sulawesi jungle. The obvious landing place was the school playground. Kids and teachers hung out of the school windows as I jumped down and ran towards them to ask the way to the hospital. The teacher I spoke to said she'd tell us the way if she could come too. Why not? So to the amazement of her pupils she hopped in and directed us a few hundred yards to a convenient football pitch. Then she walked back to work.

The hospital was a clean, modern building with nurses in spotless white and blue uniforms. An American doctor admitted Kelvin immediately and whisked him off to a private room with clean sheets and a soft bed. I stayed with him for a couple of hours, although he wasn't really conscious of what was going on. Then the senior nurse took me away for a bath with lovely hot water and scented soap before giving me clean clothes and a snack of fresh bread with real butter and ham, mango and ice-cream. I even got a raw apple and a glass of really cold fresh orange juice. Mangoes were in season at the time and while I was there I gorged myself on two or three a day. Such luxuries. When I had the chance to look in a mirror, I got quite a shock: it was the first time I'd seen myself since one of the Young Explorers had cut my hair to one inch long all over with my surgical scissors.

Kelvin was kept in hospital on massive doses of antibiotics and it was five days before we could think of returning to camp. The helicopter had left, and taking a detour with an INCO plane to Kendari before making our way home from there would take at least ten days. So we decided to walk it over the mountains.

We set off one morning at five thirty, having said farewell to everyone who had helped us. After crossing the lake by speedboat, we followed a path across the plain and through the jungle-covered hills. We'd been told by our guide that it was an easy walk, but unfortunately the recent week of intermittent rain meant that the track was a quagmire: mud, mud and more mud. After only a couple of hours we were exhausted, sometimes getting stuck knee deep and having to pull each other out. Neither of us dared let on to the other how we felt. Many times, my eyes blurry and stinging with sweat, all I could think was, 'Why am I doing this? Let's stop and sit down.' But, like Kelvin, I kept on smiling and repeating, 'We're doing fine. Keep going. We'll soon be at Betaleme [a small village *en route*].' To make matters worse, Kelvin, already weakened by his illness, was weighed down by cans of beer he'd hidden in his rucksack. There was no alcohol available in camp so he had decided to take some presents back for his friends. Eventually we had no choice but to leave them behind, Kelvin almost crying with disappointment. Our guide was thoroughly bemused. The plimsolls on our feet had soon shrunk in the wet mud and were crippling us. Not having expected to be doing any walking, we had left our boots at the camp. In the end, we had to take them off and walk for the last few hours in bare feet. What a way for Kelvin to convalesce! A few days later my big toe nails would go black and drop off – a fine souvenir.

Just as it was getting dark, and 55 kilometres later, we arrived at the village of Pono and decided to stop for the night there. We were ushered to one of the straw and wooden huts, where we were to sleep on floor mats, after being offered the usual fried plantain and sweet black tea. As I was drinking, I noticed a bottle in the middle of the table. It seemed to contain a pickled animal foetus about six inches long. After further enquiries and many gestures, we understood that the foetus was a dog's and its pickling alcohol was used as a tonic. Despite refusing it, we found the strength to complete the walk the next day.

Soon afterwards, time ran out for the Ranu Camp. So did my time with Operation Drake. I said my goodbyes and headed back to the UK. Without much of an idea of what I would do next, my first stop was, as it was always to be, with my family in the safety of the quiet Essex countryside where I had grown up, the place where I had fostered my childhood dreams and ambitions and where the seeds had been sown for all my future adventures.

6

DYSLEXIA RULES K.O.

'YOUR FATHER'S ON THE WARPATH!' THAT CRY WOULD send me hurtling into the wood at the end of the garden. I hadn't a clue what was meant by it. What war? What path? But I knew I'd be safely out of the way, hidden in the trees, until the worst was over. That's my first real memory of my childhood – peeping through the leaves to see if the coast was clear.

I remember my father as a strict disciplinarian. He loved his family absolutely but he had high standards that he'd inherited from his parents and he expected us to match them. He was a meticulous man with a fierce temper. I was good at keeping out of his way when storm clouds threatened and doing what was 'right' to keep them at bay.

My father's father, Charles (Karl) Bertschinger, had

emigrated from Switzerland to London in 1898 as a penniless twenty-year-old, to seek his fortune. My father's mother was Swiss too. She had come to England to teach French. They met, fell in love and made their first home in Elm Grove, Haringey, in north-east London, where in 1915 my father John was born, the fourth of seven children.

During the 1920s my grandfather established his own silk business. Then, at the outbreak of war, my grandparents decided to move out of London and bought Bonnyvale, a modest but elegant Georgian house standing in five acres of land in Sheering in Essex. Our family have lived in the area ever since. The city-based office of C. Bertschinger & Co. Ltd was destroyed during the Blitz, so Grandpapa transferred it to outbuildings in the grounds of the family home until new London premises were found. The family became pretty well self-sufficient, keeping hens, rabbits and bees. With Grandpapa's Swiss farming background standing them in good stead, there was soon a thriving smallholding that provided all the vegetables and fruit they needed. The country had been urged by the government to 'dig for victory', and my grandfather always had surplus produce that was sold locally in Sawbridgeworth.

My father, who had left school in north London in 1931 to study in Lausanne then do his Swiss national service, returned home and soon enlisted in the British Army. He served throughout north-west Europe after the D-Day landings. It was while he was at home on leave that he met my mother, Rene White, who was working as a land girl near by. Mummy was from the East End of London, her father having worked in Billingsgate fish market all his life. Her grandfather's name was Nightingale, and family legend maintains that we're descendants of Florence Nightingale. I'm not sure whether I believe it but I like to think it might be true.

My parents' courtship was brief, Papa proposing after only a fortnight. At first Mummy hesitated but she remembers Papa's sister Elizabeth pointing out, 'You know, if you marry John, he'll be very loyal and he'll always look after you.' It swung the balance. And the following sixty years of their married life proved her right.

They were married at the Swiss Church in London on 23 January 1944 and lived with Papa's parents at Bonnyvale, eventually building a small house for themselves in the grounds. The foundation stone is still there with the half crown underneath that they put there for luck. They called the house Little Acre and moved in just after the birth of my oldest brother Andrew in 1947. He was followed by Richard, Anne-Marie and, finally, me. By this time Papa had joined the family firm and began commuting daily to and from London.

My own childhood was spent happily in the country. A short-haired tomboy, I preferred to spend most of my time on my own, helping in the garden or playing in the forest and fields around our house. I climbed trees, tried to trap animals, whittled tools from wood, made shelters and cooked apples over wood fires. There were often orphaned animals from a neighbouring smallholding to look after. I spent at least one summer proudly taking a lamb for walks on a lead with the dog. My brother Andrew was a rebel, constantly disobeying Papa and driving him into a fury. Richard was the quiet one. He was very musical and used to disappear after school to practise the piano or violin. Away from home, my big sister Anne-Marie acted as my protector. If anyone even said 'boo' to me at school, she'd be there to bully them back. As far as I was concerned, with her long blonde hair she was the pretty, clever one. I felt I was always dancing in her shadow. I was thought of as the quiet one, the one without the looks, always seen as the 'good girl'.

My father encouraged us to be as self-sufficient as possible, teaching us to repair punctures on our bikes, to read maps and timetables, to start the motor mower and fill it with petrol, to change light bulbs and to chop wood. When I eventually started driving, he made sure that I knew how to change a tyre, check the oil and so on. These skills were to stand me in good stead throughout the years, but particularly that time in the Lebanon when I found myself stranded under enemy fire with a puncture.

Despite having been brought up in England, Papa had inherited from his parents a strong pride in his Swissness that extended from the way he dressed to the way he ran his life – and indeed ours. His suits looked continental, and even when he wore shorts for working in the garden, he always exchanged his sunhat for a beret when the weather turned cold. Practical, efficient and organized might have been the watchwords that guided him. He not only retained dual Swiss/British nationality for himself but insisted that we kept it too. Although as a child I had no idea of the significance of this, it was to be one of his greatest gifts to me, for without it, I would have been ineligible to join the ICRC, which only admitted Swiss nationals, and my life would have turned out very differently.

Every two years we went to Switzerland, all six of us piled into the car with the camping equipment packed round us. There was never any question of finding a camp-site. We'd just pull up at the side of a road and set up camp wherever we liked the look of a place, laying out a tarpaulin so that we could sleep under the stars. We cooked basic but satisfying one-pot meals on open fires when we could and on a paraffin stove when we couldn't. Sometimes we holidayed in the south of France, settling in a campsite right next to the beach. We'd spend all day in our swimming costumes, in and out of the water, snorkelling and swimming. We'd bring back sea urchins to the tent, gut them and put them out for the ants. They would stink the tent out but we didn't mind. When the ants had finished with them, we'd boil up the delicately coloured shells ready to take home. I also remember surrounding the tent with a trail of DDT powder (those were the days before its danger was appreciated) to deter the ants attracted by the smell of the dead animals and shells we'd smuggled into the tent.

Our holidays had more than a passing similarity to scout camps, with Papa as scout leader teaching us how to make fires, how to put up tents, where to situate them (not by the river but somewhere the grass was even), how to dig a latrine, how to dig a trench around the tent when rain was forecast, how to tell the time by the sun, and how to read maps and recognize foreign road signs. The most important thing he drilled into us was to leave the place in a better state than when we found it.

This love of the outdoors extended to our life at home too. During the summer, my parents had a bed outside so that they could sleep under the stars, yanking a tarpaulin over themselves if it rained. Eventually they put up a transparent corrugated roof for permanent protection. We children often camped out in the garden. I love sleeping in a tent even now. It's the smell of the canvas, the dew on the grass, the rain on the leaves. It's seeing the stars, being able to walk in bare feet outside, the air, the sound of the morning chorus. To this day, I wear shoes as little as possible and I hate being in a room without the doors and windows open.

We often ate outside too. Our diet was very Swiss, with plenty of sauerkraut, vegetables, salad, and fruit from the garden. We were never allowed sweets or snacks between meals. Grace was said before each meal, sometimes in French – the language Mummy and Papa resorted to when they wanted to talk in secret. The family had stopped speaking in their native Swiss-German long ago, during the time when the Second World War loomed.

Now as I look back, I realize that so much of what I took for granted was inherited from my father's upbringing and in some ways made us different from our friends. Our house was always surrounded by tubs of geraniums during the summer. In the garden, the grass had to be cut, raked into a straight line with a Swiss hay rake, rolled up and carried on a pitchfork to the compost heap. You didn't see anyone else doing that in England.

Petite, attractive and always very tanned, Mummy quickly adopted the role of a 'continental' wife and in fact was the one who pushed our Swissness most. She really enjoyed being different. With elocution lessons she had soon lost her East End accent. Her cousin Matilda once advised her, 'It doesn't matter about a hat. You're always dressed if you're wearing a smart pair of earrings.' It was advice that she passed on to me, and even in the roughest of living conditions and darkest times, I always wear earrings. Her favourite eau de toilette was Madame Rochas and I remember that her nails were always painted in subtle colours. Her understated chic has always been based on practicality. Soon after she got married, she earned a severe reprimand from her very correct mother-in-law for wearing trousers: 'A Mrs Bertschinger does not wear trousers.' 'Well, this one does,' she retorted, and she has continued to do so ever since.

My mother managed the family like clockwork. Papa would disappear on the eight o'clock train to the city and she'd be left running the ship until he returned at half past six, expecting us to be tucked up in bed, the house to be spick and span and supper to be on the table. She was a good cook and I especially remember her giant Swiss cheese flans and the chocolate broken-biscuit cake that she made for all our birthdays. For salads, she'd make proper French dressing with oil, vinegar, lemon and garlic – quite different to the dry, shrivelled-up lettuce leaves with salad cream that we'd get at school. I remember her delight in equipping our kitchen with out-of-the-ordinary equipment such as a fondue set, garlic press and bowls for drinking coffee and hot chocolate.

Mummy was always involved in some kind of voluntary work, whether driving old people to their club, taking them meals on wheels or helping in the local hospital shop. In the 1970s, I remember her driving off to Stansted airport in the middle of the night to hand out warm clothes to Ugandan refugees and coming back, describing their bewilderment as she struggled to find coats and gloves to fit them and their children. She has always been a great one for meeting life's challenges head on and she encouraged us to do the same. If we were undecided whether or not to do something, she'd say, 'Don't look at the mountain, climb it.' Another of her favourite sayings was, 'The goddess of opportunity only has one golden hair. Pluck it when you find it.' I still live by that.

Mummy insisted that our house had elastic sides and would always encourage our friends to stay and eat. If I excelled at anything back then, it was in doing things for her. I'd help with the washing up and the cooking or looking after the children of my parents' friends. I used to love that. With my schoolwork, it was, 'You must try harder, Claire.' But caring for babies and toddlers was where I got the most recognition and praise.

We were one of the last houses in the village to get a television and even then our watching was very regulated. The house had to be tidy first and the washing up done. Then the magic began. Seeing the film *The Inn of the Sixth Happiness* had a profound effect on me. It was the true story of Gladys Aylward (played by Ingrid Bergman), an English missionary who in 1930 travelled to China, where she became caught up in the Japanese invasion. I remember the scene of her in prison disarming a prisoner with a machete and another later of her leading a group of children across the mountains to safety. I remember thinking, 'I could do that. That's what I want to do.'

But life scared me back then. I was fascinated by it and wanted to explore, yet I hated being away from home. My mother was my security and I never wanted to be too far away from her. She did everything she could to create peace and harmony at home, including trying to do what was best for my father for his own good. This extended to hiding his cigarettes or even, in later years, burning them all. He was never allowed to smoke in the house but would surreptitiously light up a Senior Service in the garden or in the garage, where he had his workbench with its meticulously ordered rows of tools. If he heard anyone coming, he had the knack of opening his mouth and dropping the cigarette to the floor, or else he'd stand with it cupped in his hand behind his back.

One of the best things Mummy did for me was to teach me the importance of standing back from whatever you're doing and giving yourself the opportunity to 'smell the flowers'. She used to tell me a story about a friend of hers who, when they were reminiscing about their childhood, remembered one moment in particular: 'My mother was always so hardworking,' she said. 'But one windy day she was doing the washing and I asked if she'd come and fly the kite. She abandoned all her work to go and have fun with us. That's the best thing I remember happening to me.' My mother took this story to heart and, as a result, always took time to have fun with us.

When one of my brothers left the taps running and

flooded the kitchen, instead of being told off, we were allowed to climb aboard the table and pretend it was a boat, paddling for our lives. If my father was ever late home from work, we'd lay out a tablecloth by the living-room fire and have a picnic supper. There was always music in the house, whether we were playing it or whether we were dancing to it, Mother and us, just mucking around. When I eventually started going to dances, she'd design my dresses, making me twirl around so that she could approve. She loved being with her family and always made everything fun – indeed she still does.

School presented me with real difficulties. In those days, dyslexia wasn't a recognized problem, so my difficulties in learning to read and write were put down to lack of effort. It was only years later when I read Susan Hampshire's autobiography, *Susan's Story*, that I recognized her years of struggle with undiagnosed dyslexia as identical to mine. All I can remember of primary school days was the feeling of being scared. Indeed I was so scared that I was given a toy to smuggle in for comfort. One of my mother's closest friends made me a tiny monkey, about three or four inches long, of brown fluffy material. I'd always liked monkeys – in fact Papa's nickname for me was 'Monkey' – so this became my comforter and would travel to and from school in my pocket. When I got angry I'd bite its nose and paws, and they had to be regularly patched up. Since then it has gone all over the world with me – a worn but much-loved reminder of home.

I hated school. To this day the sound of a children's playground turns my stomach with a kind of fear. I couldn't read or write fluently until well into my teens. At one stage we had to write a book review every week. All I could do, given that I hadn't a hope of finishing the book, was to copy out laboriously the blurb on the flyleaf. I was constantly being told to concentrate more or to try harder. The trouble was that the words the teachers spoke were like gobbledygook to me; they made no sense at all. I spent so much time trying to understand what they were saying, concentrating on one word at a time, that I'd lose the thread completely. It was as if I were in a maze where everyone else knew where to go while I was endlessly running around trying to find my way. I never felt I got to the bottom of it. It was like being dropped into a foreign land without being able to speak the language. As a result I felt constantly frightened and insecure. Even when I understood my problem better I didn't want to acknowledge that I had the 'D'-word because of all the connotations it had in those days. I knew I wasn't lazy or stupid but it was so hard to convince the teachers. However I remember once being put in charge of a reading group of five of us. What I lacked in reading skills I made up for in being able to organize the others, telling them when to read without having to do it myself, and that made me proud.

Those days blur into a confused memory of a gang of us travelling to school on the bus or train, and a horrible feeling of disquiet all day, overhung with the smell of boiled cabbage and floor polish. I developed a facial twitch that I had for several years and was put down to my nervousness about my disabilities at school. I'd cover my face with my hands to hide it but if a teacher saw, I'd be told off, and I hated that.

Outside school, I keenly attended ballet class and Brownies before joining the St John Ambulance Brigade when I was about thirteen. I decided on St John Ambulance over the Red Cross simply because of the uniform: I fancied myself in the black-and-grey cape. Once a week, I'd go to the St John Ambulance hall, where we'd make bandages out of sheets, learn triangular bandaging, splinting broken limbs, artificial respiration and how to carry stretchers, as well as practising our marching. We'd turn up in the St John Ambulance van at local events such as the stock-car racing or the summer fête, ready for any minor casualties. I loved it, yet I was petrified every time a member of the public came in with an injury. I carried on with St John Ambulance Brigade until I was well into my twenties.

Eventually, both Anne-Marie and I transferred to Chantry Mount School in Bishop's Stortford. Anne-Marie had passed her eleven-plus exam and could have gone to the local grammar school, but my parents wanted us all to have the same holidays. My time there was no better than it had been in primary school. I was put into the reform class, which was made up of all the no-hopers from the bottom of every year. I think the school wrote us off as incapable of learning. Anne-Marie flew through school effortlessly whereas I tried so hard but achieved nothing. It was a source of regular contention with Papa, who would lean over me and try to explain the intricacies of French verbs, English grammar or some mathematical equation. Because I couldn't read, I couldn't understand what he meant. It would drive him wild with frustration and invariably I'd end up in tears. As hard as I tried, whether I was copying out tables or English sentences, my handwriting looked as if a drunk spider had straggled across the page and I remained none the wiser. My mother was the only one who could console me. 'It's all right, Claire. You did your best.' But my reports echoed one another: 'Could try harder', 'Could do better if she tried.' When the time came, I did take various CSEs but failed every one except for domestic science.

As a result, it was decided that I should leave school at sixteen – a decision that I have never regretted. By this time I had set my heart on nursing. The idea of being a nurse grew out of the babysitting and my years in the local St John Ambulance Brigade. I used to bandage my teddy and dream of going to work abroad. I never planned to stay working as a nurse in England, but I had to do the normal training before I could put my plan into action. Thanks to my aunt, we discovered a pre-nursing course at nearby Loughton College, where somehow I was accepted.

7

LEARNING THE ROPES

RED CROSS AMBULANCE TRUCKS RUSHING INTO THE action, heroic doctors and nurses saving lives as bullets whistled past their ears – the adventures I found in my brothers' comics fuelled my imagination, along with the images of Biafran babies whose faces smiled on the charity envelopes we were given for donations. On top of all that were the stories I heard from a Swiss cousin who used to live and work in Africa and from an uncle who became the General Secretary of the World Alliance of Reformed Churches. He'd return from his travels brimming with tales of the exotic places he'd visited. I'd listen spellbound, and my ambitions to nurse overseas were fed. I loved the idea of adventure, living outside in mud huts without running water or proper toilets, and eating food with my hands.

Loughton, where I went in 1966, was a far cry from all that. But if I was going to get anywhere I had to get qualified. Somehow I had to overcome my learning difficulties. The pre-nursing course was very practically based and I spent one day a week working at the local hospital. Integrated with this were O-level courses in Human Biology, English, Sociology and General Studies, which I managed much better than I had at school. Much of the work was project based or entailed drawing and labelling diagrams, which I enjoyed doing. As I got older, things did become a little easier, although writing and reading to any length continued to be a real problem for me. I had to put ten times more effort into my work than everyone else, just to get the same result. I hid my trials as much as possible so that no one would realize how much went into my work. Even today, working in an academic environment as I do, I still find it difficult to admit to my dyslexia.

I remained pretty much of a loner, as I had been at school. After college I would go straight home on the train. I did have one friend, Jeannie. She was a peroxide blonde with an Afghan coat and hippy blouses who encouraged me to dress like her but I was much happier wearing my jeans and blending in with everyone else. She looked after me and made sure I knew what to do. 'If someone passes you a joint, Claire, just pretend to inhale and pass it on. You don't have to tell them you don't smoke.'

The one time she wasn't around to advise me, I learned

a big lesson. I was harassed by a boy who started pushing me around. I didn't like it and slapped him across the face, hard. When he hit me back twice as hard, momentarily stunning me, I realized that that was the last time I would hit anyone. I knew at that moment that violence really doesn't work. You have to think of another way.

To my amazement I was one of the few on my course who passed all the final exams. Somehow I even scraped through English Language. The choice of which hospitals to apply to was straightforward. I was interested only in those that admitted student nurses without an entrance exam. Out of the possibles, I chose St Mary's, Paddington. It wasn't a new building and it didn't have the piped oxygen or suction that was on tap in the more modern hospitals. Such disadvantages attracted me because I felt they brought me closer to the conditions I'd eventually find when I began nursing abroad. At my interview I was asked about the last book I'd read. As I'd never read a book in my life, I almost panicked. But then I remembered my mother telling me during our train journey to London about the book she was reading, Irving Stone's *The Agony and the Ecstasy*, about Michelangelo. Although I couldn't for the life of me remember the author's name, I described the story as if I'd read it myself. I was granted a place.

It was a big change for me to live away from home for the first time. I had a tiny room in a grotty nurses' home in Praed Street. After years of being too timid to leave my mother's side, I found the whole experience too exciting to even think of being homesick.

The nursing school was in the old stable block behind Paddington station. Predictably, I had trouble with the written work, but I was very good on the wards. One day a sister took me aside to ask me what was wrong with one of the patients. I hadn't a clue.

'But you must know,' she insisted.

Until that moment, it had never occurred to me that I needed to know what was wrong with any of them. I had thought it was enough to wash them, change dressings and make them comfortable.

Our days were long and very routine. I'd get up early and wolf down a bowl of cereal before going to the ward. In those days, the student nurse's uniform was a checked or plain dress with a belt coloured according to your year. The starched collars were so scratchy that we battled to soften them with surgical spirit so that they didn't leave a red weal on our necks. The hat had to have a certain number of pleats, which we'd sew in before fastening it to our heads with a white clip. The final touch was the starched white apron, which was attached by huge safety pins. I'd turn up the corner of mine and use the underside to jot down anything I needed to remember. My parents bought me a Tissot nurse's fob watch for my birthday which I proudly pinned to my uniform. I've kept it ever since.

The wards were huge, with as many as forty beds. As

soon as we arrived, working in pairs we'd take pulses and temperatures. Then it was bed-pan rounds. Then fluid balance rounds. Everything was very regimented, so with my efficient Swiss upbringing I fitted in very well; I'm sure I excelled because I responded well to the routine. Some of the sisters were old dragons and sticklers for things being done 'right'. On the children's ward, when a sister inspected the way I'd tidied the linen cupboard, she snapped, 'That's no good. Everything must be folded with the pleats in the right direction,' and yanked everything out for me to do it all again. The same went for the bed-making. Perfect hospital corners were expected and all pillow openings had to be facing away from the door as you came in. What I didn't know about order before, I learned there.

I was always very touched by patients who were terminally ill or chronic cases who were in hospital long-term. I would telephone my mother in tears because I could do nothing to relieve them of their pain or make any difference to their chances of survival. I much preferred working on the surgical wards or the ENT (ear, nose and throat) wards where the patients were discharged within a week of admission. Although I had a pretty strong stomach, another thing I learned that stood me in good stead for later was that if there was anything I felt squeamish about looking at, I could divert my eyes about six inches to the right or left without having to turn away altogether. I remember the first time I saw a colostomy bag where the wound had ulcerated on one side, becoming so badly infected that it was red raw and smelling. One of my duties was to dress it daily. The patient was a Cockney woman my mother's age who was a great down-to-earth character with three bubbly children who were always in the ward visiting. I had to be shown several times by the sister how to change the bag and then I had to show the patient, so we learned together until she could do it herself and had recovered sufficiently to return home. Another patient who stood out was a young builder whose passion in life was football. He had fallen from some scaffolding and broken his back. Paralysed from the neck down, he was unable to do anything for himself. He needed to be turned every couple of hours so that he didn't get any pressure sores. I could only admire the way he joked with his distressed parents and friends, making them more comfortable with the situation. At night, I'd hold a cup of sugary tea so that he could suck it through a straw and we'd talk. I remember how gloomy he could be, although he clung to the belief that he'd be back on the football pitch within a year. I had heard the doctors talking and knew he would never walk again, but I encouraged him as best I could. I never knew what happened to him, but it was the first time I had seen such a young man's life ruined and it has always stayed with me.

After passing my final exams, I went to work in the

obstetrics ward. I knew I needed midwifery qualifications if I was ever to work for the Red Cross. But I found working with mothers and babies boring, and midwifery was too technical and involved for me to learn successfully. Just when I thought that, without this qualification, my ambitions of working abroad might be slipping away from me, I read a magazine article about the Royal Flying Doctor Service of Australia. It sounded fun – at least it would take me abroad. So I wrote to ask whether they would take me on, if I learned to fly. They replied saying they would.

Only forty-five minutes from the family home, Stapleford Tawney airfield was offering trial lessons for £5 a time. My parents agreed to give me one for my birthday. Papa and I drove there, very excited at the prospect, but at the last minute he refused to come in the plane so I went alone. It was wonderful. I was hooked, and began to put aside as much of my meagre nursing pay as possible to pay for lessons at £12 a time. I'd live on boiled eggs and baked beans, going home whenever I could on my days off to have a big meal and stuff my bag full of goodies to take back to London. Because I'm so small, I had difficulty reaching the aircraft's pedals and seeing out of the screen at the same time. My solution was to buy an armchair cushion from a jumble sale and cut it up so that I had one part to sit on and the other for behind my back. I attached handles to each part in a futile attempt to make the revolting green Dralon shapes look something like a suitcase and make me look more professional. The normal English weather conditions which led to poor visibility usually prevented me from doing more than one and a half hours of flying a month. I became completely wrapped up in learning about aeroplanes, engines, meteorology and navigation law. Whenever I could tear myself away from nursing, I'd dive back into my flying books or hang around at the airfield.

The flying club was an exclusively male domain. I tried to blend in as much as possible. I would wear my hair in bunches and not put on any make-up. I couldn't cope with being asked, 'What's a woman doing, learning to fly?' I had the best answer possible, though: I was going to join the Flying Doctor Service – that would shut them up pretty fast. All I wanted was to be accepted as a fellow pilot. During my first solo flight, I was coming in to land when I saw all the men rush out of the clubhouse to watch me, as if unable to believe that I'd make it. Once I had successfully landed, they all disappeared inside again and when I walked in a few minutes later, nobody said anything to me. Not a word of congratulation. It would have been so different if I'd been a man: I'd seen how they celebrated one another's successes, however small.

All the other women associated with the club either worked behind the bar or were the wives or girlfriends of the pilots. The one exception was an Australian woman, who happened to be the world gliding champion. She was about ten years older than me, and became my role model. She managed to combine courage and skill with a sense of fun. She was a wonderful teacher. She also taught me that it's OK to admit to feeling under the weather. I'd been brought up to believe that even if you didn't feel well, you went out and worked harder in the garden. That would cure all ills, in my father's eyes. Her sympathy towards me one day when I had stomach cramps made me realize I was allowed to admit it when I wasn't feeling 100 per cent.

Although I loved learning to fly, it had its terrifying moments. The first time I had to show I could stall an aircraft, put it in a spin and come out of it – all obligatory skills when becoming a pilot in those days – was one such moment. Another was a solo test flight to Lydd on the south-east coast. There I was, trying to navigate with my map on my lap and to fly straight and level while calculating my speed to be sure I completed the circuit in the right time. Suddenly nothing looked familiar. I was lost. In those circumstances I had been taught to fly a 'circle of uncertainty' – that is, to fly in circles until you have calmed down and located a recognizable landmark. Out of nowhere, there was a church spire and a railway line. That got me back on route, and I reached the coast at the allotted time, but then I couldn't spot Lydd and seemed to be about to fly off over the Channel. It was time for another circle of uncertainty.

'Lydd. Lydd. This is Golf Bravo Alpha Romeo Echo. I've hit the coast but can't see you. Over.'

As the control tower replied, to my relief I suddenly saw the airstrip appear below me. But the panic stayed with me until well after I'd landed.

By the time I proudly qualified as a pilot, my idea of joining the Flying Doctor Service had evaporated. I was in love. His name was Steve (or so he told me). He was another student pilot and, unlike the other members of the flying club, he paid attention to me. We spent hours talking about the intricacies of flying as we whiled away the time, waiting for our turn to fly. To gain additional flying experience, we were allowed to sit in the rear seats behind another student's lesson, so we started flying with each other.

During my three years at St Mary's the emphasis had always been on work, at the expense of any social life. We worked a shift system, so there was never much time to call our own. I didn't enjoy going to the pub. More than anything, I enjoyed returning to the peace of the countryside, being in the garden, helping my mother in the kitchen and having a family meal.

As a result I was very naïve when it came to men and I fell for Steve hook, line and sinker. He looked like a young Paul Newman and told me he had been brought up on a dairy farm in New Zealand. I loved the Antipodean twang in his voice and the fact that he'd travelled the world. He made a fairly precarious living gardening for the rich and famous. It was only months down the line that I discovered that in fact he came from Enfield in north London and had caught that romantic twang from his pregnant New Zealand wife.

I blithely moved into an attic flat in Gloucester Road with him, and helped him with gardens in Hampstead's exclusive Bishop's Avenue on my afternoons off and at weekends. But all the time we were together he was leading a double life and I just didn't see it. When he came back from being away or out late at night, he always came up with a perfectly plausible explanation – even when I found another woman's knickers in our bed. How could I have believed his story that she had simply been gardening with him, had got caught in the rain and had come here to change? But I'd been brought up to set great store by the truth. I trusted him because I had no reason not to. My working hours were as demanding as ever. I'd bicycle to St Mary's through Hyde Park every morning, past the guardsmen exercising the horses. I loved the smell of the earth at dawn and dusk, the sweating horses and the rustle of the trees. On my way home, I'd often stop off for a swim in the Serpentine. Steve had plenty of opportunities to amuse himself.

We decided to go to America together on a four-month trip. It was the first time I'd been abroad without my family and I was so excited. We flew to New York in September. We bought a second-hand Chevrolet Impala Estate and decided to travel down the east coast to Florida. Money was tight and we needed what we had for petrol, so we lived off stale doughnuts which I'd buy for $1 and fish we caught for ourselves and cooked over our Calor gas stove.

One pitch-black night in Florida we were asleep in the back of the car when the whole world lit up. I blinked open my eyes to see a gun at my head.

'Don't move. Get out of the car.'

It was the police. They allowed us to get dressed before checking us out and making certain that we weren't responsible for the shooting that had taken place a mile down the road. They advised us that the safest place to sleep was in the brightly lit parking lot of a supermarket. From then on that's just what we did. But by Christmas we were really broke. We got jobs cleaning toilets in a campsite. Steve was meant to do the men's while I did the women's. Needless to say I ended up doing both. I was thoroughly miserable, as I had also begun to realize what a liar Steve was. He embarked on an affair with a woman in the campsite and I'd be left alone in our tent.

It may seem extraordinary that I didn't leave. But I had been looking forward to travelling for years, so I persuaded myself that I had to survive the trip whatever Steve threw at me.

After Christmas we moved on, ending up in Albuquerque, New Mexico, where Steve found casual labour as a builder and I worked as a cleaner in the YMCA. God, it was tedious. I'd end up sitting in the broom cupboard reading magazines. If only I could have got work as a nurse – but we were never in one place long enough, so we worked illegally, doing whatever jobs we could find that paid cash. And of course Steve was up to his old tricks again, philandering whenever he got the chance. Our finances got worse, and we were forced to sell the car and took to 'dead-heading' cars across the country, driving hire cars back from wherever they'd been dropped off.

Despite the misery I sometimes endured thanks to Steve, the US trip was an eye-opener for me. I discovered that I had inner resources I could draw on to help me get by, whatever the circumstances. The whole experience whetted my appetite to see more of the world.

When we got home, we carried on living together. I knew by now I wanted to get out of the relationship, but I didn't really know how to extricate myself. Nursing jobs weren't easy to come by, so I worked for a time at Stansted airport as a driver for a car hire firm. We lived in a mobile home next to the airport. After about nine months, I returned to nursing at last when I got a job in the A&E department of Addenbrookes Hospital in Cambridge. With the job came shared accommodation in a flat with three other nurses. I finally had my opportunity to leave Steve. I grasped it with both hands.

For two years I thrived on the buzz of A&E and the high I got from successfully treating emergencies. The work gave me a huge amount of satisfaction, whether I was putting up a drip or preparing a body for relatives. Generally I loved the unpredictability of the job and of the people I met through it. All sorts came through the door, drunk, violent or upset. I'd make a beeline for the most aggressive or hysterical ones and sit and chat with them, calming them down. There were tramps, travellers and Cambridge University students in their black ties and ball gowns, blind drunk with vomit in their hair, expecting us to 'do something'. One girl I remember was in a fabulous silk evening dress. She had jumped from a bridge as a dare but there was almost no water below it. Fortunately, having drunk the contents of a Drambuie bottle, she was very relaxed when she hit the ground and no damage was done except to her pride. The next morning she was very sheepish indeed. I'd come a long way from shaking with fear as a teenager in a St John Ambulance van, and I was surprised and pleased to find that dealing with people in distress was something I was instinctively good at. The first time I did mouth-to-mouth resuscitation was on a cot-death baby who was rushed in by her parents. I happened to be the one standing in the corridor and had to try to revive her, even though I suspected the attempt was hopeless. I had to keep going until a doctor pronounced the baby dead. The taste and smell of death is unforgettable.

I read an article in the *Nursing Times* about a woman who had worked with children in refugee camps. Immediately I knew that that was work I'd love to do and would be able to do well. I wrote to the woman in the article, care of the magazine, and she invited me to visit her at the Institute of Child Health in London. But my hopes were dashed. When I told her I wanted to be the first on the spot whenever there was a disaster in the world as a disaster relief coordinator, she looked at me and began to laugh. 'Don't be so ridiculous. You're not trained for a job like that.'

I left in tears, disappointed but angry and all the more determined to succeed. I supplemented my work at Addenbrookes with a course in tropical diseases at the Hospital for Tropical Diseases, driving my heaterless Mini into London one evening a week, so as to do everything I could to work towards my dream of nursing abroad.

8

A LIVING HELL

JULY 1984. THE SMELLS OF DEATH, SWEAT AND SHIT MIXED with the fragile scent of eucalyptus hit me immediately as I stepped off the Ethiopian Airlines DC3 Dakota at Mekele, the capital of the Tigray province of Ethiopia. Ruth, the Swiss nurse running the feeding centre there, met me and took me to the grandly named but indescribably run-down Castle Hotel on a rise just outside town. The only 'hotel' in Mekele, it was to be my home and hers for the foreseeable future.

After returning from the Lebanon in May I had been at home for only four and a half weeks. It was just enough time to reacquaint myself with all the things I'd missed at home. Almost before I knew it, I was in dusty Addis Ababa waiting for my travel permits to come through. As soon as they did, I was whisked off with one of the ICRC drivers to Korem, another town where thousands of starving displaced people gathered, to inspect the feeding centre established there by the Save the Children Fund so that I could see for myself what support was needed in Mekele. We spent one and a half days driving on treacherous roads, over blazing hot plateaux and across cool mountain tops, before we arrived. The approach to the plateau of Korem is up a steep mountain road with one hairpin bend after another. We passed columns of people struggling to walk up the road, trying to reach the town in the hope of finding food and shelter. They were filthy and starving. Some lay dying by the roadside while others reached out, begging for help. I remember one gaunt old woman, bent under the weight of the few belongings wrapped in a cloth that she carried in her right hand. Her robes were encrusted with dirt, her beautifully plaited greying hair thick with dust, her skin dry and wrinkled. She walked alone, slowly and painfully; she had lost all her family and had no one to help or look after her. She was so alone. She summed up for me the awful injustice of the situation. It seemed particularly hard for the old people, to stand in lengthy queues, confused, not knowing where to go. I knew that families and children were catered for by the aid agencies, but there was nothing in place for the elderly. It was a terrible feeling to know we could do nothing for her as we swept by in our large white jeep.

I can only describe Korem as hell on earth. When we arrived it was raining and there was mud everywhere, and thousands of starving people were lying or sitting on the ground, many of them without shelter. They were dying of hunger – something we find hard to imagine in our ordinary lives when we thoughtlessly speak of 'dying for' a Mars bar or a hamburger. All they wanted was a handful of grain or a piece of bread to keep them alive for another day. What was so awful was knowing that food was plentiful in the rest of the world but not for them. Four thousand children under six years old were registered at the centre, some of them so thin that they were only skin and bone and covered in sores. They all exhibited the symptoms of severe malnutrition – stunted growth, loss of muscle mass, brittle hair, mottled dehydrated skin, a large, protuberant belly. Their decreased immunity meant that almost all of them were sick in one way or another. A mouthful of teeth disproportionately large for their body told you when they were as old as four or five. Seeing all this was my preparation for Mekele. It was terrible, but it made me angry. It made me want to fight.

The situation at the Korem centre struck me as being one of 'organized chaos'. Two doctors and two nurses from Médecins sans Frontières were working flat out in the medical centre, aided by local volunteers. But they were under-resourced and overwhelmed by the numbers needing their help. They had medical supplies but neither food nor sufficient water – the two pillars of emergency assistance. What's the use of providing antibiotics for a child with a chest infection or dysentery when their body's too weak to cope? These people were dying of hunger and dehydration. Seven children died in the intensive feeding centre during the night I was there. If a child recovered enough to stand, however shakily, it was immediately sent to an outside shelter so that another could take its place. I was there for only a few hours but in my mind's eye I can still see a baby girl who had just had a drip removed because she had stopped vomiting and was able to take fluids by mouth. Her grandmother carried her to another shelter, moving mechanically, looking dazed, as if she couldn't believe what was happening to them. I was to see that look so often. The ground was shin deep in mud and the displaced people went barefoot and in rags, waiting, hoping. When the rain stopped, vultures circled overhead, and at night you could hear hyenas howling at the edge of the camp.

Back in Mekele, I lay in my bed in my room at the Castle Hotel, listening to the hyenas and wondering how I was going to cope with what was to come. Mekele was remote, 485 miles north of Addis. The government had blocked all the roads into town, deeming them 'hostile' and dangerous, so we weren't allowed free passage. It wanted to prevent rebels from moving in and out of the towns and the possible exchange of information and arms. One of the problems was getting in the dry rations for the displaced starving people, who were arriving at the rate of up to two or three thousand a week. Our most regular supplies were flown in every six weeks or so by an old Hercules plane. After only two and a half days I wrote home: 'First impression is "My God. However am I going to stand it for six months let alone a year?" I hope that in a few weeks I'll look back and laugh at that statement.' Not a chance, as it turned out.

The hours were long and exhausting. We'd leave the hotel at about seven o'clock and drive the four or five kilometres to the feeding centre. Our route took us through the dusty African town, past simple houses with grass roofs or, more luxuriously, corrugated iron ones. The townspeople, dressed in traditional Telfi white robes decorated with colourful embroidery, walked purposefully through the streets going about their business, while the displaced people shuffled desperately between our supplementary feeding centre for children, the ICRC warehouse on the other side of town which distributed dry rations, and the centres run by the Don Bosco Society and the Daughters of Charity, according to where the rumours said there was food. The roads were dirt tracks, but there were no cars apart from ours and the two belonging to the Daughters of Charity and the priests of the Don Bosco Society. All the lorries belonged to the military, who maintained a heavy presence in town and surrounded it with checkpoints. We'd pass a few local stores selling the barest provisions –

soap, a pencil or a lined notebook – and the open market area, where locals sat on the ground to put out their wares – four bruised tomatoes in a pyramid, old farm tools, a family heirloom such as a hand-made silver cross or a few coloured beads, a couple of scrawny chickens. Sometimes we'd see a mother or father sitting with a baby in the middle of the road, begging us to stop. At other times, as we drove towards them, desperate parents would put their baby down on the ground before running away. They would have to be called back and encouraged to pick up their child again. We couldn't take in abandoned children just like that. We didn't have the resources to cope with them then. I could imagine the utter despair that would lead parents to do such a thing and was saddened that we didn't have the infrastructure to help them.

Day after day it was the same. During the day displaced people drifted into the town, hoping to find food. Their faces were blank, their glazed eyes betraying bewilderment and exhaustion. It was terrible seeing adults lying where they'd dropped in the streets. I remember one old man lying by his wooden stick while his wife sat dazed and despondent waving the flies off him, waiting for help they both knew wouldn't come. The townspeople ignored them. I soon learned that it was pointless my trying to help. In my first week, I picked up another collapsed old man, dragging him into the back of the van with his wife. I left them in the waiting area at the hospital. I went back twice but couldn't find out what had happened to them. The third time, I found the man sitting alone outside the hospital grounds. He'd been kicked out because he didn't have any money. This time I took him to the ICRC distribution centre to get some dried rations. I never saw him again. I talked to Ruth about him and the others, and she made me see that we simply couldn't help everyone. We had to concentrate on those we could help. I felt hopeless, and angry about the injustice of it all, but I had no idea what more I could do except throw myself into our work with the kids.

As we arrived at the centre in our Land Cruiser each morning, there'd be a ripple of movement through the huge crowd already surrounding the centre as the worst cases were brought forward to be shown at the gate, hoping to be let in. Inside was a large corral surrounded by corrugated iron sides. On one side was a small staff room, a kitchen and a store. There was no proper chimney in the kitchen, just a hole in the corrugated iron roof to let the smoke out, so our eyes were always stinging. The feeding areas were open, partially sheltered by lean-to corrugated roofs on opposite sides with an open area in between. Along the other wall was a washing area and a wood store. We had two oil drums of water, one by the kitchen and one by the washing area, which we'd fill with water using a hosepipe from a nearby standpipe. Outside crowded hundreds of displaced people whose children hadn't been chosen for the feeding programme, who gazed into the corral at those luckier than themselves.

The chosen mothers and children would file in and sit down for the feeding as the cooks prepared the high-energy milk drink that we were to give to the children, made from butter oil, dried skimmed milk, sugar and boiling water. Beyond the gate, a member of the local Red Cross would talk to those waiting their turn about hygiene, illustrating her talk with drawings to drive her points home. When the children had been fed, the mugs were collected for washing up in four more oil drums – cold rinse; warm water with Omo to help wash off the butter oil; second cold rinse; storage – while the children filed out with their parent or guardian, and we'd prepare for the next group. With this routine, we managed to feed about 350 children three times a day (1,050 portions), increasing the numbers over the weeks to nearer 500 (1,500 portions).

At sunset, the displaced people were all herded out of town by the government soldiers to stay in an area called the 'political camp'. The vast majority slept outside under the stars, huddled together in small groups of five or six for warmth. When I first got to Mekele, there wasn't anything they could use to make a shelter, although some of them tried to make small windbreaks with stones and others wandered for miles looking for a few bits of wood to make fires so that they could cook the meagre rations the ICRC gave them.

In those first days, Ruth had me supervising the Red Cross youths, who were each assigned to a group of mothers and children. It was better that way because the children were often scared stiff of an unfamiliar white face and some of the little ones screamed blue murder if I went near them. Some of the older children were braver and let me play with them, so I got to see them smile. The worst part of the job was getting the reluctant children to feed. Sometimes we had to virtually force-feed them the first few mouthfuls, holding their hands and feet and waiting until they opened their mouth so that we could spoon in some milk. Some of it would go down or it was spat straight back. Although they were starving, they had lost their appetite. My heart went out to them.

Engrossed in such a hopeless situation day in and day out, I almost forgot how normal children looked and behaved. Then, *en route* in an old Ethiopian Airlines DC3 from one of our monthly meetings for ICRC medical staff in Addis back to Mekele, engine trouble meant we had to make an emergency landing at Bahr Dahr, a small town on Lake Tana, far from the famine. It brought me up short. Children were playing on the landing strip that doubled as village green, football field, sheep and cow pasture, chicken run, sports ground – and swimming pool as there was about a foot of rainwater on the ground. As we came in to land, the children and animals scattered. Two days later when the engine had been repaired, we took off, the tougher children dashing into the slipstream of the propellers, falling over themselves in the force of the wind and having a whale of a time in the muddy waterlogged grass. Seeing them made me realize how sick the children in Mekele were. Surrounded by so much suffering and sickness, we tended to take it as normal.

Within a very short time, Ruth and I both realized that we were not cut out to be the perfect team. She was in her mid-fifties and was of the old school of relief nursing, and I was overawed by her age and experience. Unlike me, she had worked in other African feeding centres and knew what she was doing. However, before being sent to Mekele, I had been told in Geneva and again in Addis that the children weren't being discharged quickly enough from the centre and the feeding regime had to change: the ICRC wanted the children to recover faster so that we could treat more of them. Ruth had strong ideas but I was young, enthusiastic and desperate to take some responsibility for the running of the centre. Our different trainings separated us and the pressure of the situation intensified our differences. In any other circumstances, I'm sure we would have been able to sit down and clear the air, but there was never any time and we were always either too depressed or exhausted.

Apart from differing over the best way to select which children should be fed, Ruth and I also disagreed over the feeding regime. In Geneva, I'd been told that the ICRC felt that the portions she advocated were too bulky, with not enough calorie intake, but Ruth preferred to supplement the high-calorie milk drink with either a bowl of rice, flat bread or sometimes porridge. The feeds were quite close together and we were concerned that at the second sittings, some of the children weren't hungry and would either refuse to eat or, when persuaded to eat, would vomit up the first feed. It took a little while to institute the new higher-calorie regime that Geneva wanted because we were both working under enormous pressure. Whatever our differences, our motives were the same: we both wanted to do the best we could to help.

When after a couple of weeks Dr Pierre, the medical officer in Addis, asked me to reorganize the medical care at the centre, I was glad to have a project of my own at last. I set up a clinic in a tin hut in a corner of the compound, which operated after the feeding. I was always rushed off my feet, seeing as many as ninety-five patients during an afternoon. With a two-inch paintbrush, we'd paint the ones with scabies from neck to toe in brown benzyl benzoate lotion for three days in a row. We gave oral rehydration salts to children with diarrhoea and vomiting. The ring-worm sufferers got covered in gentian violet, including the inside of their mouth if they had thrush. Sometimes I'd have to lance boils, because often antibiotics weren't enough to shift them. I remember a ten-month-old baby being brought to me with boils the size of ping-pong balls on his back, his groin and his leg. The poor little thing screamed as we held him down so that I could lance the first of them, giving him immediate relief. On the third day, I was anxious because I only had a razor blade and a bit of alcohol left. I had to release all the pus in the last boil or else the boils would keep coming back, and the baby was in great discomfort during the procedure; but afterwards he was much calmer and happier.

Many of the children were covered with flies that buzzed up from the dirt on the ground and often infected their eyes. It was a joy to see a mother's reaction when our field worker, Asmara, showed her that if she gently splashed water on her child's eyes from the drum of water outside, the eyes would unstick and the child would be able to see again. Our supplies didn't run to the luxury of cotton wool or sterile pads but this was something positive that we could show them. Because many of the children were under threat of blindness from a lack of vitamin A in their meagre diet, we snipped open a capsule of vitamin A and dripped the contents into the mouth of every child newly admitted to the centre. This prevented the onset of blindness in many, although for some it came too late. If I had to administer a course of antibiotics, I'd fold scraps of paper from exercise books or magazines origami-style into little bags that would hold a daily supply of two or three tablets, so that some of the mothers could dose their children themselves before returning for more the next day.

Often it was a question of educating the mothers in how to care for their babies in this situation. One who sticks in my mind came to the centre with her three-month-old twins, one plump and cheerful, the other starved and weak. We discovered that she was feeding only the plumper one of the two, as she thought she didn't have enough breast milk for them both. She wanted us to bottle-feed the twins but I explained to her the benefits of feeding her babies herself. A bottle-fed baby is twenty-five times more likely to die from diarrhoea where water supplies are unsafe. I explained that to bottle-feed them would be like putting a bullet to their heads. We gave her extra food so that her body would produce more milk and encouraged her to feed them little and often; and we supplemented her efforts with spoonfuls of oral rehydration salts. It was fantastic to see the mother's pleasure as the second twin filled out and how, two weeks later, he smiled when I tickled his tummy.

As the weeks went by, I built up my contacts at the local hospital where I took the more seriously ill and eventually wheedled the doctor in charge into opening up a twenty-two-bedded ward and a couple of medical offices in the grounds as paediatric wards that would take a hundred cases – a real achievement. In exchange I provided the medicine and food necessary to support the children. Mothers and children were packed into the bare rooms with bars at the windows, as many as two adults and four kids squeezing on to one bed or a mattress on the floor. There was barely room to turn around, but at least it was somewhere they could be cared for.

However, I soon realized that the children still weren't receiving the medical treatment they needed. I had arranged for the hospital to receive equipment and boxes of assorted drugs to treat the most common illnesses, and so I was surprised to be asked for a stethoscope and other basic equipment that I knew we'd supplied a couple of months earlier. When I asked the nurses what had happened to it all they told me they'd never seen it. One of the doctors had apparently kept it at home, partly because of its rarity value and partly to treat his own private patients; the supplies never reached the children. I felt powerless against this sort of abuse by the hospital authorities. Likewise I found it impossible to ensure that the supplementary food supplies I organized reached those they were intended for when I had no control over the hospital's distribution of them.

I visited the wards every day to check how the children were getting on. One day, I saw a mother I had brought in a few days earlier with her son, who had a chest infection. She was sitting with him on her lap. He was limp and fighting for breath. She told me he hadn't been given any medicine. I immediately went in search of the medical director but couldn't find him anywhere. I talked to the nurses, who helplessly said, 'Yes, yes,' but shrugged their shoulders in defeat. Without the right supplies all our training was useless. The next day I arrived to find that the boy had died. I was devastated. It was a totally needless death.

In August I wrote home:

The main problem is getting the dry rations for the thousands of starving people here. Only this week, another 2–3000 appeared – many with marasmus (a form of malnutrition causing muscle wasting). We [the ICRC] just can't get the rations into the area to feed them. The ICRC can do it easier than anyone else – other organizations aren't allowed into the combat zone. So you see all the money in the world doesn't help.

But it wasn't all misery. We made our own fun, chasing the giggling recovering kids around the shelter and dancing with them on feast days. Sometimes a friend of one of the Red Cross workers from the town would come and play a strange home-made stringed instrument that twanged monotonously. He'd make up songs about us and have the local people in gales of laughter. Whenever I asked them to translate for me, they were laughing too hard to do so. We'd sing with the children to the accompaniment of the ululating mothers. They were all fascinated when I whistled old favourites such as 'This old man, he played one' or 'Whenever I feel afraid, I whistle a happy tune'. They also loved stroking the hair on my head, arms and legs as it was so different from theirs. When I went for a pee in the pit latrine, they would play peekaboo games through the holes in the sacking that acted as a not very good screen. The angrier I got, the more fun it became for them, so I ended up trying to ignore them. They would follow me around, imitating the way I spoke and laughing at their own efforts. I often felt like the Pied Piper as dozens of children scrabbled to hold my hand or hang on to a bit of my skirt wherever I was going. With all the children clambering all over me – snotty, shitty, bug-ridden and generally unwashed – I would get filthy but I couldn't resist cuddling them whenever I could, and I often had one perched on my hip or riding on me piggyback.

Once we got hold of a camera and I bought some black-and-white film from one of the street vendors. We set up shots of the kids and of the local Red Cross workers, who wanted pictures of themselves with me or Ruth. In one of the photographs, a little girl with an enormous stomach and skinny legs, wearing a ragged sacking dress, is grinning and holding two gerbera, one orange and one pink. I'd found them in the gutter round the back of the hotel and she was thrilled to have them, smiling from ear to ear. She dragged them round in the dust, refusing to let go of them for the rest of the day. In other photographs a mother sits with her hand supporting her sitting child as she washes him with water from an old kettle, pouring it slowly over his head. He sits patiently, wearing nothing but a string of beads round his neck. An almond-eyed Afar woman, her hair neatly plaited in cornrows and strings of cowrie shells around her neck, holds up her child, who is so thin that its skin bags like loose underpants round its bottom. A squatting child screams as she's painted with benzyl benzoate. A little boy smiles, proud of the Western clothes I'd given him. A father cuddles his daughter, who hides her face shyly from me, while his baby son sits on his hip, looking out boldly. Two children, one in a long T-shirt with beads around her neck and another in a floral dress, gulp their high-energy milk drink unaided. Everybody was thrilled when, thanks to our field worker Asmara knowing a young man in town who had a dark room, we got the photographs – a few snapshots of a typical day in the centre – developed and could give them out. A simple present but one that meant a lot.

A little relief came each evening when I returned to my room in the hotel. The peeling walls were painted a gaudy shocking pink with creamy yellow and mauve touches. Defiantly I had pinned two posters on the bathroom wall – one a picture of a cream slice oozing cream and jam announcing 'Already she was more deeply involved than she cared to admit' and another of a jammy doughnut with the slogan 'After this, she could never go back to muesli'. Looking back, I find these tasteless, but at the time I felt I wanted to balance the horror of the situation with something that would make me smile. I'd get back absolutely filthy, itching from fleas, lice and scabies. The first thing I'd do was throw off my shoes. Then, if I didn't have a bucket of water in my room, I'd go downstairs and find somebody to get me some water to wash in from the local well. Washing my hair once a week became a real luxury, although I was never really able to do it properly so I kept it very short. I hated washing in cold water in the chilly evenings but it was essential. When I felt cleaner, I'd have my cup of tea and, if I was lucky, a bite of a Crunchie or Mars bar that I'd saved from my parcels from home. I'd ration them over weeks until I got new supplies from my sister. Every month, she'd send me a rolled-up magazine with chocolate packed inside, and sealed so that the customs didn't realize that the chocolate was there.

Sometimes, in the evenings, Ruth and I might make ourselves a soup of a few green leaves, a carrot and a fresh tomato, if one of us had been lucky enough to find them in town. Otherwise we might have a tin of sardines or tinned fruit that we'd brought from Addis. As we were the only people staying at the Castle Hotel most of the time, it was lonely for both of us, so we were thrown back on each other's company, and we made the best of it. Sometimes we went down to the empty hotel restaurant. Cooking was done on a wood fire, but only if we asked. Then the hotel staff would have to find wood, and kill an animal or buy something from the market. Otherwise their larder was bare. If we ordered them in advance, we might have fried eggs or some leathery meat, usually goat or chicken. The local dish was *injera*, an enormous sour-dough pancake eaten with the fingers and dipped in a chilli sauce mixed with beans or goat meat or, if you were very lucky, pieces of offal cut into strips – the intestines and gall bladder being favourite delicacies. It was enough to make anyone a vegetarian for life. However, although the food we were served was pretty basic, I couldn't help but be aware that it was so much more than the displaced people had.

I didn't go out in the evenings. There was nowhere to go, and anyway I wanted time to myself, time when I wasn't the constant centre of attention. Whenever I went out, people were always staring at me, coming up to me, begging and touching me. At night I would write my diary and letters to my family while listening to the fuzzy BBC World Service on my short-wave radio, a lifeline to the rest of the world. I'd snapped off the aerial once when I was closing my suitcase and used a broken fork poked into the hole to improve reception. The quality was unreliable, depending on the conditions and time of day. My other lifeline was the letters sent to me by my mother, who provided me with more support than I think she knew. I treasured her letters, reading them over and over again, imagining the wheat harvest in the field beside my parents' house, the may blossom, the yellow fields of rape and how busy my father's bees would be. I'd think of how much I was missing my young nieces growing up. At times I would cry in frustration or despair for what I had or hadn't done that day. I was frequently ill with diarrhoea and vomiting, and suffered from boils and terrible flea bites. My cotton track-suit was scant protection against the bedbugs that I periodically saw marching defiantly across the sheets at night, immune to any insecticide. My last resort was a tip from my mother: I would throw back the sheets and hit the bugs with a soft bar of soap, and some of them would get stuck to it – never all. But I was comfortable enough at the hotel and, although I lived out of a suitcase, I made it my home.

One thing that made the situation more difficult for me was the lack of other people I could talk to. Most of our local helpers didn't speak good enough English to become really close friends. After working flat out all day, they usually wanted to get home before the curfew. The one exception was our field worker, Asmara. She was my right hand. I couldn't have survived without her. We discussed everything and she advised me on how I should go about setting up projects in a way that would fit in with local customs. If a doctor at the local hospital refused to admit a child, Asmara would calm me down, whispering that this was just the way he could show his power, and that there were more subtle ways of getting round him and getting treatment for our children. An Ethiopian man would never lose face by giving way to anger, so I had to be patient. 'Claire, in Switzerland you have watches,' she'd say, 'but here in Africa, we have time.' I learned that things got done in their own time. The only solution was to adapt to African time, be patient and wait. It usually worked and eventually the doctor would come round. Asmara taught me so much. She was my ears and eyes for what was going on and a barometer for the moods of the people. She was incredibly quick to learn and worked hard.

Soon after I'd met her, Asmara took me back to her house to meet her family, who were somehow related to the Ethiopian royal family. As we walked through the streets, she took my hand and I remember feeling very awkward at first, although it seemed to be what everyone there did. We walked and sang together and I made myself kick off my Western inhibitions and enjoy the moment. She took me to a wooden shack with a corrugated iron roof and windows without glass. We entered the only room, where I met Asmara's mother. I knew that she looked after Asmara's baby daughter while she was at work. There was a strong smell of eucalyptus wood smoke, incense and cow dung from the cow tethered outside. The room wasn't very big and Asmara, her baby and I sat on the one bed that they all shared, while her mother squatted by the open wood fire preparing coffee. It was an intricate traditional ritual that took over an hour. First she fried green coffee beans in an open pan, and then she brought the pan over to waft the aromatic smoke in our faces while we inhaled deeply. After roasting them for a little longer, she ground the beans with a wooden pestle and mortar, boiled them and sieved them through a piece of material. Then she carefully served the coffee in tiny china cups without handles. Tradition and politeness demanded that I drank three cups. It was very bitter and tasted nothing like the coffee I was used to at home. Asmara's fourteen-year-old brother and fifteen-year-old sister stood by, giggling. Her mother generously offered me a glass of milk straight from their cow. I hesitated, thinking about tuberculosis and brucellosis, but I couldn't refuse. We ate *injera* that was cooked over the fire in a large blackened terracotta plate while the lentils and animal entrails bubbled in a saucepan alongside. We went out to the back of the shack where chickens scratched in the dust around the cow and I saw that the family possessed the luxury of a pit latrine. They seemed very poor to me, but with Asmara's wages from the centre they had a lot more than many of their neighbours.

I had friends in Addis who I enjoyed seeing when we gathered there about every six weeks to coordinate the medical programmes throughout the country. I would arrive there exhausted, and recharge my batteries, sleeping, lying by the hotel pool, eating well and chatting, getting ready for the next onslaught in Mekele. My letters home describe the food in mouthwatering detail – especially the chocolate mousse. I remember decadently lying in a steaming bath for hours at a time. I even allowed myself two in one day and felt very naughty but it was such a treat. When

I was in the thick of it at Mekele, I'd feel I could hardly get through the month until the next meeting, but once I'd had a few days in Addis, I was happy to return to the field.

The return journey was often fraught with mishaps. A burst plane tyre and a violent storm once threw me into the company of two sisters of the Daughters of Charity and a brother Jesus from the Don Bosco Society in Mekele. On our way from Addis we were re-routed for an emergency landing at Axum, the centre of Christian religion in Ethiopia and at that time out of bounds for tourists because of heavy fighting in the area. After we had landed, and seeing that the military were about to search us, one of the sisters whispered to me that she had hidden some home-made blackberry wine in a castor oil bottle in her bags, and was desperate that her colleague shouldn't find out. So would I help by diverting her attention at every baggage check? I thought it was hilarious and had great fun trying to help.

The town was famed for its sixteenth-century church of St Mary of Zion, built on the site of a fourth-century church that is said to house the ark of the covenant. It's also known for its tall, carved granite obelisk and the palace of the Queen of Sheba. We were escorted round the town by the one town guide, the local Red Cross and of course someone from the security services to make sure that we didn't go anywhere or see anything we shouldn't. They opened rusty gates and dusty tombs and we got excellent bargains at the boarded-up, dusty souvenir shop – not having seen a tourist for ten years, the owner had no idea when he'd next sell anything.

After that I often used to go and visit the nuns for tea or to share a frugal meal with them in the convent in Mekele. One of them, Sister Gabriel, was nearly ninety but she still worked in the clinic. She was the sort of woman you didn't say no to but she was also kind and ready to dispense motherly advice, particularly when I was feeling despondent about the injustice of the suffering we saw every day. The nuns had a small collection of English novels which they let me borrow, although with little time to read it took me ages to finish one. Twice I was invited to a meal with the brothers of the Don Bosco Society, and each time we had wine with a proper European meal of meat and vegetables. The brothers were extremely entertaining. One of them was so young and handsome that I couldn't believe he was throwing his life away to be a monk – but I was young and naïve then and didn't understand about the rewards of a spiritual life.

By October I was feeling very low. Our stores were empty. We'd been promised a new feeding station on the edge of town but completion had been delayed until January. We were promised more food but there were problems with transport as rebels attacked the supply convoys and many of the roads were mined so we never knew when the next supplies would arrive. We were cut off and alone. Meanwhile starving people continued pouring into Mekele, and conditions were getting worse. By this time we had over five hundred children in the centre and the death count was growing daily. The situation was out of control. I was working ten-hour days for eighteen-day stretches without a break. I was tired of seeing more people die than I could help. I was tired of the pressure of deciding who to take in and who to leave outside to die. If I put a protective shield around myself and turned my back on those I couldn't help I felt guilty later about not having done enough. But if I didn't, I'd feel hurt and useless, and that made it impossible to go out and do my job. I cried myself to sleep with anxiety every night.

At one point the new man in charge of the Red Cross relief department flew in from Addis to see how we were doing. A visit from headquarters was rare. As I drove him around, we passed a man lying dying in the road. As we went by, he opened his eyes and gestured towards us.

'Aren't you going to stop?' asked my shocked passenger.

'Why? What could I do if I did?'

'You must go back. We should help him,' he insisted.

'I can't stop for everyone,' I explained as reasonably as I could. 'I pass a dozen or more old people like that every day and there's nothing I can do for them. It's pointless taking them to the hospital because they're only interested in caring for the wounded military there. I've tried it. They'll just kick him out. He needs food but we don't even have enough to keep the children alive. There isn't any to give to people like him. There are thousands more just like him beyond the town's boundary. We need tons more dried rations to feed them all.'

He just looked at me and I felt worse than ever. He was the one in charge of sending us the food supplies and, despite the reports we kept sending, he seemed to have no idea how bad it was in Mekele. He made me feel as if I wasn't doing my job properly. I felt a failure, but I also felt angry. What more could I do, given the impossible conditions in which we were working? The situation seemed hopeless.

9

SAVED

JUST AS THINGS HAD REACHED CRISIS POINT, I RECEIVED A telephone call one evening from the head of the ICRC delegation in Addis. A call was in itself unusual, because although there was a telephone in the hotel, it rarely worked. I was told that a team from the BBC was coming to Mekele and I was to show them around, explaining what we were trying to do. I was surprised, because if the ICRC ever made any public statements, they were always issued from a higher diplomatic level, not by the field staff.

The next day, the BBC foreign correspondent Michael Buerk and his cameraman Mo Amin turned up at the gates of the feeding centre. He'd seen the starving people on the roads and been to the camps elsewhere in the country and now he saw the selection process in the feeding centre. He followed me as I was trying to feed the kids. While I was surrounded by desperate skeletal and malnourished children who were screaming and shouting, and pulling at my hands, Michael tried to ask me questions and get me to stand where they would get the best shot. Then he asked me if making those life-and-death decisions over who should be fed did anything to me.

What a question! I was indignant. What on earth did he think it did to me? For a moment I didn't know whether to take him seriously or not, but in the end there was only one reply I could give: 'Yes, of course it does. What do you expect? It breaks my heart.'

And then they'd gone. For me, their appearance was just a blink in the day. I remember that day because I took a baby with a dangerously low haemoglobin count to hospital. After chasing around town to find the laboratory technician, who'd knocked off early, I discovered that I was the same blood group as the baby, so I gave a unit of blood for him (without telling the mother). While I was recovering, a number of casualties from the fighting outside town were brought in to the hospital, some of them with nasty abdominal wounds. I asked the hospital staff why they weren't giving blood transfusions and was told there wasn't any blood. At the time, I bit my lip, but the next day I cornered the doctor in charge.

'You make me laugh. Here we are in a town of around

fifty thousand people and you say there's no blood. It's about time people realized how they could help. I'll get you some blood.'

He looked at me, a slip of a girl in her cotton dress, and smiled in disbelief. 'All right, then. As much as you can get.'

Ten minutes later I was back with ten 'volunteers' from the military camp on the edge of town. How could they refuse when I told them that I'd given blood myself, and me just a woman? The technician and I spent the next hour taking blood, while Asmara went to get some bread and tea from the feeding centre to help them get their strength back. Usually these war casualties would have remained hidden from us but as I'd happened to be there I wanted the hospital to understand that the Red Cross would help save any lives in emergencies. In return, I knew that this would make it easier for me to get my sick children admitted. That night I consoled myself that I had done something worthwhile that day.

I was so caught up in our daily horrors that I virtually forgot about the BBC. It didn't occur to me that their visit would make any difference. Then on 29 October I got a telex from home.

ALL HAVE SEEN AND HEARD REPEATED BROADCAST REPORTS BY BBC TELEVISION AND RADIO PLUS NATIONAL PRESS ON HORRIFIC CONDITIONS IN WOLLO AND TIGRE

PROVINCES. YOUR INTERVIEW WITH BBC NEWS TEAMS IN MEKELE AND ADDIS ABABA [By then I'd also been interviewed by the BBC Africa correspondent, Michael Wooldridge] MOST IMPRESSIVE. MANY PERSONAL TELEPHONE CALLS RECEIVED EXPRESSING ADMIRATION OF YOUR WORK WITH ICRC IN MEKELE

And the telex listed everyone who had called. I couldn't understand it.

Then I got a letter from my mother saying that the telephone hadn't stopped ringing. Family friends and acquaintances had seen the interview and wanted to say how shocked they were by the situation and how they related to it by knowing somebody who was in the thick of it. It simply didn't compute. I couldn't understand how a few minutes of television reporting could have had such an impact. If anything it made me angry that everyone was saying how proud they were of me when they hadn't a clue what I was doing and didn't understand what was really going on. How could they?

But then things changed dramatically. Ten days after Michael's visit, in the absolute still of the early morning, I stood on the roof of a lone building in the dirt field outside the town, breathing in the air and the smells, watching the cattle and sheep grazing on the makeshift runway. I'd had to wake the soldiers at the checkpoint so that I could get here for the time I'd been told to arrive. Then, in the distance I heard a noise, and a dark spot over the mountains grew bigger and bigger as it got closer. It was an RAF plane. All I could think was, 'We're saved. We're saved.' Help from this quarter was so unexpected, and I was very emotional. The plane landed in a hail of dust and stones, with the crew smiling and waving. They asked me into the cockpit and gave me a hot cup of tea and Marmite sandwiches on delicious white bread, apologizing that it was all they had with them. To me, it was manna from heaven. When they opened the doors at the rear of the plane, I saw that it was full of food.

I was unaware then that, following Michael Buerk's broadcast, international charities were flooded with donations from the public. Relief supplies had finally poured into Addis, but no one had thought how they would get from there to Mekele. One of the European Red Cross organizations sent Mercedes trucks to transport them, but no one had taken into account the fuel rationing and so the convoys took months to get through. Eventually they hit on the idea of flying the food in. Within a week, loads more planes arrived. The runway was soon damaged by so many planes landing, and everything had to be temporarily halted while it was regraded and a warehouse built to store the supplies. People forget that relief efforts have to be about much more than just sending supplies; the organization of transportation and distribution is every bit as important. Nevertheless within a couple of weeks we were able to double the numbers at the feeding centre and a whole town of tents began to mushroom on the barren plains, providing much-needed shelter for the displaced families against the cold winter winds.

The best day was when I came across a lorry carrying the crew of an RAF Hercules that had landed with supplies. They'd managed to drive from the airport to Mekele without any permits or passes, just smiling and waving at the checkpoints, who let them through so that they could deliver everything to the brothers of the Don Bosco Society. They had some medicines and two large boxes of apples, pears, melons and sliced loaves of white bread, which they gave to me, having seen me raving about the sandwiches I'd been offered when the first plane arrived. I hadn't seen an apple since leaving Europe and dashed round to the nuns to share the haul with them. I took the RAF crew through I don't know how many checkpoints to show them round, so that they could see the starving people and the feeding centre – the reasons they were flying the food in every month. It was quite different from a tour by the authorities, who often judiciously omitted the most distressing and horrifying sights because they didn't want to reveal the extent of the suffering and concentrated on showing visitors what was being done, not what still cried out to be done.

By this time many other reporters were arriving, from all over the world. I felt like a Cook's tour guide as I showed round various news crews. A light bulb had gone on in my head and I now realized how the press could be used to raise public awareness, raise money and bring in proper relief supplies. My name was the one that was given to the journalists as a contact when they arrived in Addis. I soon understood what they wanted: a picture of a young English-speaking white woman working in these terrible conditions, with whom their readers could identify, as well as pictures of starving children. That was what would get the public to put their hands into their pockets and contribute. I didn't mind being that young woman if it would get us the food and medical supplies we so badly needed.

One day, a Swiss photo-journalist working for the ICRC's public relations department came to take pictures, but she was too upset and horrified by what she saw to do what she had come for. I took her round the feeding centre, suggesting various shots. 'Why don't you take a picture of this baby? She's very weak and won't last the night.' Or 'What about this toddler? He's blind from Vitamin A deficiency.' All she could say was, 'Oh no, I can't. I'd feel awful if I did.' She just didn't get it. She didn't understand the effect that images of these children could have on the rest of the world. I felt that her scruples about exploiting the misery of the children were misplaced. She was aghast at our living conditions and the lack of clean water. I don't think she cleaned her teeth or washed her face for the couple of days she was there and I suspect she didn't dare sleep on her bed after I'd warned her about the fleas and bedbugs. Fortunately other visitors were less squeamish.

All sorts of visiting dignitaries and celebrities, among them the British Ambassador, Senator Edward Kennedy and Cardinal Basil Hume, started to come out with the relief supplies, all wanting to do something to help. However, not all of them got it right. Robert Maxwell arrived with a much-publicized planeload of donations from *Daily Mirror* readers, which included masses of stuff we couldn't use – baby formula we couldn't make up without a clean water supply or bottles and teats; out-of-date drugs, including contraceptive pills, hypertension pills, diabetic tablets and slimming tablets in one big bag – a complete waste of money; toilet rolls for people who didn't know what they were for. One week we held off distributing blankets to hundreds of refugees because we were told that some new ones were coming in. When they arrived they were beautifully hand-crocheted baby blankets – utterly useless against the freezing nights.

It was the smaller donations that were the most affecting. I remember that a Sussex newspaper donated enough to charter a plane filled with full-size blankets. The journalist who came with them was tickled pink to find that within an hour of arriving they were being distributed to the needy. He was able to take home some great shots for the readers who had made donations. There was a small six-seater piloted by Air Southwest that made a dramatic flight via Rome and Cairo through sheet lightning and storms, restricted airspace and more storms, and finally arrived at Addis without any landing permits but with some much-needed medical supplies. The adventures people undertook in order to bring aid to Mekele were wonderful.

Perhaps what touched and amazed me most were the letters I began to receive from all over the world from people who had seen the news footage. Envelopes addressed only to Sister Claire, Red Cross, Mekele, Ethiopia, found their way to me. I even began a correspondence with a church minister from Georgia, USA, who wrote asking how her church could help and offering their love and support. One that particularly moved me came all the way from California. I imagined an exhausted businessman coming back to a hotel room after a day making money, throwing off his jacket and sitting down to watch the television news. Seeing what was happening in Mekele, he realized that there were more important things in life and was motivated to scribble a letter to me on hotel notepaper:

Dear Sister Claire,
You said on the news just now that letters from home helped you cope during this famine. I've sent money through CARE; let me merely send you one more letter to let you know people all over the world are inspired by you. If you could hear us rooting for you – think of the

loudest roar you ever heard from the fans in a football
stadium for the solitary player carrying the ball for them
– if you could only hear us it would overwhelm any cheer
you ever heard. Please keep carrying the ball for us, Sister.

Getting that, and letters like it, made such a difference to
me.

Just as things were beginning to improve, as food and
shelter were beginning to get through, Dr Pierre flew in
from Addis to see how things were going. He told us that
the ICRC were opening a new feeding centre in Maichew,
405 miles north of Addis. He knew that Ruth was particularly attached to Mekele, having been there for so long,
and besides, her contract would soon be running out, so
would I be interested in transferring there? I didn't have to
think twice. Always ready for a new challenge and with the
attractive prospect of having to get things up and running
dangled in front of me, I leaped at the chance.

All I knew about Maichew was that it was a government-
controlled military base on a mountain surrounded by the
Tigrayan People's Liberation Front (TPLF). The only way
in and out was by military convoy. I had heard that lorries
would be loaded and then have to wait for weeks for the
green light. The military would go ahead to de-mine
the roads and post soldiers on the hilltops. Then the convoy
of lorries would roll by, followed by the ICRC vehicles a
good five hundred metres behind so that we wouldn't be

directly associated with the military. As soon as the last car had passed, the road was closed again. Hans-Peter, the ICRC delegate who worked in Maichew, said he always put on walking shoes, just in case. Accommodation would be basic and food scarce. At least in Mekele I'd been able to buy tomatoes and onions and had an emergency escape route by plane. Hans-Peter was trying to construct a runway within the military camp – the only safe place – but Maichew was surrounded by mountains so any pilot would have to risk a spiralling descent or take-off. The only contact we'd have would be through an HF radio via the Relief and Rehabilitation Commission in Mekele. It all sounded very much my sort of thing. I couldn't wait.

As Christmas approached, I was curled up in bed one night when I heard a song, 'Do They Know It's Christmas?', crackling over my short-wave radio. There was some sort of fuzzy explanation about how it was for Ethiopia. Getting completely the wrong end of the stick, I was incandescent with rage. Who was this Bob Geldof to capitalize on the misery of the displaced people of Ethiopia? I had no idea that through the song and his charity Band Aid he was raising millions for their benefit. I thought that everyone involved was taking a percentage and making a quick buck for themselves. Isolated in Mekele, I knew nothing of the extraordinary work he was doing.

All I knew was that my time in Mekele was running out

and, though anxious that I might have burned myself out, I was looking forward to the next challenge of setting up the centre in Maichew and providing much-needed aid in another part of the country.

10

STARTING FROM SCRATCH

NINE HUNDRED PAIRS OF EYES LOOKED UP AS THE FURIOUS buzzing noise grew louder. Suddenly a white speck seemed to jump over the mountain tops before gliding down into our dusty, drought-ridden plateau. Someone described the place as like an extinct volcanic crater, because it was surrounded by mountains on three sides; while on the fourth there was a sheer drop to the village of Mahoni and the parched plains two thousand feet below. As the speck got closer we could clearly make out the two distinct red crosses on its wings. It was 'Gussie', a small single-engined Pilatus Porter aircraft, with Bill the Dutchman at the controls.

Gussie (short for 'Augusta' because she reminded us of an eccentric elderly aunt who'd arrive at odd times of the year bearing gifts of all sorts) was old and ugly but very dignified. She looked as if she'd been stuck together from orange boxes and her nose was too long for her body – but we loved her. After all, she was our main exit route from Maichew, apart from the irregular military convoys that came in and out by road. She could carry in up to one ton of relief supplies at a time or ten passengers, or the seats could be removed to fit in any wounded on stretchers for evacuation. At 2,640 metres above sea level, Maichew was so high and the newly built runway so short that only Gussie knew how to land there. Being in an area in south Tigray where the security situation was extremely unstable and the roads in and out could be 'shut' for days or weeks at a time, without Gussie we'd have been helpless.

As for Bill, the pilot, he was in his sixties, plump, jovial and as experienced as they come. Because it was surrounded on three sides by mountains, our valley was often shrouded in cloud when he made his first early-morning flight. We'd hear Gussie buzzing like a wasp above the clouds looking for a hole to dive through. We'd watch anxiously, scared silly that he'd crunch into one of the mountainsides. But he'd keep on trying, and all of a sudden he would find a gap and down Gussie would swoop, to land on our makeshift runway despite the crosswinds and the trees along one side. At one stage, we had to ask the military to move one of their defence points as it was in danger of being clipped by Gussie's tyres as she landed.

Six years earlier, the area around Maichew had been green and luscious, but by the time we arrived, like the rest of Ethiopia the ground was brown, cracked and dry and whatever rain came never seemed to soften it at all. Maichew itself had become a government stronghold amid countryside controlled by the TPLF. A few mud shacks with corrugated iron or straw roofs straggled on either side of the main dirt road. The only place to buy anything was the weekly market on the outskirts, but few peasants came now and those who did had only a few leaves to sell, a pile of prickly pears, a couple of eggs, the odd family heirloom or an old cooking pot. But because of the presence of a military base, the village was deemed a safe place to establish a feeding centre.

Thousands of malnourished men, women and children had been herded into a camp beside the site of the new feeding centre on the edge of town. These displaced people had been driven out of the interior of Ethiopia by the civil unrest and the desperate need for food. Conditions in the camp and centre were much as they had been in Mekele. But now that relief had begun to flood into the country in earnest, soon after I arrived things began to improve. Tents were brought in relatively quickly, each of them big enough to shelter ten people or two families. Food was more of a problem because the convoys were few and far between and Gussie couldn't carry enough for the number of people camped there. Every morning, we heard the familiar sound of chanting and wailing accompanying the bodies on their way to be buried. But when we first went into the camp to weigh and measure the children, we were thrilled to find that everyone had at least been getting some rations, however small. We set to work, concentrating on the children under five who fell under the 75 per cent weight-for-height ratio. These were the ones who urgently needed to go on the same supplementary feeding programme of oral rehydration salts and high-energy milk drink that we had supplied in Mekele.

Four of us ICRC workers had come to work here. Hans-Peter was a Swiss delegate who was in charge of liaison with the local authorities and the logistics of organizing the deliveries of food and supplies to the town and their distribution to the displaced people. He was a vet by profession and back home he ran a farm. An old hand with the ICRC, he always returned to Switzerland in the spring in time for the cherry harvest. I remember him for the way he made such an effort to get on with the locals, going out of his way to talk to them and help them. For example, he paid out of his own pocket for our cook to have a false leg to replace the leg blown off by a landmine. Max was a lively, hardworking, typically French thirty-something doctor who was never far from his Gauloises. He had years of working with Médecins sans Frontières under his belt. He understood the difference between the theory of providing emergency relief and the practicalities of doing it in the field. For instance, instead of using charts, he got the mothers to draw charcoal lines on their child's arm to show how many cups they'd drunk; and he taught the local workers that soap and water was as good as any other disinfectant. The other nurse, Helen Staunton, was Irish, my age and red-haired; she was quick-witted, fiery, and made us laugh. She'd just returned to the field after several weeks recuperating from being shot in the chest when her car was ambushed in Uganda. We made a great team and morale was high. I was happier than I had been for months and I found myself working with people who became good friends.

The new feeding centre was completed by the beginning of February 1985. We'd had to order everything necessary from scratch, from corrugated iron to plastic sheets. We had even mounted an expedition to the market in Addis to buy five hundred teaspoons, plastic cups, cooking utensils and washing-up liquid. What a different set-up it was from the one I'd known at Mekele. We had six large three-sided corrugated iron shelters with mud floors covered with plastic, which could each accommodate 75 to 100 children plus a parent or guardian. There was also a large kitchen shed, a stores shed, a de-lousing shed and pit latrines built on the leeward side.

A project like this always took time to set up because each local worker had to be trained to do their job. Often they couldn't read or write and it didn't help that we didn't speak their language. Showing them what to do took a while because everything was new to them. So it was a real pleasure to see that within days Raya Bellay, a local Maichew man whom we appointed as our administrator, was running the day-to-day routine of the centre single-handedly. I was always there to make sure that all was running smoothly and to help with any problems, but his appointment left me free to coordinate, recruit and set up training programmes. He'd never had this kind of a job in his life before but had dabbled in this and that – anything from labouring to trading in the market. We picked him because he'd finished his schooling and spoke good English. He was thirty-one years old, older than the rest of the staff, and he had a warm smile. When we interviewed him, he recited the entire history of the ICRC front to back – not bad, considering he'd had only twenty-four hours to bone up before the interview. I don't think any of us would have claimed to know the full history of our own organization with dates thrown in.

I found that being dyslexic helped me when I was trying to explain something because it was natural for me to convey my meaning in pictures. Take hand washing. When I talked to our local workers about germs and bacteria and the importance of using soap and water to prevent the spread of infection, they'd say, 'Yes, yes, yes,' but then I'd see them just running their hands through water. However, I found that if I acted out what happened when they chopped chillies, dipped their hands in water and then rubbed their eyes, and then told them, with Raya translating, that 'bad germs' were like chillies, too small to be seen, they understood very clearly why hands had to be washed properly.

Training the cooks fell to Helen and me. We cooked using wood in clay ovens that were designed to take an oil drum filled with water. The first day we got into a terrible muddle and got the quantities of the ingredients for the renourishing milk drink all wrong. Hardly surprising given that most of the cooks couldn't understand a word we were saying. So I drew the quantities on sheets of paper which I pinned up by the mixing area, using butter oil tins as a measure – three tins by the sacks of dried skimmed milk, two tins by the butter oil and one tin by the sugar. Nor could they quite grasp the idea of having to boil the water before stirring in the mixture until I drew an oil drum of boiling water with bubbles overflowing the sides. My imitation of the sound of boiling water had them rolling about with laughter. Then I drew a picture of the bucket with the pre-mix of milk powder, butter oil and sugar alongside four buckets of boiling water – cue more laughter – and showed how to mix them. They got the message and a few days later all was running smoothly.

We started feeding on 4 February and by the end of the first week had admitted about seven hundred children. We'd been advised by the medical division in Addis to take it easy and start off with about 150, gradually increasing the numbers as the staff became more experienced, but when Max saw the situation at Maichew, he said, 'Bullshit! [his favourite English word] We feed all the children who need supplementary feeding.' And that's exactly what we did. We made our selection of the children in the camp and fed them four times a day with the high-energy milk drink. But many of them were weakened by dehydration and diarrhoea so within four days we had introduced a system of pink cups to be given out by the health assistant to all those who needed a drink of oral rehydration salts before the high-energy milk drink came round. Once they were tolerating the milk drink, which was usually after a couple of weeks, we could wean them on to porridge made of the high-energy milk drink plus flour, their first solid food. When we first dished up the porridge, it was as if we were doling out ice-cream. There was a mad dash by about thirty mothers in the feeding clinic, all hitting and shoving one another out of the way to get at the porridge bucket, even though there was more than enough for everyone. My pleasure in seeing how much they enjoyed it was tempered by my feeling of sadness as I saw how people lose their dignity in their struggle to survive.

What was so encouraging was that we quickly saw good results. The children's bellies and faces grew fuller, and some were soon running around on their matchstick legs. There was even a smile or two to be seen. To begin with we were nervous about discharging anyone too soon, anxious that they should not return days later as starved as they'd been in the first place, as I had often seen in Mekele. But our hopes for good results were not disappointed and after several weeks we were confidently able to let some go and to admit about a hundred new children on a weekly basis. The death rate dropped by half.

At the beginning, there was a lot to organize. For example, there was the scabies programme to get going. Many of the children had infected sores, spread by scabies mites, all over their bodies. Their whole families needed treatment since they all huddled together to sleep, and the problem was never-ending. We'd soak the children in a barrel of warmed-up potassium permanganate solution, often several at a time. They hated it and, to make matters worse, the water never stayed warm for long. After about fifteen minutes we'd wash their hands with soap and paint them with benzyl benzoate solution. One little boy in particular turned out to be a help to us. He was among the group of the worst affected whom we treated first. With infected lesions all over his body, he stood huddled with several others, all shaking with fear. After three days, it was heart-warming to see him running around trying to escape the third and final treatment. After he'd had it, though, he went round encouraging the others who weren't keen on the treatment, showing them how much better he was. But the reality was that we were fighting a losing battle. Scabies is highly contagious and the living conditions made it impossible to treat everyone. We steamed all the clothes and blankets of the children we treated as well, but it was never long before they returned, re-infected by someone else in their tent.

Max and Helen were great to work with. We were trained in the same school of thought: if you help people to help themselves without becoming dependent on you, you minimize the need for outside assistance. We all understood that because of the precarious security situation, Maichew could be taken at any moment by the TPLF. It was imperative that in such an event, the feeding centre should be able to continue its work without us. Max taught me to ignore theoretical rules when they didn't make practical sense. We often saw children over the age of five who needed feeding. He would say, 'Admit them and we'll deal with the admin later.' He taught me not to panic when a child came in with a prolapsed rectum, a condition that can be caused by diarrhoea, and showed me how to put it back. We didn't use rubber gloves because we wanted the mothers to learn to do it themselves if it happened again: we had to teach them in a way appropriate to the conditions in which they might find themselves in the months to come, so we couldn't have them thinking gloves were a must. He taught the local Red Cross workers how to examine the children to diagnose pneumonia and bronchitis, and then prescribe antibiotics according to a regime he'd set out. But it used to make Max laugh when he asked Raya for something from the stores and he replied, 'I'll just ask Sister Claire if it's all right.' Doctor or no doctor, Raya always saw me as the boss. It was Raya's attention to detail and his efficiency that kept the centre running so smoothly.

My role was to oversee everything, rather like a matron, and to coordinate the operation. We put up charts that recorded attendance each day as well as any deaths. Each youth worker was responsible for fifty children, registering them at each feed and, if they hadn't turned up for the first feed at 08.00, going to find them under the piece of sacking they called 'home' to see why they hadn't come. Often the parents hid their children if they thought they were dying in the belief that devils would get them otherwise. Raya interviewed would-be workers with me, acting as translator. He kept the staff in line but asked me to discipline them if ever it was necessary. In one instance he advised me to sack a deaf-mute cleaner for stealing food. I felt dreadful because I knew how badly the cleaner must need the food, but all the staff knew that stealing was against the rules and Raya thought I should make an example of him. Raya knew the locals far better than I did, so I had to trust him.

We also were able to open a primitive clinic for in-patients. It might not have been up to Swiss standards or those of St Mary's, Paddington, but it was well above what the Ethiopians were used to and it worked well. We could accommodate up to ninety starving children who were so close to death that they needed intensive feeding. We couldn't offer intravenous therapy but fed them by spoon and then cup. The most severely dehydrated would receive oral rehydration salts and there was medical treatment in the way of antibiotics and other drugs. We also had a daily average of about sixty out-patients, all under five years old, on regular medical treatment for complaints such as diarrhoea and chest or eye infections. They had to come to us daily for whatever dosage they were taking. That was the only way we could be sure they took it. Giving a course of antibiotics to a mother without a watch who didn't have three regular meals to feed her family a day meant that the pills often got forgotten or, when the patient seemed better, she would share the 'magic' tablets with someone else in the family or sell them in the market to buy food.

We found that the hardest thing to explain to the mothers and to our auxiliaries was that the food we gave the children was as important as the medicine, or even more so. They didn't always understand that they had to continue making their children eat and drink after they had been discharged while continuing to take the medicine too. It could be so frustrating. Too many of the children who died were starved to death by their mother's lack of understanding. Looking back, I sometimes think I may have been naïve in wanting to save them all, but I couldn't accept any child dying when we were doing all we could to help them.

Although there were so many children in the centre, there were inevitably a few who made themselves particularly dear to me. When asked who I was, the children would say I was their mother. I still remember Abuhanna, a two-year-old girl from an Afar family, part of a nomadic tribe from the Danekel area, who was cheeky and full of beans. Like many of the other children, when she was sufficiently recovered to follow me around she'd sit on my lap and try to slip her hand down the front of my dress to get to my bosom so that she could have a drink. This was very normal in a culture where children often feed from whichever woman is holding them. Being a reserved Westerner, I never allowed her to get that far with me.

Asofu, the little Afar girl I am carrying in the picture on the cover of this book, was brought in by her exhausted father. They'd been walking for three weeks from the Danekel. Her brother had died just days before they reached Maichew. She was a skinny little thing in a red T-shirt with a few blue and white beads on her wrists. Her skin had no elasticity and looked as if it was dripping off her. She lay very still and completely silent in her father's arms. I very slowly spoon-fed her some watered-down milk drink, handing the spoon to her father to take over. I showed him that although it was dribbling out of her mouth, we had to keep trying and that eventually she would start swallowing it. When I returned a couple of hours later, he had given up, telling me through an interpreter that she wasn't hungry. Once again, I gently explained that although she might not want the drink, she needed it to survive and that he had to keep going. They stayed at the centre for the whole day and I encouraged them to return the next. By the morning of the second day she was drinking from a spoon, by the afternoon from a cup. By the end of the week she was running around on her own, and coming up to me to stroke my hair, so different from her own. Not long afterwards, I saw her father and some friends eating a slaughtered goat, sucking its liver as if it was a sponge. Offering me a bit as a thank-you for saving Asofu, they found the horrified look on my face hilarious.

Hagos, another favourite, was a four-year-old boy who never stopped talking and giving me kisses, always with a runny nose. As soon as I arrived in the centre, he'd run over calling out, 'Mama Clear, Mama Clear,' giggling and talking ten to the dozen. He'd follow me around, hanging on to my skirt, asking me for a blanket or extra clothes if I went to the store. It never bothered him that neither of us could understand a word the other said. When I spoke to a child who wasn't eating properly or a sick child I was worried about, he'd happily chat away to them too. Heaven only knows what he said. I loved these children dearly. It really brightened up the day to have them around.

Starvation wasn't the only problem we had to deal with. Every ailment was exacerbated by the conditions. Complaints that for us would have been relatively minor, in normal living conditions with good food and rest, took much longer to recover from here. If anything more serious happened, we had a problem simply because we were so cut off from the rest of the country.

One day in March, a high-pitched scream cut across the babble of children's voices in the centre. I looked up and saw that Almaz, our chief cook, had somehow been accidentally knocked into the 100-litre barrel of boiling water. Luckily I was only a hundred yards away, and I dashed over to drag her out, screaming and fighting. I got her to the water tap, stripping off her dress and drenching her in cold water. Her burns covered her thighs, buttocks and arms. Although extensive, they looked fairly superficial, but I was worried about the danger of infection. We didn't have enough dressings, so I drove her to the village health centre. Within five minutes of getting there I was sorry I'd bothered. We were shown into a filthy room where the health assistants came in with dirty hands, dropped the gauze on the floor and still wanted to use it. They were sympathetic and really wanted to help, but not only did they have no supplies, they hadn't a clue what to do. I was horrified. I realized that it was up to me to save Almaz.

I decided to take her to her home, but on the way I stopped at my room and picked up some clean sheets (we'd had to bring our own, as well as mattresses, from Addis) and spare tubes of antiseptic cream from the paediatric boxes. They were meant for nappy rash but as our children went without nappies, fortunately we had dozens of tubes spare. She couldn't direct me to her house by car, so with me supporting her, we somehow walked for ten minutes to the mud room she shared with her mother, three sisters, brother, brother-in-law and baby. Inside, there was a rickety chair and a bed made from logs lashed together with a lattice base made of raw hide, with no mattress. Where they all slept, I couldn't imagine. I put some antiseptic cream on Almaz's burns and got her to lie down in the clean sheets. I managed to put up a saline drip and encouraged her sister to give her regular sips of oral rehydration salts to try to prevent her going into shock from dehydration. Two hours later, I took Max to see her. Poor Almaz was in agony, her back, buttocks and arm raw and blistered. We had no specialized supplies for such large burns and we agreed that the only thing we could do was give her antibiotics and sedate her while we arranged to evacuate her to hospital in Asmara or else she would die from an infection. We gave her a shot of painkillers and some Valium to calm her for the night.

Next morning, at 08.30, we had a radio check with Mekele, but for the umpteenth time no one was there. It was often a case of 'out of sight out of mind'. Luckily I knew Ato Hailoo, the village radio operator, and I explained the severity of the situation, asking him to arrange a telephone patch (that is, use the military HF radio network used only for official information). With his help the ICRC delegation in Asmara was alerted and broke off Gussie's day of maintenance so that she could fly out immediately. Another radio check at 10.30 confirmed that Bill was on his way. Almaz was in terrible pain, vomiting and dehydrated. I arranged the stretcher with more of my clean sheets to wrap her in as soon as we heard Gussie approaching. Suddenly I remembered we needed security travel permits for Almaz and her brother, who was going with her. No one was allowed to move outside the village without permission from the security forces, signed and stamped in triplicate. The military security office closed in twenty minutes but we managed to get the necessary documents and Almaz was dispatched, with 50 birr in an envelope marked 'Buy yourself a dress before returning'. As an ICRC employee, she had medical insurance, so she could be admitted to the Italian hospital in Asmara, where she was cared for by the nuns. What a party we had when she returned six weeks later, healthy and fit, in her new dress. She was lucky that she got away with minimal scarring.

11

EPIDEMIC

FOR THE SIX MONTHS I WAS IN MAICHEW WE STAYED IN A hostelry in the village. It was a single-storey building with walls made from mud, dung and straw, and painted white on the outside. It was used mostly by truck drivers and I was fascinated to see the local girls enter one room at night and leave another in the morning. 'Comforting the drivers' was accepted as completely normal. Our rooms were each the size of a horsebox, with the doors opening on to the outside courtyard. They were just big enough for a bed, chair and bedside table – there were no cupboards or shelves. I kept most of my things in a suitcase, although I banged a nail into the door for my toilet bag and hung a small mirror beside it. There was no glass in the window, just an ill-fitting wooden shutter. A lone 15-watt light bulb lit my surroundings, but when the generator failed (which it did frequently), or once when I changed it for a 60-watt bulb and fused the entire hotel, three candles worked almost as well. I regularly sprayed the vivid green walls with insecticide but apparently without effect, largely I suspect because I was being bitten by fleas that I picked up in the centre.

A woman collected the water for the hostelry from a well in town and carried it in a big earthenware container on her back. Water for washing in my room was brought in a bucket by the cook, and the supply was irregular. Sometimes we got what looked like ditch water to wash in and sometimes nothing at all. When the supply ran out, we'd bring water in jerry cans from the feeding centre. I became used to standing in a small washing-up bowl filled with cold water and, if I was lucky, a splash of the cook's water which he kept on the boil for tea. I soon worked out an efficient strip-wash routine using minimum water. However the other hostelry in town boasted 'hot shower for fifty cents'. We'd warn the owner that we were coming the day before so that he could buy wood, and then Helen, Max and I would all go over together to drink sweet tea and play Yahtzee, cards or I-Spy while taking it in turns to shower. It was the highlight of the week. Just the pull of a string made the hot water fall from the tank into the tiny, smelly wooden cubicle alive with spiders. Mmm, it was good.

The smell of ammonia from our hostelry's latrines was so pungent that my eyes watered and smarted whenever I went near them. The locals didn't always use the hole, so you'd have to negotiate turds in the dark, careful not to touch the shit-smeared wall. When Hans-Peter and I both got severe food poisoning, using those latrines was no joke. It happened one night when we were offered tripe instead of the usual goat meat with our nightly *injera*. Helen sensibly sniffed it and refused to have any, but Hans-Peter and I were too hungry. Even though we had only a few mouthfuls, a couple of hours later we were both stricken with diarrhoea and vomiting. Those latrines! I had to squat, feeling weak and dizzy but not wanting to support myself with a hand on the wall, while my trousers dragged in the mess. Flies rose up from the shitty ground, landing on my face faster than I could brush them off. We were both so ill that we could barely get out quickly enough for the other. I kept replacing the fluid I was losing by drinking a solution of oral rehydration salts which tasted awful, nothing like the 'tears' they are meant to resemble. Hans-Peter felt too nauseous to drink, so he became extremely dehydrated despite the drip that Helen put up for him. By the morning we were both in such a weakened state that we were airlifted out by a military helicopter to Mekele and taken from there by a C-130 Hercules to the Russian hospital in Addis. Hans-Peter had to be medevacked back home to Switzerland. I escorted him and took the opportunity to fly from there back to the UK and have a weekend at home before returning alone to Maichew.

For our own security we were confined to living quarters from nightfall till morning, so there was nothing much to do in the evening. We'd arrive back for our supper, almost always delicious *injera*, eaten, like everything else, with our fingers. There was no fruit and the only vegetables we had were locally picked leaves that tasted a little like spinach. Occasionally someone found a tomato in the market, but that was a real treat. I usually hit the sack exhausted at about nine o'clock, only to be woken early by one of the cockerels that scratched about outside, crowing on my window sill. I rigged up a system of strings so that I could pull open the wooden shutter without getting out of bed and lie watching the changing colour of the mountains as dawn approached. How do you stop a cockerel waking you on Sunday morning? Yes, I know – eat him for Saturday dinner, but it didn't work for me. If ever we ate chicken for dinner, we never seemed to eat the right one. Apart from the cockerels, there was always the bustle of farmyard noises as people and animals began to rise with the sun. Every few days someone would slaughter a goat in the shed next to my room. I'd wake hearing the goat's cries of terror as it was dragged in and hung upside down by its legs, and then had its throat slit. It sounded so like one of our children in pain that my stomach would turn over every time and I'd block my ears until the noise stopped. It didn't prevent me from eating stewed goat, though.

Once, as I was groping my way towards the heavenly smell of the latrines, I looked up and noticed how bright the stars were. And there it was, right in the place where I'd been looking for it every night for the last two months – the Plough. I'd been able to identify Orion and the Seven Sisters before but the Plough had stayed stubbornly below the horizon. I was so thrilled – it was like finding an old friend from home.

Within a short time after we moved in, two of the village children seemed to adopt us. One of them was aged about five and I think had suffered from polio. She was grubby and grey with dust, and she pulled herself along on her arms, dragging her dead leg behind her, through the dirty streets, rain or shine, clad in a tatty shirt that hardly reached her belly button and shorts held up with a bit of tied red material. She went everywhere with her big sister, who was about ten (though she looked six). They relied on other people to give them something to eat. In the morning, I'd give them some bread and a glass of sweet tea. Sometimes we'd eat prickly pear together, the only fruit that grew on the mountainside. Considering their circumstances, they were very healthy and the younger one had a lovely smile. We had a little game in which I used to shake her hand and we'd say hello, she in English and me in Tigrinian. Once I bought her a toy plane just like Gussie, made from the remains of a butter oil tin with red crosses torn from a cigarette packet on the wings. All the children in Maichew and at the camp were fascinated by planes. They had never seen one at close quarters till the arrival of Gussie. They'd make planes out of sticks, old cans and cardboard. A sure sign of their recovery was when they started wheeling round the feeding centre with their arms outstretched, making engine noises. It was a joyous sight. I'd almost forgotten how it felt to see children happy and playing till then.

Soon after we arrived in Maichew we were able to set up a satellite feeding centre at Mahoni. Flying down the 200-foot drop from our plateau was a heart-stopping experience, like leaping off the side of a precipice, but it took only eight minutes in the fearless Gussie. In Mahoni, the malnutrition among the displaced people was dreadful. These people were too weak to make it up the mountain road to Maichew. While I continued to look after the Maichew centre, Helen soon had the one in Mahoni up and running. She and I covered for one another whenever we managed to take a break, so occasionally I'd have to go down to Mahoni. Between Mahoni and Maichew, we could care for 1,100 children at a time. We heard that in Mekele they now had five ICRC nurses and a doctor for the same number of children in a new feeding centre while we were only two nurses and a doctor. But we managed very well indeed.

Things were going well in Mahoni until Helen returned to Maichew one evening, reporting a case of cholera. Having been in an outbreak before, she recognized the symptoms immediately and knew what to do. Without panicking, she raised the alarm with the medical co-ordinator in Addis. It was imperative that the infected people were given fluids as quickly as possible, but to save them and to prevent an epidemic, we had to improve sanitation. Max swiftly negotiated for the road to be opened and we all headed down to Mahoni, our Land Cruiser loaded with intravenous (IV) infusions and oral re-hydration salts as well as the sanitation expert who happened to be visiting us. Fortunately there were already two enormous hospital tents set up for the feeding centre and we laid the sick in these. They had dark sunken eyes, dry skin and lips and rapid shallow breathing; some were unconscious and all had profuse diarrhoea and vomiting. Our sanitation expert saw to the water supplies by dis-infecting the well, arranging for new latrines to be dug and explaining to the people how to use them, as well as spray-ing the living areas against flies. He even tried to make 'cholera beds' – a piece of suspended plastic with a hole in the middle and a bucket underneath – but they were a bit too elaborate for our 'bush' way of working and most of the patients just lay on plastic sheeting spread on the floor. We didn't have any proper cannulas for attaching to the intra-venous sets and running the fluid through. We had only the butterfly type for children and babies, and they were too small and slow-running to give sufficient fluid to adults. As a result, we had to follow the local health centre practice of putting a needle straight into a vein and strapping it in place. It was a painful procedure and the patient had only to bend their elbow a little and the needle would pierce through the vein and the fluid would dissipate in the surrounding tissue – useless.

What I remember most was the terrible smell as we struggled to make the patients more comfortable, working flat out, our legs aching, backs straining, each putting up as many as forty drips in a day. We were surrounded by children and adults soaked in the distinctive shit of cholera victims, whose stools were like rice water. We'd be kneeling in it to put up a drip on a child while her mother cleaned up with her shawl which she'd then wrap around her healthy baby. To my Western eyes, the hygiene arrangements left much to be desired, but of course these people hadn't been taught anything different.

We tried to impose order on the growing chaos. We called the patients in one by one so that we could keep reasonably organized – in, take their history, get the IV up, one relative only, next. There were three-month-old babies too weak to cry, whose small veins kept tissuing as we tried, oh so carefully, to put in a drip, not once or twice but five or six times, trying different sites – forearm, front of elbow, scalp, feet – and not stopping to feel anguished about trying so many times when there were no veins to see. As the child hyperventilated, its eyes glazing over, what could we do but keep trying? One of the assistants who was the most helpful in putting up drips happened to be the man who kept the latrines clean. The hygiene!

I felt I was moving in a nightmare. Trying to put up a drip and realizing that the patient was already dead. Shouting at mothers when a drip tissued because their child moved their hand. Crushing tetracycline tablets for children to swallow and having them vomited back in my face. Mothers emptying potties (old butter oil tins) under the plastic and hastily pulling it back so that we didn't notice, leaving those bacteria to multiply in their new lovely warm home. One of the guards trying to clean the plastic by splashing water everywhere and then mopping up with his hands, spreading water and dirt all over the place. Trying to wash my hands in a cup of water. The army bringing in one of their comrades on a stretcher. Helen screaming at them to get their bloody guns outside the Red Cross centre. One of our guards on the gate, who knew the regulations, confiscating a gun but absent-mindedly wandering round the centre with it – Helen screaming again. Oh, the language! A whirlwind dust spout on the horizon coming closer and closer, blowing dust everywhere, all over the patients, in our eyes, noses, mouths, on cotton-wool gauze, inside boxes. A visit from the Red Cross medical coordinator and local administrator: 'How are you getting on? Fine, fine. Jolly good. Keep going. Don't let me disturb you.' Idiots!

Inside the tents, it was sweltering hot. There was no time to stop for a break; we just took a moment every now and then to grab a cup of water (brought from Maichew) and a piece of bread. Outside, young mothers who had been brought in moribund with dehydration but who had revived within two hours of receiving several litres of liquid sat under the trees drinking oral rehydration salts while getting registered and braceleted for follow-up treatment. Then to cap it all, a ferocious storm broke, bringing torrential rain and flooding. Patients with drips lay in six inches of water, some supported by their relatives, while outside, the three-metre pit we'd dug for emptying the potties was overflowing everywhere. Water and shit – lying in it, walking in it, working in it. If it hadn't been such a serious life-or-death situation, it would almost have been funny. But laugh about it we did that evening – what else could we do? We came back to Maichew cold, soaked and stinking, but at least we could change our clothes, and have a hot drink, some food and shelter. The displaced people we'd left behind had nothing, nothing, nothing.

In the end, once we'd organized clean water and adequate sanitation facilities, the cholera burnt itself out. We'd managed to give sufficient fluid replacements promptly enough to avoid any deaths. Thankfully the outbreak didn't spread to Maichew, and we avoided catching it ourselves by taking doxicycline prophylaxis and making sure that we drank only clean water and that our food was cooked thoroughly. One month later, the feeding centre was back to normal.

Another potential crisis was narrowly averted, but it left me very shaky. Several times a day children would dash in front of the ICRC Toyota at the last minute as I drove the mile between the hostelry and the feeding centre. Even mothers carrying babies on their backs did it. It scared me stupid. The four-to-six-year-olds were the worst, not really understanding the danger. I had fifty fits that one day I'd kill one of them. Raya explained that they believed they had the Devil chasing them and that if they ran in front of the car at the last minute, he would be killed behind them. When Raya was with me, he would make me stop the car so that he could chase after them and tell them off. But one day, I was driving alone when a little boy ran out in front of me, throwing a stone as he went, oblivious to any danger. I pulled up sharply, leaped out and told him off in my pidgin Tigrinian before turning back to the vehicle to continue my journey. But to my horror, I realized that I hadn't put on the handbrake properly and I saw the Land Cruiser gathering speed as it rolled down an incline towards the tented shelters below. I ran after it but it was too far away for me to catch up. Fortunately some strategically placed trees forcibly stopped it only feet from the camp. I was relieved but horrified. There I was trying to save as many lives as possible under very difficult conditions and I could have killed God knows how many innocent women and children. The thought shook me up so much that I couldn't talk to anyone about it or write home about it for several weeks, and I certainly never got out of my car to tell off another child again.

We were always very aware of the military activity in the area. It was hard to ignore it. Gunfire frequently reverberated as close as a couple of kilometres away. Sometimes army recruits were being trained in Maichew, squads of them being drilled first thing in the morning, singing their marching songs and doing exercises round the streets. We would hear the sound of running and sometimes the noise of helicopters thudding overhead as they prepared to land on the football pitch to pick up any wounded. We never officially knew the details of what was going on. Our job was to carry on working to alleviate the suffering of the people and not to involve ourselves in the politics of the situation.

We all got on well and when not too exhausted could be found playing Yahtzee or Monopoly with our puzzled but delighted local colleagues, who had never seen a board game before. One day I let the girls who worked in the hostelry henna my hands and feet so that I looked as if I had a terrible nicotine habit – as Helen fondly pointed out. Occasionally I would cook something for myself if Gabriel, the one-legged hotel cook, would give me a few hot coals.

I'd wedge myself squatting in the corner of cockroach-ridden squalor that passed as a kitchen with chicken giblets spattered on the floor and last year's dirt on the chopping board. A little boy would fan the coals so that I could knock up something simple like scrambled egg in butter oil, if I'd been able to find eggs at the market.

When we had time off, we used it well. Some of the ICRC personnel went to Kenya on safari or to the beach. My favourite escape was still the Addis Ababa Hilton. What was the point of going on my own to an identical hotel in Kenya? It seemed to me a waste of money to go there, even if there were a few lions thrown in. Happiness for me at that time was lashings of hot water, flush toilets, chocolate mousse, and unlimited fruit and vegetables. That was all I needed.

One evening after the cholera outbreak, we held a party for all the guards, cooks and auxiliaries, and the local dignitaries from the town. It was also to mark our farewell to Max and to Doug, our sanitation expert, whose contracts were up. We'd bought two hundred bottles of Coke and beer that had been brought in by convoy and Raya organized the food – *injera*, naturally – and a few presents. There were fifty or so guests coming and the servants in the hostelry were busy slaughtering goats and chopping meat all day. Raya told me that I was expected to make a speech, along with everyone else. I wrote what I wanted to say in English and he translated it into Tigrinian and read it to me, clearly enunciating every syllable so that I could write it down phonetically and then learn it parrot fashion.

We were honoured by the attendance of the local Maichew dignitaries. The tall 20-stone administrator arrived, accompanied by the skinny, slithery mayor, the small, shifty-looking secretary of the Workers Party of Ethiopia and of course the two officers in charge of the military camp. The first three left after an hour, but it didn't take much pressure to persuade the officers and the chief educational director to stay on. After we'd eaten, given presents and made our speeches (mine had gone down well and I was told they loved my accent), a few local people started dancing in the local Tigrinian style, shaking their shoulders while keeping their head and hips still, to the accompaniment of the women ululating. But our staff clamoured for 'disco dancing'. They knew that Max had brought a tape recorder and some tapes from France. It was a bit too early for most of the expats to get up and dance without a few more drinks inside them, and the dance area under the grapevine in the courtyard remained embarrassingly empty. Then Max spoke up. 'Miss Claire,' he said (they never dropped the Miss, however hard I tried to get them to), 'I think I'm going to be obliged to ask you to dance a rock with me.' He looked serious, as if it was the last thing on earth that I'd want to do. But my feet had been tapping since the music came on. With a good partner, I can dance the night away.

We danced, and it was wonderful. All the guests loved it, clapping and cheering with every double twirl. It got them all going. The beer gave way to whisky, brandy and gin, and everyone wanted to dance with Max. The men asked him, and the girls asked me. In the end we dragged everyone up to dance, however shy, even the two majors, despite their refusal to take off the civilian overcoats hiding their military uniform.

Our curfew was at ten, and the generator stopped on the dot. But we kept going by candlelight for at least another hour. By now, everyone was pleasantly drunk, as we'd expected given that the locals couldn't afford to drink alcohol normally. Then, as we gave two of the female workers a lift home in the car, we were nearly fired on. It was dark and the soldiers at an impromptu checkpoint couldn't see who we were. Their guns were cocked and ready until we switched on the interior light and they could see that we were Europeans. The local girls explained the situation and they soon waved us on, allowing us through on the return journey without any trouble.

By May, things at Maichew were changing. Max had been replaced by Lillia, another French doctor, who had trained in paediatrics in Uruguay. I was by now totally used to the makeshift way we often had to run things if we were to cope with the numbers, but I could see that, coming from a more conventional hospital environment, she was shocked. It was hard for her to grasp just how basic the treatment that we gave people had to be. Either the children were sick, in which case we'd give them antibiotics and sometimes put up a saline drip, or they were hungry, in which case we had to encourage the parent to feed them. There was no room for anything more sophisticated here. I felt for her, but I realized how well Max, Helen and I had worked together and I missed our old team. We had raised the level of care in Maichew to an excellent standard for the area, saving thousands of lives despite the pretty primitive conditions.

Suddenly our group was dispersing. Our sanitation engineer had gone and so had Hans-Peter. Gussie's pilot Bill had been replaced by Walter, half Bill's age. His bright orange baseball cap and zipped flying suit soon earned him the nickname Flash Gordon from Helen. His daredevil flying style was occasionally alarming but thrilling as we dropped down over the edge of the mountain, almost close enough to pick off the cactus flowers, following the road to Maichew.

By June 1985, my own contract was coming to an end too. A year trying to help the Ethiopian people had taken its toll on me emotionally and physically. I began to dream of home, of walking down the Back Lane, looking at the green trees and ripening crops in the fields, being able to eat a fresh crisp apple, turning on the light at the flick of a switch, having copious running hot and cold water, helping my father in the garden. What would I do first – go on holiday, get fit or sleep outside in the tent in the garden as I had as a child? I went over and over the options in my head. I longed to be able to walk outside without everyone in the street pointing at me or calling my name, without thirty or forty children running up and pulling at my clothes and wanting to shake hands. I wanted to be free to come and go without having to observe curfews or be hemmed in by checkpoints. I wanted to be in the English countryside. I wanted not to be constantly fighting illness and exhaustion. I wanted some time to myself at last. And I needed to think. I couldn't wait.

12

SINGING SILENCE

HOME.

Fresh green grass. Trees in leaf and fields of sprouting crops stretching into the distance. Bees madly harvesting the oil seed rape flowers scenting the air. Silence and calm in the wood at the end of the garden. Lying in my expedition hammock between the trees, soaking up the peace and quiet. Supermarket shelves overflowing with fruit and vegetables and rows of superfluous food. Motorways. The roar of traffic. Men and women, smartly dressed, heading off for work, or for an enjoyable day out with their family. Healthy smiling babies. Rosy-cheeked children running about, shouting in the playground, dressed in expensive-looking clothes. Life went on.

And on the other side of the world, people were starving to death.

It was impossible for me to reconcile the two. I found it hard even to enter a supermarket. How could anyone justify the abundant varieties of cat and dog food on sale? I couldn't flush the loo because the idea of wasting ten litres of water each time was shameful to me. I couldn't bear the sight of food left on plates to be thrown away. I'd hoard food that was past its sell-by date, refusing to let my mother get rid of it. In fact, I still do.

The second week after I returned from Ethiopia, I was travelling in the car with my mother, my sister and Sophie, my plump baby niece. When Sophie started screaming, Anne-Marie asked me to hurry up because the baby was starving hungry. I could feel my anger suddenly boiling up inside and I rounded on her, shouting, 'How can you say that? You have no idea what it's like to be starving. Look at her, the great fat thing. No way is she starving.'

Dead silence, even from Sophie, who had stopped crying as we all took in what I'd just said. My poor sister didn't know what to reply. Of course she hadn't seen what I had. How could she be expected to behave any differently?

I was exhausted and could cope with the culture shock only by withdrawing into myself. I just wanted to be quiet. I wasn't interested in what I ate, what I wore, the weather. My friends and family would come home wanting to hear about Ethiopia. I still had no conception of the impact of those four or five minutes of Michael Buerk's news footage. I had never seen it. All I wanted to do was to go off by myself and take the dog for a long walk.

Friends and family bombarded me with questions. 'What was the weather like?' 'Was it hot?' 'What was the worst thing you saw?' 'How did you get by without shopping?' 'How did you cope having a period?' I wanted to shout, What's that got to do with anything? People wanted to hear about my life there, about what seemed to me to be the irrelevant details of my lifestyle, rather than what I saw as the real problems. Perhaps those questions were easier for them to ask because they could relate to the answers. But it was also because they could not conceive the suffering I had seen, the life-and-death fight for survival. Quite understandably they could think only in terms of their own comfortable lives and those, by Ethiopian standards, were ridiculously luxurious. I believed that nobody could have any real idea of the suffering that still went on in Ethiopia, or understand the shame I felt over my role in denying life to so many of those starving children. I felt despair that we had done so little to help the old people in Mekele and Maichew who had had a life of hard work behind them and now were too weak to care for themselves. I think I felt particular empathy for them because I could relate to them through my own parents.

Whenever I came home from any of my stints abroad,

my mother and father would sit me down at the table with my favourite meal of sausages in home-made gravy with carrots, leeks in white sauce and roast potatoes, followed by home-preserved Rivers plums. 'Tell us all about your trip,' they'd say. This time was no different for them, but I found that I couldn't. I couldn't face explaining the suffering to them and I saw that it was impossible for them to relate to what I did try to tell them. Yes, they heard the words, but they didn't understand the experience and that was what I couldn't express. I could talk about the smells and sounds, the suffering and my role in it, but doing that didn't convey what it had really felt like. I blamed my own inarticulacy and ended up not saying anything. It was easier to do that.

The local school saw a newspaper article about me and rang to ask if I would talk to the students. I apologized and said that I couldn't. Why not? I tried to explain the pain I was feeling and why I found it impossible. But the person I spoke to seemed angry and shocked, saying didn't I realize how important it was? I felt terrible letting them down.

Although people praised me for what I had done, I knew that I was far from being a heroine of any kind. In my eyes, I had sent people to their deaths. It was as if I was in mourning for something but I couldn't explain what, and no one was able to empathize with me – except perhaps my father. He knew that I'd lived through war, just as he had so many years before. He understood how horrendous the reality of war is for everybody. I had never heard him talk about his wartime experiences either. Like him, I battened down the hatches. For the first time, he treated me like an adult. He was kind to me. He listened without interrupting or arguing. He encouraged me to do things in the garden – always his cure-all. Together we started planting the flower beds and vegetable garden, putting flowers in the tubs, cutting the lawn. It was tremendously therapeutic. Now that I knew the fragility of life first-hand, I seemed to be so much more alive to everything I was experiencing, the smells of the garden, the cut grass, the leaves, the flowers, the rain on the earth.

I had never been particularly religious but when I was in Lebanon I had written to my father asking him how to pray. In his reply, he had advised me to set aside a quiet time each day in which to think and be thankful and pray for the good things in life.

Firstly we must ourselves be convinced that an eye for an eye and a tooth for a tooth is not the way to bring about a solution. The only solution in the long run is LOVE . . . It is very difficult to love your neighbour as yourself. It is probably impossible for an ordinary human being – unless he has some 'outside' help – Richard [my brother] says it is 'inside help' from the inner man that is needed . . . The proven way to sort it all out, and to reach for Faith, Hope and Love is simply to be quiet and listen. Some call it prayer, some meditation ... The essential thing is to be quiet inside and listen with an open (clear and clean) mind ... You are a true child of your forefathers (and mothers) and you possess the true Spirit – it bursts out of you all over. It needs to be controlled and directed for the good of mankind – and for inner peace. Much love, Papa.

I had tried to follow his advice but never thought of going to church until an old school friend, William, contacted me. He was in the local church choir, and I went along to services with him. I don't know how I expected them to help me but I was looking for support of some sort. I had begun to look for the answer to the question 'Why?' What was the point of a world where resources were so unequally divided? What was the purpose of such needless suffering? William also introduced me to Transcendental Meditation – although I noticed that while I tried to achieve some inner peace all he used to do was go off to sleep. I was given my one private word as a mantra (for which I paid a great deal of money) but I didn't feel it had much effect. I stuck at it for only the few months I was in England, for William's sake.

I was running on empty, but William, although unable to empathize with what I was going through, helped me by taking me out and about. We went sailing together, and to the last night of the Proms and other concerts. That was exactly what I needed to do. I had lost contact with most of my old friends because life had taken us in such different directions. There was only so much I could take in about their husbands and children, housing and schooling, and my experience was equally alien to them.

However, I couldn't escape Ethiopia. My brother Andrew told me about a concert called Live Aid and even tried to get me tickets. But I didn't want to go. I had no reason to be there and didn't really understand what it had to do with Ethiopia, let alone with me. How could a concert make a difference? Surely the musicians were using one nation's disaster to line their own pockets? I didn't understand how it worked. I'd never been to a rock concert and had no idea what the fuss was all about. It seemed so surreal that this event was happening for the sake of Ethiopia. I didn't understand that Michael Buerk's interview with me had been one of the catalysts for Bob Geldof to produce Band Aid then Live Aid. I didn't want to look back at reports of what had happened. I knew first hand what it was like and that was enough. I really didn't need reminding.

I remember that the Live Aid concert took place on a scorching hot July day. I sat alone on the settee at home, watching the television with the terrace doors open, looking over the green fields and feeling numb. I saw the bands and the footage of the tragic Berhan, one among the many starving children, and her father pleading for her life. I saw all the emotion emanating from millions of people in the name of Ethiopia. Tears poured down my cheeks yet, although I knew that the emotion was there inside me somewhere, I couldn't feel it. I felt completely detached. It was so strange. I felt as if I had just landed on the planet and was trying to make sense of what I saw. Then suddenly I felt terrible pain and I broke down completely at the memories of all I had witnessed and lived through.

I've been told since that I was suffering from post-traumatic stress, but at the time that wasn't a recognized complaint for an aid worker. My circle of colleagues all thought that to admit to such stress was a sign of weakness. As far as I was concerned, I would never admit to being so weak as to be affected by what I had lived through. It didn't occur to me to seek help. All I knew was that I had to move on, keep busy and continue to face new challenges, helping people less fortunate than me. There was so much suffering elsewhere in the world and I knew I could help relieve it.

Before I'd left Ethiopia, I had looked at other organizations such as Médecins sans Frontières and Save the Children, investigating their mandate, what they did and how they employed people in the field. But every time I came back to ICRC as the organization for me. I could go along wholeheartedly with its aims and objectives. However, I knew that if I were to stay with them, I had to learn French. Although English is an international language and the ICRC did use it, if there was something they really wanted to get across to their staff, they always said (or wrote) it in French. I also badly needed a change and I needed to have some fun. So I started applying for nursing jobs in the French-speaking part of Switzerland, taking advice from the ICRC medical coordinator, who gave me two or three names of hospitals near the ski slopes. One of them was the hospital at Sion in the Valais. Luckily, when I was being debriefed by the senior ICRC nurse in Geneva, he said he knew the chief nurse at Sion and would call him to arrange an interview.

No sooner said than done. I went out to the hospital in Sion and was offered the job of a nurse in the A&E department. And what a fantastic hospital it was. The building was contemporary, round, and in a stunning setting. Everything was modern, from the automatic doors to the latest medical technology. Helicopters landed on the roof, bringing in ski injuries from Zermatt, Verbier and the Crans Montana areas. All patients were treated as soon as they came in; they were seen by the relevant specialist and all the necessary tests were sent for without delay. The results came back in a matter of hours. It was extremely efficient and the level of care was excellent. The three-course meals on the wards were fantastic and came accompanied by wine. Each patient in A&E was assigned to a private cubicle with their own nurse in a crisp white uniform. Working there coloured my view of healthcare for ever. I realized that it needn't be the norm for patients to be forced to wait if they needed emergency treatment, as they were in the UK, where people with a fractured wrist or leg often had to wait hours for an X-ray and pain relief.

Just as I arrived, another nurse was leaving, and her studio flat was going begging. It was in a little village halfway up the mountain in a modern wooden chalet-style building among apricot trees and grapevines, with a spectacular view of the valley. There was a sofa bed in the main room and there was a small kitchen where I could sleep under the table if a friend came to stay. It was warm, clean and had everything I needed. Nelly, a French nurse on the paediatric ward, lived in the same building and shared my love of walking. Whenever our days off coincided we'd go into the mountains together, the more testing the terrain the better. Sometimes I went to a tea bar in the afternoons when the English-speaking club met and made friends with local Swiss people who wanted to perfect their English. I did classes at the local Migros supermarket in jazz and ballroom dancing and, of course, French. I joined the church and even went to Bible study classes, where I made more friends. I was still looking for some comfort in the face of my experience in Ethiopia, but all the classes showed me was that calling on God, an outside force, didn't work for me. It didn't give me the answers.

Not long after arriving I received a wonderful letter from Raya in Maichew:

Dear Sister Claire

... I am very happy of your new job; since you go I was so very much worried to know if how you are leading yourself. Our feeding center has six meals, the children are going good. Now the whole shelter people have gone to their homeland taking their seeds as well as dry ration. We are left only with 340 children in our feeding. We have some tents left for them. Now it is very easy to check our children, because they are so few in number ... I have kissed Hagos for you but Abuhanna is discharged. She has gone to her homeland with her parents ... Maychew is green by now there is rain. It was nice if it can last long ...

I was overjoyed by the news that the centre was running as well as I had hoped it would and that the rains had come, reducing the scale of the famine so dramatically. The fact that the Red Cross were distributing seeds meant that people were ready to return home to grow their own crops and become self-sufficient again.

I threw myself into my work at the hospital. We were constantly busy with interesting cases and I was very happy. After the first year, when a friend on nights was leaving, I jumped at her job. If I worked eight long days with night duty, I could have six days off at a time to go up into the mountains skiing in the winter or walking during the summer. Whenever I had any spare time, that's where I went.

Looking back, I can see that my addiction to pushing myself to the limits, to finding and facing the next physical challenge, might stem in part from my childhood, when I was that nonentity, 'little Claire', who wasn't much good at anything and struggled to keep up at school. I needed to prove to myself that I was better than that. Nobody expected anything of me except myself. So on the ski slopes, I was as mad as they came. I teamed up with an English guy, Nigel, who'd come over for the season, and was working as a night porter in a hotel and skiing by day. Once my sister, Anne-Marie, came out to stay with me and we had two wild wonderful weeks with Nigel and friends of his who worked on the Saudi Arabian oil rigs. For a week, Anne-Marie slept in my bed while I worked. I'd arrive home in the morning with chocolate croissants and climb into bed while she went off skiing for the day. The second week we spent together, skiing and partying.

Nigel and I always skied off piste. I would carry a backpack stuffed with a space blanket, a change of clothes and a large plastic bag that I thought would keep me warm if I was stranded and climbed into it. Fortunately, I never had to put it to the test. I remember best the day we skied on a glacier below Mont Blanc, the Vallée Blanche in Chamonix, one of the most famous ski runs in the world. When Nigel had suggested the trip, I'd replied, 'Why not?' thinking it was just another ski run. When he mentioned ropes, ice axes and crevasses I began to realize that it was a bit special.

When the alarm rang at six o'clock in the morning I groaned before remembering that this was the day of our expedition. The stars were shining when we took to the road, which meant that we had ideal weather conditions and the glacier would be frozen hard. The La Forclaz pass between Switzerland and France was open and reasonably free of snow and ice. As we approached Chamonix, we noticed that many of the large pine trees had been snapped in two and branches and twigs were littering the snow. One of the hitchhikers we picked up told us they'd had tremendous storms the previous week with gale-force winds causing many avalanches in the area.

On arrival at the cable car at Chamonix we asked for one-way tickets to the Aiguilles du Midi (3,842 metres) but were told firmly, 'No guide, no ski.' We had planned to follow a guided party's tracks in the snow and if there weren't any, Nigel was to be our guide – he had skied the Vallée Blanche before. Other skiers with rucksacks bulging with ropes, crampons and ice axes were being turned away too, so we went for a coffee, waiting to see if a guided group was going up that morning. At ten o'clock we decided to go up anyway, and slipped past the ticket collector, who thought we were travelling with the four other people with skis in the cable car. We hadn't come all this way on a beautiful day for nothing. The trip up was disappointing for Nigel as there wasn't enough wind to make the cable car rock and sway around, but I was quite happy watching the needle-sharp peaks flying by below us, contrasting sharply with the smooth velveteen whiteness of Mont Blanc.

At the top, the air was noticeably thinner as we passed from one peak to another by a short bridge and then into a labyrinth of tunnels through the rock until we reached the exit carved through the ice. A small ledge held about a dozen people who must have come up on the eight o'clock cable car. They were roping up to climb down the first thirty metres – a narrow ledge with sheer drops on either side.

'All right?' asked Nigel, without looking at me, as he strode past the first guided group on the ledge, his skis in one hand and sticks in the other, and his boots digging out small footholds on the way down. I launched my inflexible ski boots into each of his steps and only just managed to stop myself from sliding too far by digging my skis into the foothold below.

'Feel the altitude, can you?' Nigel shouted over his shoulder.

My mouth was dry, my head spinning, I was shaking all over. Breathlessly I answered, 'Just a bit. But I'd rather not think about it at the moment, thanks.' I made it safely to the bottom of the climbing phase and a vast white cushion of snow opened up ahead of us.

We lanced off down the side of the mountain and within seconds I was sliding on my backside. Eventually I managed to stop, but the experience had taught me not to take this venture lightly. Then we were off again and the great expanse of pure white glacier seemed to swallow us up. We were like two rolling pebbles on an enormous desert of snow. The warning notices in Chamonix had predicted temperatures of −20°C and the need to wear warm clothing, but I had already peeled off one layer as well as removing my hat. I suddenly realized that despite the blazing sunshine, I could no longer feel my ears and my eyelashes were freezing together. I took a look at Nigel and saw that his nostrils had frozen up.

Around midday, we dug in our skis and sat down, getting out the map and deliciously squidgy pizzas we'd bought earlier. We were surrounded by the Aiguilles du Chamonix, having taken the route down through the Vallée Blanche via the Mer de Glace before descending the mountain to Chamonix.

After lunch, we continued to follow the tracks of a guided party who had passed that way earlier – at least we hoped they had a guide. We crossed narrow snow bridges over gaping crevasses, avoiding the enormous chunks of pale blue ice rising out of the snow. It seemed strangely unreal. At times we made virgin white tracks through deep fresh snow, only to be suddenly thrown off balance and sent tumbling by a sheet of ice or rock hidden beneath the snow. Occasionally we had to get over and down a large step of pure ice where nothing gripped. I wanted to take off my skis and creep across these bits but Nigel pointed out that I'd slide just as much and at least my skis might stop me from falling down a crevasse. Small comfort – but I took his advice. I just took a deep breath, hoping for the best and knowing I'd eventually stop but not which way round I'd be.

We criss-crossed the glacial valley. Often it seemed to me that we'd never find the route through those gaping holes. Sometimes the tracks we tried to follow seemed to stop, but that usually meant that there was another blue ice flat to cross. Once when the tracks disappeared, we found they continued on the other side of a waist-high ice wall. The only way over – without damaging ourselves – was to sit on top of it and slide over backwards, landing with a bump and our legs spreadeagled skywards. A strong wind started to blow up and, glancing over our shoulders, we saw a wall of white cloud obliterating the view behind. The tracks we were following became fainter as the wind-driven snow covered them and we hastened on as best we could to keep ahead of the cloud. I really didn't fancy being lost out there.

The end of the glacier was marked by a climb out of the valley. Once again we sat and rested in the blazing sunshine, finishing our bread and cheese before skiing down the snow path to Chamonix. Tired but elated, we made it safely. The only real trouble of the day was trying to find the car in the Chamonix car park.

That was the kind of adventure and beauty I thrived on through the winter months.

An hour away from Sion, my cousin Pierre owned a chalet called 'Le Silence qui Chante' (Singing Silence), in the alpage of Breona in the Val d'Hérens, where the cows went up the mountain to their summer pasture. He couldn't use the chalet as much as he would like, so he let me go there whenever I wanted. In the summer, I'd park the car at La Forclaz above Les Haudères, eat steak, chips and salad in the little café at the bottom of the mountain, buy a piece of cheese and a couple of large slices of apricot or plum tart, and walk up the mountain for a couple of hours, following a small zigzag footpath to the chalet. The road was too precarious to drive, although I remember that the cowman at the time had a battered Volkswagen Beetle that had only reverse gear, so he drove up and down the mountain backwards. Not for me. I'd pass the cowsheds and breathe in their pungent smell, which immediately reminded me of holidays as a child – it always gave me the most glorious relaxed feeling – and made my way through the lush meadows scattered with flowers. In winter, I'd take the ski lift from La Forclaz to a neighbouring mountain then ski off piste as silently as possible across an avalanche plain before heading down to the chalet, where I'd have to use my hands to dig away the snow from the door. At last I'd arrived at 'Le Silence qui Chante'.

The chalet had once been a cow shed, and one end was

tucked neatly into the mountainside while the other gave way to an almost sheer drop, with wonderful views. Part timber and part stone, it had a slate roof with a chimney, wooden shutters and a solid wood front door. To its left was a meticulously stacked log pile, and to its right a big table with a wooden bench, always bearing a jam jar of wild flowers. Inside, there was a *pierre ollaire*, an enormous round stone fireplace that absorbed the heat when a fire was lit on it and then radiated out heat throughout the night – ideal for melting snow in a saucepan to make tea in the morning. Plenty of duvets meant that there was always something to wrap myself in when I curled up to sleep on the floor on a mattress by the fire. There was no water or electricity, just the glacier stream tumbling past outside and candles for light. I usually got up and went to bed with the sun. Or, in the spring, I'd be woken by the cowbells as the cows slowly made their way up the mountain, followed by the cowherd with a flower in his mouth, his floppy felt hat, a shepherd's crook and his dog. At night it was freezing cold, with the wind whistling outside; by day the sun shone. For me, it was a pleasure not to have the comforts of twentieth-century living but to find myself so at one with nature. It provided me with all I wanted.

I never needed to eat much but would pick nuts and fruit where I could. I got to know my mushrooms really well and gathered them to make *croûte aux champignons*: bread soaked in white wine with mushroom wine sauce and a bit of cheese, baked in the oven – heaven. If I was there for longer than a couple of days, I'd eat local fare – a few potatoes, mountain cheese, dried meat, gherkins and chestnuts roasted by the fire. There were always plenty of local apples and black rye bread with nuts in it that would keep in the cellar all winter. I couldn't help thinking back to Ethiopia when we had so little and every bit of food was so good. It made me value what I had.

Otherwise, I didn't think about my life, where I had been or where I was going. I simply loved being there, bathing myself in silence. I bought a camera and started learning about F-stops and depths of field as I practised taking photos of a flower, a leaf or the bark of the tree until I got the right colours and degree of focus. I walked for hours, sometimes stopping to draw. I had a little book of alpine flowers and whenever I saw a species of gentian, eidelweiss, anemone, wild orchid or moss campion I hadn't seen before, I'd mark the date and the place I saw it. I'd bought a small pair of lightweight binoculars and could sit for hours outside the chalet, spying on the chamois, trying to spot the marmots whose distinctive whistle I could hear near by and watching the eagles circling the mountain tops. On a clear day I could make out the Aiguille de la Tsa (3,668 metres), a spectacular mountain peak whose summit I had climbed the first winter I had gone there. At night the stars were so close and distinct that I felt that if I reached up with my hand I could pick them out of the sky as if they were apples on a tree. I spent many happy evenings identifying the constellations and making wishes on shooting stars.

Although alone, I was never lonely. My friends at the hospital worked different shifts, so I didn't have any choice but to come on my own. I was happy in my own company, and I found a much-needed sense of peace and happiness. I felt comfortable here, surrounded by the strength and beauty of the mountains and nature. Mike Christy's words, spoken as we swung high above the jungle floor years earlier in Panama, came back to me. 'Lift up your eyes to the mountain – there you will get your strength.' There was no question that I owed some of my appreciation of the power of nature to him.

One day I met Pierre at the chalet and we hiked up to visit the cowherds spending the summer higher up the mountain. Their chalet was filthy, without running water, and there was a wood fire over which they made cheese in an enormous copper cauldron. After that I'd occasionally go up there on my own to get milk warm from the cow. I could drink it by the gallon without worrying about my health, as I had done in Mekele. Wonderful. Sometimes I went up and joined them for a raclette or a fondue. But mostly I kept to myself.

My other favourite spot was the *cabane* or hut owned by the Geneva University Alpine Club on the Aiguilles Rouges (2,810 metres). I'd climb up the mountain with a spring in my step. Despite the breathlessness and slow pace, I felt such happiness. I followed the rocks marked with a splash of red paint to arrive four hours later at the hut, where a cousin of mine was the warden. I'd bring up the mail, extra groceries or whatever they wanted. Bernard, my cousin's son, would get up at 04.00 when the glacier above the cabin was still frozen solid. His job was to serve breakfast to the climbers staying overnight in the hut, watch them go out and count them back again. Once he and a friend took me across the glacier to Pont du Vouasson, where there is a stunning view of the Matterhorn. We left at 03.00 and climbed by a highly dangerous route, crossing back over the glacier before the sun was high. That was the kind of exhilarating challenge I loved and that I faced time and time again in my two years there.

It was once reported in a newspaper that I'd retreated into the mountains to live without creature comforts as some kind of penance. Quite the contrary: living in Switzerland was a pleasure. I found both peace and my ability to have fun again. It gave me back my emotional stability, my happiness and my balance. It was one of the best times of my life.

13

THE PEARL OF AFRICA

IN THE FIRST PRISON I VISITED IN UGANDA, WE'D GET locked in with the prisoners every day from 09.00 to 12.00 and 14.00 to 17.00. In between shifts, we left only so that the jailers could do their head count. It was an enormous, rat-infested Victorian building, a labyrinth of filthy, damp, unlit passages with dirty corners stinking of urine. It had originally been built by the British and was intended for about five hundred prisoners, but now well over a thousand men were crammed into it in appalling con-ditions. They were crowded into cells just sixteen feet square, without toilet facilities and often without water. The taps had no handles, so when the water was on, it spurted everywhere, and when it was off, nothing. The latrines had been bunged up for months, so there was shit everywhere. The prisoners walked in it, lay in it, ate in it, washed in it. There was one central courtyard to which they had access in relays, depending on the whim of the guards. The food supplies had been inadequate for months too – if lucky, each prisoner got one meal of rice a day. The prisoners were skeletal figures in varying degrees of distress, most were filthy dirty, many had diseases associated with malnutrition, and scabies was rife. The place reminded me of nothing less than Auschwitz.

I started caring for the prisoners in the intensive supplementary feeding yard. It was hard. My experience had taught me that starvation makes one feel too ill to want to eat, so I had to use gentle encouragement. All the prisoners had been tortured and none had seen the outside world for years. To the worst cases we gave seven meals a day (high-energy milk drink, porridge, rice). The rest were given two meals a day by the prison authorities: rice or pochow with vegetables or beans.

Illness was rife. One of my other jobs was to explain why the prisoners should keep their cells clean and praise them when it was done. Some cells were less filthy than others, depending on the cell leader. We tried to screen everyone for tuberculosis in every prison we visited – difficult when everyone was coughing and spitting everywhere – and finally whittled the suspects down to those who were spitting blood and having night sweats after a two-week course of antibiotics. We couldn't send the sputum for analysis because the prison authorities wouldn't let us use the prisoners' real names. We clinically diagnosed a few men with leprosy and they were referred to the prison hospital in Kampala. We were aware of the danger of cholera, which was already endemic in the area. Despite seeing a few isolated cases of profuse watery diarrhoea, we were relieved not to have to deal with an epidemic.

As they began to recover, many of the prisoners began to regain their dignity, refusing to show me 'below the belt' when we were scabies hunting. That was such a change from when they had been so weak and demoralized that they had stripped off their rags to stand in line for a piece of soap and a bucket of water to wash in without complaint. I liked and respected the prisoners I worked with and if we often found supplies missing, I could perfectly well understand why they tried to pinch as much as possible in order to survive. I'd have done the same.

In July 1987, Uganda was still in some turmoil after the National Resistance Army had taken control, ousting General Okello the previous year and replacing him with Yoweri Museveni. In some parts of the country tribal wars continued unabated. Part of the ICRC's role under the Geneva Convention is to visit prisoners of war and political detainees, to monitor their welfare and, where necessary, to improve the conditions in the prisons. In Uganda, men were dying because of the inhumane conditions in which they were kept, many of them 'hidden' prisoners whose whereabouts were unknown to the outside world. Believed to be rebels against previous regimes, they had 'disappeared', having been taken by the militia, imprisoned indefinitely without charge and simply forgotten. In some prisons, political prisoners were locked into a VIP area where they received some privileges, but elsewhere they coexisted with murderers, thieves and rapists. Our team of ICRC delegates and nurses were brought in under an oath of strict confidentiality as neutral intermediaries to establish feeding centres within a number of prisons, improve the sanitation arrangements and try to organize a link through ICRC messages to relatives on the outside. The ICRC believes that the best way it can prevent or halt torture and ensure decent conditions of detention is by getting repeated and unrestricted access to prisoners, talking to them about their problems and urging the detaining authorities to make any improvements that may be necessary.

In one of the prisons, the prisoners had rioted, got hold of some guns and barricaded themselves in, refusing the prison officers entry. However they let us in so that we could provide the basics – food, water, sanitation, blankets and medicine. In another, one of the first things we gave the prisoners was a football. The look on their faces will stay with me for ever. Those lethargic, disinterested expressions were transformed by laughter. It was wonderful to see. All of a sudden a subdued prison of about 3,000 men came alive as they planned a football league and started to play every day. They wrapped filthy grey bandages or strips of cotton round ankles and knees to look the part despite the lack of shoes, and games were vigorously lost and won to the sound of shouting and cheering. It was the first time I remember hearing noise in that place despite the overcrowded conditions.

I had left Switzerland in early 1987 when my mother became housebound with arthritis and I wanted to return home to care for her. I couldn't bear seeing her in so much pain, so nauseous and crippled. I wanted to help her in the only way I knew at the time, by giving her anti-inflammatories and other medication. However, my father wanted to put her on a regime of raw onions, boiled liver and charcoal tablets as he didn't believe in conventional medicine. Papa and I clashed dreadfully over this, and after a couple of months I decided I had to get away. I was booked to start a training course in operating theatre techniques in London in the autumn, so could only spare two to three months, but I called the ICRC anyway. They immediately asked me to do a short-term cover for one of the ICRC nurses in Uganda who had broken her leg.

Before leaving the ICRC in Geneva, I had been warned that the situation in Uganda was very dangerous with robberies, muggings, thefts and rapes rife in Kampala, where I would be based. One of the female ICRC delegates had recently been raped there. As a result the ICRC had offered to withdraw all women delegates from the country, but those who were already out there were adamant that they wanted to stay and continue their work. Everyone asked to go there was given the option to refuse. Sure, I was nervous, but I wasn't going to let that stop me. Those of us going were thoroughly briefed about personal security. We were to live in groups with guards and floodlighting protecting each house. The ICRC were having VHF radios installed in each one as a precautionary measure in case of attack. We were never to travel alone.

When I arrived, I was overwhelmed by the smells and sounds of Africa. Unlike the towns I had seen in Ethiopia, Kampala was busy, colourful and vibrant, full of well-fed people, food, noise, bicycles and cars. There were even green trees and bushes in the city. During the day, the streets of central Kampala overflowed with people, dilapidated old cars and pavement stalls offering everything from rubber stamps to radio repairs and food. In Ethiopia there were few shops and no supermarkets so it was impossible to get even a tin of peaches or a piece of fruit, whereas here you could buy in the markets almost any fruit or vegetable you might want. I'd also buy fresh Nile perch that were so big that they couldn't be carried by the little boys who brought them into town balanced on the seats of their bicycles.

Nevertheless, the economy of the country was near collapse and its infrastructure crumbling. Understandably the people seemed to have had enough of being poor and under the thumb of the dictators, Idi Amin and then Milton Obote. Just being white was enough to make targets of us, as their memories of colonial rule were not much better. The local people were very poor and lived off their wits with whatever they could beg, borrow or steal. We had heard that there had been house raids, so we were careful about leaving things lying around, making sure that bags weren't visible and doors and windows were locked.

My base in Kampala was the 'Big House', which was very big, with seven bedrooms, and empty to begin with because the secretary I was sharing with didn't often come home. Being the only one in the delegation who was over thirty, I found life rather lonely at first and I didn't feel comfortable at the wild parties held by the younger delegates and nurses. But it wasn't long before I was joined by Alan, a jolly nutritionist who brushed his hair across the bald bit and wore bright psychedelic shorts for leisure; Yves, a burly red-haired sanitation expert who was always up for a joke; and then another experienced field nurse, Elizabeth, who joined us in August. We'd often eat out together or go out as a team on our days off. With the house came a mad dog with streaming yellow pussy eyes who howled all night long, and a mangy cat who one evening did Alan the honour of having kittens in his bed. Every window and door, including the thirty-foot partition doors in the downstairs lounge, had heavy metal concertina gates like old-fashioned lift gates. They were pushed open and shut with great difficulty and were held closed with large padlocks. I had the biggest room (big and empty) with a lovely balcony that got the evening sun. I could sit out and watch the hummingbirds – something I hadn't been able to do since Panama – as well as storks, herons, swifts and wonderfully exotic parrots that flew past the huge rubber tree and bougainvillea in the garden. All I needed for company was my trusty radio, my diary and my well-travelled photocopy of a poem, 'The Green Eye of the Little Yellow God', that Mike had given me in Panama. I had learned all eleven verses by heart and would recite them to myself when I needed something to pass the time. Challenging myself to remember it all in the right order kept my mind active.

After dark two armed guards, one an ex-policeman who carried a Kalashnikov, patrolled the garden. Whatever next, when even the ICRC needed protection? One night we were woken by an alarm from one of the other houses (nicknamed PPF after the procaine penicillin injection given against venereal disease). Luckily the guard there wasn't asleep and had spotted some intruders. He set off the screech alarm that all the guards carried, waking the occupants, who set off the siren fitted to the roof and radioed for help. As our house was the closest, Yves and Alan grabbed their trousers and, taking our armed guards with them, dashed round in the car, making as much noise as they could when they arrived at the scene. They got the guard to fire some warning shots into the air. That was enough to scare the raiders off. Then Alan and Yves came home and finished off the bottle of Glenlivet that they'd begun earlier that evening. I'm glad to say that that was the nearest we came to getting attacked, although other white people's homes around us were frequently raided.

As for strict personal security – at times it seemed a joke. Many of the ICRC delegates routinely travelled between Kampala and Jinja without radio contact and with their car doors unlocked. It took the ambush of a priest's Land-Rover, complete with a red cross on its side, when four people were killed by machine-gun fire, to make us more wary. I remember driving Klause, a newly arrived, very green delegate, down a lonely road in the jungle when we were flagged down by a little old man with a 'broken-down' lorry. Klause couldn't understand why I didn't stop. He thought I was being selfish and uncaring. It didn't occur to him that it might be an ambush.

I had worked in dangerous places before, but in Uganda I learned what it was like to feel real fear in the face of aggression, more than once. On the first occasion, we'd been working hard in one of the prisons, setting up a feeding centre. One of the courses of treatment we offered to some of the prisoners who were suffering from pellagra and beriberi was a concentrated dose of vitamin B. It worked, with dramatic effect. I was in one of the dank corridors when one of them came up to me. He towered over me as he thanked me for helping him and said, 'Now I can feel myself coming alive again here,' and he gestured at his crotch and made a move towards me. I froze. We were alone and I was scared stiff. Just then, some other men rounded the corner and I was able to make a quick get-away. After that moment, I became very aware of looking over my shoulder all the time and making sure that there were other people around wherever I was working. As long as they were ill, the prisoners were no threat, but as soon as our feeding programme began to work, I occasion-ally found that being the only woman among these men, who had been cooped up together for months if not years without sight of a female, could be slightly uncomfortable.

Another time I was to travel to Jinja and then on to Mbale with a driver. We were about to leave when I remembered that I'd left something behind. I ran back into the house to pick it up. When I got back into the truck, I immediately knew that something was wrong. I sensed the tension in the air and could smell the driver's sweat. This was the smell of someone who was worse than scared: I could feel his terror and, much worse, his hatred. It scared me to death. At first I had no idea what had happened in the few minutes that I'd been away. Then I realized that my bag was lying open on the seat. It was obvious that he had taken some money. I didn't know what to do in the face of his obvious hostility, especially since we had a long ride ahead of us. I remember clearly the smell in the truck, the atmosphere. He was an ICRC employee and I was urgently expected in Jinja, so I felt I had no choice but to go with him.

In the end, I blurted out, 'Oh, my bag's come open.'

'No, it hasn't. It was always like that,' he spat at me, his eyes challenging me to contradict him.

I knew of the killings that happened across the country, how ethnic conflict and banditry were rife and the ease with which some people eliminated anyone who stood in their way. I didn't want to have my life ended so abruptly, thank you.

Just shut up, Claire, I told myself. Don't say anything.

Side by side we sat for the longest three hours of my life. I was constantly anxious that his obvious loathing would turn into aggression if I said or did the wrong thing. Never have I been so relieved to reach my destination. I knew that I hadn't been wrong about that driver and I made sure that I never travelled with him again.

Jinja is the second largest town in Uganda. It sits on the banks of Lake Victoria (full of bilharzia in those days), the source of the White Nile. We'd stay in the pretty but faded Sunset Hotel, aptly named for its beautiful view westwards across the lake, towards Owen Falls and the dam with its hydroelectric station. An enormous viaduct spanned the water and you could see an old diesel train with two or three coaches chugging its way across several times a day. The area was full of familiar sights left over from its colonial past: old red English telephone boxes, all burnt out and destroyed; the blue light of the police station with 'POLICE' written in English; wonderful colonial mansions with filigree ironwork, now run down and looted, occupied by squatting displaced people, chickens and dogs, and surrounded by once magnificent grounds now abandoned and overgrown. Thirty years earlier, it must have been lovely.

Only a few hundred yards up the road from the hotel was a British war cemetery with beautiful gravestones standing to attention with a bougainvillea-clad memorial to those who'd given up their lives in the Second World War. It reminded me of a British cemetery I used to visit in Saida in the Lebanon which stood right next to the hellhole of shacks that was Ein Helweh Palestinian refugee camp. Although the country around it was bombed out, the cemetery had been kept pristine by a gardener who mowed the lawns and tended the roses. Sometimes I'd go there to sit on the bench and be at peace. When I saw the one in Jinja, I hoped it would offer the same sort of escape, and I went to explore it on my own. I hadn't been wandering long through the brambles and grass, trying to get a better look at the graves, when I realized that I was being followed. There were footsteps close behind me whichever way I went. Two young men wearing rags were following me, laughing quietly and whispering between themselves. All those reports of rapes and warnings about personal security were racing through my head. How was I going to get out of this one? How stupid to let myself get into this situation! I should never have gone there alone; I knew far better. My days in A&E flooded back and I remembered that I'd found that the way out of a tense situation was by talking, saying something off-hand to a threatening member of the public when it was least expected. So, instead of screaming and running away, I steeled myself to turn to face my followers, asking them to help me get back to the hotel, making a joke out of being lost. They stopped in their tracks and looked quite taken aback. My heart was pounding but I made a supreme effort to appear perfectly calm. I walked quickly past them, saying to myself, Keep chatting, keep walking, keep chatting, ask questions, get out. It worked. Too closely for comfort, they followed me to the gate, where I firmly said goodbye with the hotel in my sight, and made my way back there in one piece.

But all the fear and unpleasantness I experienced was counterbalanced by the friendly and hospitable people I met. For instance, when my car broke down on my way to Mbale, as I was walking along the road through the rainforest I met a woman and her two children. My mind was back in the rainforests of Panama and Sulawesi when they broke into my daydream, smiling and inviting me in to their home, speaking a little English. The woman wore a brightly coloured sarong with her hair tied back from her face, showing its delicate bone structure. Her children were barefoot and dressed in rags. Their house was open on three sides with palm fronds for a roof. It was only about six feet square, more a shelter than a home, with no furniture and just a torn rush mat on the floor. The woman made a tiny fire with a few sticks, boiled some water in a tin can and made tea with leaves, no milk, no sugar. This was obviously a luxury for them and it was an honour for me to be asked to share it. We sat together on the ground talking in pidgin English about the children, their school, their father who was away looking for work and the problems of their beautiful country. There's great dignity to be found in such poverty. We could have been sitting on a sofa in one of the mansions in Jinja. Despite the language barrier and the differences in our lives, we connected and managed to convey to one another that we were at one over life and its problems.

By the time the rainy season began in the middle of August, I had worked in several prisons. My last posting was back in Kampala. This prison was the largest I'd worked in but its problems were common to all the rest. It was holding more than four times the number of prisoners it had been built for. Among them were convicts and remands, but the majority were 'lodgers' – that is, political prisoners and those 'forgotten' by the military authorities. The conditions in which they lived were appalling. The medical dispensary had only a few beds. Medicines were non-existent and the bare essentials such as soap, blankets, disinfectants, brooms and pots weren't readily available. Proper facilities didn't exist for the diagnosis of diseases, and typically diseases were identified only when they'd spread to epidemic proportions among the inmates.

Although the authorities had been making efforts to increase the quantities of food for the prisoners, there were still plenty of problems with the way they were fed. The one and only electric boiler was always out of order, gas was rarely available for the gas cookers and firewood was in short supply. Unless they could afford to have their own cups and plates, prisoners had to make do with rusty old tins they found in the rubbish or had to simply eat from the ground. The kitchens were indescribably dirty and overrun with cockroaches.

The cells were crammed with men. There was no running water for washing and no electric light. Most of them slept on the floor with nothing to cover themselves. The prison had given up providing blankets or uniforms, so during the day the men went half naked, perhaps clothed in a torn shirt or a torn pair of trousers. Most of the sanitation system was blocked, and there were nowhere near enough toilets to support the population. What toilets there were had stopped flushing long ago so were always overflowing and, of course, stank terribly. Some cells without toilets had oil drums or barrels which overflowed and leaked, and sewage flooded the floors.

My reaction to seeing all this was practical. I made a mental list of things that I had to do to sort things out. In fact it was quite simple to get the water running again and the toilets unblocked. It didn't cost a lot and was fairly easy to arrange in a few days if you had the influence and some money to do it – which we did. Compared to dealing with the badly wounded needing specialist treatment, this was a straightforward if rather smelly problem to cope with.

I began working in the sick bay, trying to get things ship-shape there, setting up a supplementary feeding clinic, and giving out vitamin A capsules, benzyl benzoate and any necessary medicines. I always wore my jeans to visit the prison – when you have a few hundred murderers and rapists around you in dimly lit corners of a maze of corridors, it's as well not to be too feminine in your dress. Once again, though, my preconceptions were proved wrong, as I found the prisoners to be human and warm and, although they played tricks, thieved and cheated with the prison officials, they didn't behave like that with me. I loved being among them. I started up a nutrition clinic for malnourished prisoners and slowly, as they realized that I wasn't there to poison them, more and more came, until the numbers doubled. They'd eagerly eat all they were given and come back for more. It was so rewarding to see their condition rapidly improve. I remember one who had pellagra, his skin dry and discoloured, shake himself out of his lethargy to the point of asking me for some coconut oil to put on it. I took it as a good sign that he had begun to take an interest in himself again. Otherwise, a renewed interest in playing football was a sure sign that they were beginning to pick up.

It was in one of the prisons that I learned my most valuable lesson. Shortly before I was due to go back to England, I was approached by two of the prisoners in a dark, dark passageway smelling of urine and damp bricks with cells on either side. They asked me to follow them. Feeling trapped, I went with them nervously, not knowing what to expect. They led me to a tiny, dank cell with a small barred window too high to see out of and gestured for me to go in.

A prisoner who seemed to be in charge was waiting and, after they'd shaken out a dirty piece of cloth and laid it on the ground, he invited me to sit down. Despite the grim surroundings, to my relief it became immediately clear that they were all acting with great respect. I sat on the cloth as invited. As if from nowhere, one of them produced a cup of tea with the flourish of someone who had served as a head waiter in the finest of restaurants, despite the cup being chipped, stained and without a saucer. The tea was sweet and made with condensed milk. Where they got it from I have no idea; we certainly hadn't brought it in with our supplies. They presented it to me as if it was a ritual. There wasn't any for the others who'd gathered around, standing or squatting, so I drank alone. Then the headman made a little speech and presented me with a large wooden cross they had made in the workshop, thanking me for everything I'd done for them. I realized that this was a tremendous privilege and a momentous occasion. As I took it, he turned round and started picking away at the mortar round a brick in the wall. Very slowly he managed to free the brick. From behind it, he pulled out something wrapped in a dirty bit of cloth. Shaking off the dust, he unwrapped a grimy piece of Mars bar, and presented it to me, saying 'We would like you to accept this with our thanks.' This was clearly the ultimate honour. They wanted to give their precious secret stash of chocolate to me. I had to eat it and as I did, I felt awful, knowing that while this was a prize to them to me it was something I could get any time I wanted from a market stall in town. But I was profoundly touched too. I was reminded that it's not the size or the cost of a gift that matters but the reason for it and the way in which it is given.

14

DESERT CHALLENGE

TRAVELLING FROM NAIROBI (FOR TWO AND A HALF HOURS in a light aircraft), we left the green and luscious land of the Kenyan Highlands behind as we dropped over the Rift Valley and entered a different world. The country looked dry and inhospitable, and the further north we got, the drier it became. It was June 1988, and we were heading for Lokichokio, a small frontier post in north Kenya by the southern Sudan border, surrounded for hundreds of miles by desert. It was a quiet, dusty one-street township. There were a few shacks where you could buy only the very basics and a number of *manyattas*, groups of mud- and straw-walled huts, arranged in rough circles. This was Turkana country.

Like their country, the Turkana tribe is harsh, cruel and

solitary. Survival is their main occupation. Known as the 'shepherds of the desert', they live off their camels, cattle, sheep, goats and donkeys, moving on as each waterhole becomes dry. Their only other preoccupation is the tribal tradition of cattle raiding their neighbours. A Turkana man cannot receive the honour of tattoos on his back and chest until he has killed five men. Until recently the raids had been carried out with sticks, spears and wrist knives, limiting the casualties. But armed conflicts in neighbouring territories had brought an influx of guns and ammunition, and cattle raiding had now become a seriously bloody business, with potentially as many as a hundred deaths in one raid.

I'd been asked to stay on in Uganda but I had been committed to returning home after three months to take up my place on the training course in operating theatre techniques at St Mary's, Paddington. When I got there, however, I panicked. I had no idea that so much study and writing would be involved. I can't do this, I thought. I can't write essays. I can't study. I knew I'd have enormous trouble doing all the required reading and that my writing and spelling would let me down. Within two weeks, I'd chickened out and dropped out of the course. I knew I wanted to go abroad again. I had risen to the challenge in Uganda and found that working for the ICRC could be worthwhile without it having to knock my physical and emotional well-being sideways as it had in Ethiopia. This time, the ICRC asked if I'd like the post of medical administrator of Lopiding field hospital in Lokichokio, which had been set up as a base for ICRC relief operations across the border into southern Sudan, a country ravaged by civil war since 1983. I leaped at a new challenge and a promotion.

The hospital had been set up to provide emergency medical assistance for the war-wounded of the conflict zones in southern Sudan, where medical services were severely reduced or non-existent, and for wounded rebel soldiers of the Sudanese People's Liberation Army (SPLA). We were just a mile into Kenya from the border because the Sudanese government wouldn't allow the ICRC to build a hospital in its country. In the same way as they are doing in Darfur today, at that time the Sudanese authorities were trying to destroy the infrastructure of the rebels in the south.

Those seriously wounded in the conflict were evacuated by the SPLA and brought over the border to us. They might have been travelling for anything from a few days to a few weeks to reach us, without any proper first-aid treatment. They came in any available empty commercial truck, thrown in like sacks of grain and then driven for miles over unmade roads, an experience close to being driven over ploughed fields. Most of those wounded in the chest or abdomen didn't survive the journey. The wounded who were still alive by the time they arrived were heavily infected and it wasn't unusual to see maggots crawling out of a bullet wound. However, if our patients had survived the journey, they usually survived our treatment and were soon putting on weight and smiling again. Getting the healed fighters back to their homeland was not always easy. It depended on the mood of the truck drivers, who sometimes refused them. And under no circumstances would they transport corpses. We needed to transport them back for burial in their own soil, and so we had to forge an arrangement whereby the ICRC could repatriate the bodies in our own vehicles to Narus, a border town in south Sudan – which was time-consuming and unnecessary, given the number of non-ICRC vehicles that regularly took the route.

The hospital itself was basic: three solidly built brick rooms with forty to fifty beds and a covered yard. If many more patients arrived they had to be accommodated in large tents outside. There was one operating theatre with two tables. We often re-used the surgical gloves. To begin with we had to use water piped from the Lopiding Turkana settlement while we bored holes until we found our own water supply and could make a well. The showers and toilets were admittedly rudimentary but we were surprised that within a few days of opening the toilets were already completely blocked. We didn't know that the local custom was to use a few flat stones to wipe your backside before throwing them away – in this case, blocking the toilet. It was always difficult to persuade the patients to use any of the 'Western' facilities because they were so used to going under a nice clean bush beneath the open sky. The only solution was to dig trench latrines instead and put two local men in charge of them, and things improved after that.

To begin with, the work was hardly overwhelming. We were waiting for our 'bush team', or field workers, to get permission from the Kenyan and Sudanese government authorities to fly into Sudan and begin surveying the situation to assess what was needed. Until then our patient count remained low; there were fifty-five when I arrived. As medical administrator, I ran the hospital, ordering everything from food and cleaning materials to medicine and medical supplies, as well as hiring and paying the staff, stock taking, setting up a stock-card system and making sure that everything ran smoothly. The bulk of our supplies came from Nairobi, a two-day journey by lorry, although this was to speed up with the completion of a new tarmacked road.

I hadn't been there long before my skills were significantly tested. I had gone with a Dutch surgeon, Jan, and a young Finnish anaesthetist, Tom, to survey the hospital in neighbouring Lodwar. On the way, we stopped at the mission hospital in Kakuma where, in the absence of a full-time doctor, Jan was asked to examine some patients, one with an appendix abscess, the other with a ruptured hernia in the groin. He decided that the two of them needed urgent operations, and that we would return the next day. I was going to have to act as operating theatre nurse, as no one else was available to fill the role. Was I scared! I explained that I was pretty rusty in my theatre skills (I didn't admit how green I was), but he brushed my concerns aside. We used mostly our own drugs and intravenous infusions and were given sterile gowns although we worked in bare feet. There were blood and guts everywhere. Jan turned out to be a patient teacher and even let me suture the skin afterwards. The work was rewarding and I thoroughly enjoyed myself. We returned home that evening tired but happy, having left the patients convalescing comfortably.

We lived in a compound about four kilometres from the hospital. There I shared one of the circular palm-roofed huts with a Danish nurse. Like everything else, it was pretty basic, with just two bedrooms, but we had a shower and basin between us, and we even had the luxury of a flush loo, but as water was so limited we had to ration ourselves to flushing it only once or twice a day. A larger hut served as a dining room, where we ate together on its open verandah. When things were quiet, we'd sit gossiping late into the night. In such a small insular community, everything was news and discussed endlessly. There was a good bunch of doctors and nurses from all over the world, most of whom would grab any opportunity to party, and I soon found myself a couple of willing rock'n'roll partners. Indoor space was a bit limited, and when I was teaching a six-foot-tall Finnish nurse, Marcus, how to pull me through his legs while turning me in mid-air at the same time, I crashed into the arm of a chair and split my knee open. I couldn't have been in better company, with a choice of professionals competing as to who would stitch it up best. I lay on the kitchen trestle table and let them at it.

The one resident of the compound it was impossible to ignore was Alice, the pet ostrich. After a year, we discovered that in fact she was Alan. She used to chase us across the compound, kicking and flailing her wings. Her other bad habit was eating anything, including my red knickers. When they went missing, the washing woman told me that Alice was the culprit. Yeah, yeah, I've heard that one before, I thought. Until, to my disbelief, I saw Alice sneak up to the washing line, pull a pair of knickers off and swallow them. She'd also gobble up anything from nail brushes to plastic bags and cigarette packets.

I spent some of my working life in the compound overseeing our warehouse, which was big enough for about four double-decker buses. Bernard was my warehouse man. He was a Turkana nomad who had been taught some English by the missionaries based in Lokichokio. When he came to work, he dressed as he thought was appropriate for his position, discarding his normal sarong for a pair of black nylon trousers about three sizes too small and a dirty old T-shirt. Like all the other locals working with us, the first things he bought with his wages were a pair of Western dark glasses and a transistor radio – prized items indeed. He couldn't read, write or count. But he showed me that he could differentiate between the boxes of supplies by looking at the outlines of words and that he could count in fives by marking four lines and then striking them through. If I needed to know how many boxes were in the store, all I had to do was count his lines of five. For him, anything above about ten was 'lots' or 'many', yet he knew exactly how many of our boxes or his cattle went missing. When I questioned why he never stacked the boxes with the arrows on the outside pointing the right way up, he looked at me quizzically. I suddenly realized that as far as he was concerned an arrow was shot horizontally, not up in the air. The marking meant nothing to him. As for the wine glass and umbrella symbols marking fragile goods or things to be kept dry, they were meaningless to him too. Despite these failings, Bernard was the best and most honest store man I have ever had.

Like many of his friends, he was fascinated by the things we brought with us. With the new road from Nairobi came the intrusion of the 'civilized' world. How it would ultimately affect the Turkana we would have to see. In the short term, just building and staffing our hospital had already helped change the once-prolific bartering of goods into trading with money, as a large number of the population were employed by us. While we were there, telegraph poles started to sprout among the mud huts and along the dirt tracks, and a telephone box was installed in the village. Bernard and I once walked there together. I put in some money and called Nairobi. As I chatted, I noticed Bernard walking round me, looking up, looking left and right. Even when I tried to explain, he couldn't grasp why I was talking into this thing. He'd never seen anything like it. I imagine that if I were to go back today, such technology would all be taken for granted.

I remember Bernard's reaction when he had his first piece of chocolate. I had spotted a Mars bar for sale in the village.

'Look at this, Bernard. Let's have a Mars bar. Mmm.'

'Yes. Let's have a Mars bar. Mmm,' he echoed.

I bought it, took a big bite and gave it to him so that he could do the same. Mmm. Then his face dropped. He obviously wanted to spit it out but didn't want to be rude. Stupidly I hadn't realized that he had copied my words and actions without having any idea what the Mars bar would taste like. Of course it didn't taste anything like the fresh meat he was used to eating, and he wasn't used to anything sweet. What I had thought would be a treat tasted disgusting to him.

Bernard was one of about fifty hard-working local staff, most of whom, unlike him, always turned out in crisp shirts despite living in hovels. I noticed that one of them,

Margaret, had got quite large and seemed to be slowing down a bit.

'Margaret, I wonder if you might be pregnant,' I suggested quietly one day.

'No, no, I'm not pregnant. No.' She was adamant. She was adamant right up to the birth of her baby daughter a few months later. Even then, she claimed not to know how such a thing could have happened. Several of the nursing aides who had been trained and employed by the missionaries had been dismissed when caught living with someone of the opposite sex out of wedlock. Margaret obviously believed that she'd lose both her job and the baby if she admitted her pregnancy. In fact she did neither, and I was delighted when she named the little girl Claire.

Although it was a quick drive to the hospital from the compound, it was much nicer to walk across country, on dirt tracks. I'd pass five or six small groups of straw huts surrounded by felled acacia trees to keep the goats and sheep in and to provide a barrier against wild animals or the Toposa, a neighbouring tribe who frequently raided. The Turkana women went topless and tied an animal pelt round their middle, long at the back to sit on and open at the front. They wore lots of bright bead necklaces which they never removed, three or four hoop earrings in each ear and a large metal labret in their lower lip, sometimes as long as two and a half inches and sometimes with an amber stone at the end. The babies would pull it out and use it as a teething ring. Both men and women covered themselves in oil and red ochre, particularly liking to use the butter oil we gave out to them to make their skin shine. As a result, they often smelled strongly of rancid butter. The men usually went naked apart from a blanket over their shoulders reaching to crotch level – not for modesty but for style. Many of them wore a circular blade around their wrist for fighting and they always carried a little wooden stool to use as a pillow so that their hair, which was artfully matted with red clay and if they were really wealthy decorated with an ostrich feather, wouldn't get damaged when they lay down.

We were accepted by the local people and they often greeted us with a handshake. There were always dogs following them, each child apparently being given a puppy at birth that would grow up with them, looking after them and keeping them clean by licking their backsides. I also saw dogs lick the legs of women who were menstruating. The result of this close relationship was the spread of hydatids, internal cysts in humans caused by worms carried by dogs – hence the need for the work being carried out by the local research station run by the African Medical and Research Foundation, who treated not only the people but also the dogs.

As I passed, the birds cried and sang, the crickets chattered and the goatboys called out 'Ajok' in greeting. Sometimes I'd see a dik-dik, the smallest antelope there is, running out of the way. Hornbills flapped across the sky and there were always the horrible black cacti that reeked of rotten flesh.

One morning I was greeted by a little group of naked children, aged about four to six, all wanting to hold my hand and say hello. Chattering and laughing, they pulled me towards the bushes to show me something with great glee: a dead wild dog covered with flies. I made appropriate noises and beat a hasty retreat. Some time later, I was driving a jeep back to the compound and found all the little darlings sitting by the road watching. They had strategically placed the dead animal right in the middle of the rutted track and were giggling in anticipation of the wonderful spectacle when we drove over it. They found it just as amusing when we tried to avoid the animal and of course got stuck in the soft mud of the river bed and had to dig ourselves out. That provided them with their entertainment for the day.

What coloured the first few months of our stay there was the uncertainty surrounding our work. To begin with our South Sudan Survey Team were stuck at Lokichokio waiting for the go-ahead, which was held up for security reasons. Finally, after a number of attempts, they made it to Kongor on 13 July and began their survey, despite it being the middle of the rainy season, which made travel and transport extremely difficult. Patients were beginning to be brought out to us more frequently, although the roads got so muddy that often the trucks couldn't get through. A new surgical team arrived of Esko, a Finnish surgeon, and his wife Sirkka, an operating theatre nurse. He was tubby and a very energetic worker. He was particularly strict on hygiene and patient care at the hospital. He also loved dancing and making the most of his time off. She was petite, always smiling, and saw to his every need. One day he demanded a particular surgical power tool, for repairing fractures. I had to explain that the pilots said it was too dangerous to fly compressed air cylinders in a light aircraft. He wasn't used to not getting what he needed. So I was straight with him. 'Don't think you can order whatever you want because you're the most important person here, because you're not. The most important people working here are the cleaners. Without them the infection rate would be horrendous and then you really wouldn't be able to do your job. You're going to have to make do with the equipment we have here.' To his credit, he took the point.

A major setback to our work occurred in August, when we lost contact with one of the teams working across the border in Yirol. There was a field nurse, a delegate, pilot and co-pilot, none of whom I knew well. At first we heard nothing and feared the worst. Then we lost contact with the plane sent in to see if they were OK. There were five days of silence before we were contacted by a member of the SPLA, who told us that the team were safe and that they should be able to leave. There was an agonizing silence for another couple of days. We kept twenty-four-hour radio watch, every day hoping that we'd hear news or the sound of a plane. Eventually, after two weeks, they were released. They had been held in a one-roomed mud hut under armed guard. Thankfully, they all emerged unharmed. They assured us they had never been in real danger of losing their lives. The ICRC immediately pulled all personnel out of southern Sudan and once again we were back in the unsettling position of not knowing whether our projected work, supporting the existing local medical infrastructure, would be able to go ahead.

In the meantime, casualties kept trickling through, depending on the weather and the road conditions. One day, Tom, the anaesthetist, and I were left in charge of the operating theatre lists while Esko and Sirkka went on leave after many weeks without a rest. We received a message warning us to expect two trucks of wounded, but not giving any numbers. They finally arrived at 23.45 – thirty of them with gunshot and shell wounds that hadn't been cleaned, swarming with flies. Any dressings they had were filthy. They were all covered in dust and smeared with blood, sweat and tears. Most of the wounded were badly shocked and dehydrated, and certainly hadn't eaten for days. God knows how they survived the journey without painkillers. Imagine travelling for several days in an open truck with two fractured legs and a chest wound. All I could hope was that most of them had remained unconscious.

We sorted the wounded out as best we could as they lay higgledy-piggledy on the floor in our covered yard. Our Pilatus pilot, Gerard, helped by getting beds from the store and setting them up. Then we set about removing the dressings. We'd rigged up a hosepipe so that those who could walk could shower, while the others were carried to the water and strip washed. We dealt with all the wounds, scraping away maggots from the gangrenous stumps of amputees, giving patients intravenous antibiotics and tetanus shots, and roughly dressing the wounds before putting the patients to bed. We had put up two large tents outside to accommodate them so that we could clear out the yard for the next lot. All the wounds needed to be cleaned up and the dead tissue removed under general anaesthesia before being sutured at a later date when the risk of infection had passed. Many of them needed regular irrigation and cleaning under anaesthesia as well; the deep bullet wounds were too painful to be treated without. One soldier had an arm in plaster but when the plaster was removed, we found that gangrene had set in and the arm had to be amputated. Esko and Sirkka weren't due back until the next day and in the meantime Tom and I had to do our best.

I acted as theatre nurse. Tom had taught me to administer Ketelar, a light anaesthetic that doesn't put the patient out completely, so I was able to help speed things along. One poor young man, with the distinctive markings of the Dinka tribe across his forehead, had had the lower half of his leg blown off by a mine. When we started to remove his dressing, his flesh seemed to ripple. On closer inspection, we saw that it was heaving with maggots. Jumping back, we brushed them off our gowns and the sterile towels surrounding the wound, stamping on those on the floor. Neither of us knew what on earth to do. One of the nursing auxiliaries dashed out for a can of fly spray but it only made the maggots more active. In the end we had no choice but to scoop them into a bowl by hand, pouring bleach on them to kill them. I could feel them crawling all over me for days afterwards. After weeks of cleaning the wound and giving him antibiotics and nutritious food, our patient made a good recovery and was to be seen hopping about on his good leg playing volleyball and laughing.

Another hideous result of injury was tetanus. I saw this for myself when one of the wounded soldiers started having muscle spasms. Between attacks, he remained quite lucid, and it was obvious that he was aware of what was happening to him because he had seen others suffering the same thing. He faced his fate stoically. We did what we could, injecting him with tetanus immunoglobin and antibiotics to fight the infection, but we didn't have a respirator, so once he started fighting for breath we could only stand back and watch as he slowly asphyxiated.

Esko and Sirkka got back the next day to find that we had successfully made all the wounded as comfortable as we could. The surgical team got on with the operations, while Tom went back to work as anaesthetist and I returned to my administrative duties.

Not all our patients were wounded soldiers. We were occasionally called on to treat local people. One was a thirteen-year-old boy who'd been bitten by a snake under the bush where he'd been dozing, looking after his father's goats. His father brought him in. They had travelled for several days and the boy's foot was black – not from the bite itself, but from the effect of the tourniquet that had been left on his leg since it happened. Our only option was to amputate. The instruments were prepared but the surgeon was spared the job when, as I was helping to lift the child on to the operating table, his foot began to come away from his leg. The sweet rotting smell from all that necrotic tissue was unbelievable. I was horrified, but I swallowed hard and tried to appear as calm as if it were an everyday occurrence. On another occasion, two young girls were brought in, having been bitten by hyenas in separate incidents. We gave them antibiotics, antitetanus shots and rabies vaccine before transferring them to the hospital at Kakuna for follow-up care. Of course problems associated with childbirth occasionally cropped up too. We were called to Kakuna hospital when a Turkana woman was having a difficult labour. As the hospital nurses were all busy, I was asked to accompany the surgeon. Fortunately the sisters at the hospital had the operating theatre ready and, as they prepared the patient, we gowned up for an emergency Caesarian. As the mother's abdomen was opened, what seemed like a bucketload of fluid and blood erupted, drenching us from head to toe. We didn't even have plastic aprons, so were soaked through to the skin. I'm glad to say that mother and child both survived very happily.

Until October, the weather was unpredictable, often with huge storms that transformed the dried-up river bed by the camp into a raging torrent and the roads into ribbons of mud. One time, three other nurses, Nikki, Franz and Marcus, and I took the inner tubes from some lorry tyres, inflated them and floated along the river from the compound down to the hospital, shrieking our heads off. Muddy brown water, broken branches and fallen trees swirled about us. We arrived frozen and blue but high on adrenalin. Both my shoes had been washed away on the journey. The hospital staff thought we were mad. Perhaps they were right.

During my time in Lokichokio, there was a constant coming and going of staff as one by one they fulfilled their short-term contracts, which were often for as little as three months. In less than a year, we had nine different surgeons working in the hospital. As the patient count went up, more staff were sent in. As a result, it was hard to make lasting friendships, although those we did establish were always very intense, cut off as we were from the rest of the world. Tom, the Finnish anaesthetist, and I had immediately clicked. He specialized in A&E emergencies and had already spent two years on a full-time flying squad emergency rescue unit. We spent lots of time together in the camp, having a drink with the others, chatting at night over our secret store of chocolate and listening to music. We pledged to each other to learn two K'swahili words a day, with the result that by the time we left we could just about make ourselves understood to the locals.

Tom and I had a strong common bond. We settled for being good friends; our relationship was strictly platonic. We relied on each other's support in our work. He was inexperienced in bush medicine so, when he was promoted from anaesthetist to medical coordinator and had to travel and work in very basic conditions, he counted on my advice. In return he supported me in managing the hospital and field teams, something that required more tact than came naturally to me, especially when people got into disputes. He was a quiet type (until he got a few drinks inside him) and his diplomacy neatly balanced my no-nonsense way of sorting things out.

Finally, at the beginning of December 1988, as the weather was getting hotter, dustier and drier, the mission in south Sudan got off the ground and after that we were run off our feet. Planes flew in and out of south Sudan three times a day, but they weren't big enough for the amount of relief goods they had to carry. Thousands of people in southern Sudan were crowding around the major towns, driven there by conflict and famine as they are again today around Darfur. The planes flew in medical supplies for the ICRC-supported dispensaries as well as stocks of maize and blankets. Part of my role was to make up emergency first-aid kits. I was kept constantly busy taking stock of what went and came back from the southern Sudan mission and liaising with Tom, who now spent four or five days at a time in the field. Every day was full of administrative work, organizing and running the busy camp and hospital, with many new faces arriving, until we had a permanent expat staff of around twenty-five to thirty people. Although I missed working with patients, I really enjoyed rising to the challenge of running the warehouse, recruiting people and sorting out disputes among the staff, however stressful I found it.

Habari sucuo cuo – Happy Christmas in K'swahili. Although a long way from home, we celebrated Christmas in style, starting the day with a breakfast of Swiss star biscuits, home-made Finnish biscuits and chocolate sent by Tom's mother, as well as other treats sent to the others. While we were eating, a group of villagers appeared in our compound. The children sang and stamped their feet, rattling tin cans full of bottle tops and other bottle tops that were tied to their calves. About thirty men followed them into the compound, each with a wonderful ostrich feather adorning his clay-plastered hair. They did a strange kind of hopping dance, bobbing their ostrich feathers at us as they passed. Suddenly they all crowded as close as they could around me. The smell of the rancid animal fat they had rubbed into their skin was overwhelming. Without warning, they grabbed me, hauled me into the air and danced around the huts, carrying me on their shoulders and singing. I was a bit startled, but soon we were all laughing and, by the end of it, my Sunday-best clothes were smeared with grease and red ochre from their skin.

Work went on as usual that day, except that we found a bag of bullets under an empty bed in the hospital. We questioned all the patients but everyone denied all knowledge of them, scared of being accused of smuggling them out of the Sudan, for which they could be sent to the firing squad. Later in the day Åke, a Finnish male nurse, said there was a Christmas present for me and handed me a bag. When I looked in it, I found more bullets, newly arrived with the latest patients. I began to build up quite a store of them in my office. We decided to return them to one of the visiting SPLA commanders, asking him to remind his men that guns and ammunition weren't allowed over the border, and certainly not on Red Cross property. It may not have been the most politically correct way of dealing with the issue, but at least the ammunition disappeared from the compound quickly.

That evening, we did nothing special. We'd had our Christmas Eve dinner the night before, a superb barbecue cooked by the Portuguese/Angolan chief pilot with the rest of us helping. Instead we had a good old gossip in the hammocks on our verandah – Tim, the English plane mechanic, Åke, Tom and myself. We sat up well into the night, until we were suddenly interrupted by the sound of shooting. We flicked off the lights and hid ourselves beside the thick old concrete sink until silence fell. The next day we heard that the police had been chasing some cattle rustlers – a pretty regular event.

After Christmas we were able to get a programme going in south Sudan to vaccinate children and mothers against measles, tetanus and polio. I was responsible for maintaining the 'cold chain', ensuring that the vaccines were kept at the correct low temperature during their journey from Nairobi via Lokichokio to the clinics in Sudan. If the insulated cold boxes and ice packs were neglected and the temperature in which the vaccine was stored rose above 8°C, it would lose its potency and be useless. The clinics in the field didn't have electricity for fridges so for everything to be kept at the right temperature they had to be re-supplied with ice blocks every four days. At one point, I was sent out with another nurse, one of the Swiss delegates and Tom to assist with one of the first mass vaccinations in Kongor. Several weeks earlier, we had used the local grapevine to inform the mothers in the area that we were coming. We got there a few days before the mothers and children were due and enlisted the help of the local school teacher and health worker. I gave them a crash course in how to give injections, and we worked out a routine where one person would give an injection in the left thigh and another in the right arm, while someone else administered the oral polio vaccine. We settled into an efficient routine like clockwork and it all went pretty smoothly. However, I caught some of the older children sneaking under the roped-off area to pinch some syringes. I chased them round the village, and ended up having to explain the danger to the headman. He gave them an earful but they just went off giggling.

The only downside to this mission in Kongor was the house we were given to stay in. Before we even got to the front door, we were knocked back by an acrid smell. Bats! We'd already noticed a large tree that stood darkly alone in the centre of the village. When a religious parade marched by, we had seen a great black cloud of large bats lifting off into the sky and sweeping round, up and down before landing in the tree again. It was like something out of Hitchcock's film *The Birds*. Inside the building, there were hundreds of bats in the roof, smaller cousins of the ones outside. The house stank and the stench of ammonia stung our eyes. We had no choice but to move our hammocks out on to the verandah. We'd be in bed by six thirty, when stars were already twinkling against the velvet-black sky. Beyond our mosquito nets (a handy deterrent to stop the bats getting tangled in our hair), the village was quiet apart from the squeak of the bats and the cawing of the crows that began as dawn eventually broke.

In February 1989, I was sent back to south Sudan to repatriate the remains of two American pilots killed in an air crash at Christmas. It was arranged that I would collect the bodies for the ICRC on behalf of the families. Spiralling down to avoid being shot at by the local militia, who might mistake us for enemy aircraft, our pilot flew me into a little village, where the local commander of the SPLA met us and greeted us with great dignity and respect before taking us into a blood-spattered mortuary. On the slab were two metre-by-half-metre packs of the pilots' body parts, which the commander had identified and separated as best he could and wrapped beautifully in much-needed crocheted blankets that had been sacrificed out of respect. With the smell of death filling the cabin, we flew them back to Nairobi, where I had the sad duty of presenting them to the grieving widows and the US diplomats.

A couple of weeks later, I was asked to return to Kongor to conduct a survey of the medical needs of the village. I went alone with the pilot because none of the medical staff was available. While I was there, a convoy of trucks carrying wounded men heading for Lokichokio arrived. But Lokichokio was several days' drive away, depending on the road conditions and the fighting, and at least twenty-five of the wounded were lying in terrible pain, dehydrated, covered in dust and blood, and urgently needing treatment.

We had only a small Pilatus plane. The pilot had to calculate his fuel against distance and weight carried. He worked out that we could take only eight wounded men. I remember one soldier in particular, a young man who had been shot in the back and was paralysed from the waist down. Although he was badly injured, I made the difficult decision to take several other wounded soldiers instead, including traumatic amputees who had a better chance of quality of life if they survived. Being paralysed in a nomadic environment was not a good viable option. A few days later when the convoy finally arrived at the hospital, I was shocked to see that he had survived the journey. He died within a short time of our admitting him.

In spite of such tragedies, I enjoyed life in Lokichokio. I liked the people I worked with and I loved the work. By the time I left, after one year, we had 142 in-patients and were carrying out approximately 94 operations each week. The foreign staff in the hospital had doubled, and the number of local staff had increased from 47 to 66. Organizing all those people and the supplies had appealed to my Swiss efficiency and I felt that I had really achieved something in helping the hospital grow to accommodate larger numbers of wounded.

In April 1989, I returned to England, where I bought a small house in a village near my parents and did six months' basic nursing at the neurosurgical unit at Addenbrookes, which was obligatory if I were to qualify for an A&E course I wanted to take at Whipps Cross Hospital. This time I didn't run away from it. The reason? I had discovered computers. The difference a computer made to my written work was a revelation. It meant no more of my spidery scribble, which neither I nor anyone else could easily decipher. It meant neat straight lines of legible words that I could move around easily to make a proper sentence without having to start from the beginning again. It meant I had Spellcheck to help me. The result was that I began to relax and enjoy studying.

And yet I didn't feel totally at peace within myself. I was still haunted by my time in Ethiopia, and I found myself looking again for a spiritual framework that would help me make sense of the world. It was at this time that I heard a programme on BBC Radio 4 about alternative funerals. It talked about humanism and utilitarianism. Both philosophies sounded interesting to me, since neither relied on an outside force or any sort of deity. Humanism particularly seemed to reflect my own ideas, and I liked the suggestion that the individual has to take responsibility for his own actions and work with others towards the common good. I duly joined the British Humanist Society and even went to a couple of its meetings. However, without being able to put a finger on exactly why, I knew that humanism still wasn't quite what I was searching for. It made me think, but I didn't feel that there was a deep philosophy to which I could connect.

But before I had made any commitment either way, my life changed direction once more. While completing the A&E course I was able to experience the simple pleasures of living at home again, but as soon as it was over, I was ready to go abroad once more. This time I was to go to Afghanistan.

[faint mirrored text from previous page, illegible]

15

BROTHERS IN ARMS

OUR AFGHAN FIELD OFFICER, SHER AFZAL, LOVED DRIVING fast. He'd brake only at the very last minute for each of the many potholes or road-blocks, ignoring my protests about wanting to transport the wounded without inflicting any more damage. On a typical day in December 1990, he, my Norwegian co-worker Halvor and I, shrouded in a white chiffon scarf, headed north out of Kabul, crossed the government front line, and drove through no-man's-land, a desolate barren stretch of land where, for security reasons, all the fruit orchards had been decimated by invading Russian forces years before. At every one of the six or seven checkpoints we passed through on the way, each belonging to a rival mujahidin commander, we stopped for a quick '*assalamu alaikum*' (peace be with you) with the soldiers, who bristled with guns and grenades.

On arriving at Mir Bacha Kot, a village some twenty-seven kilometres north of Kabul, we backed into the courtyard of the old fort that was now the ICRC's first-aid post (never drive in forwards – always be prepared for a quick getaway), where we were warmly welcomed by our staff. They were all local men culled from each of the various mujahidin factions in the area. Finding that there were no patients waiting for us, we joined them for lunch. Sitting around on long checked floor cushions and resting against the bare walls of the communal room, we drank tea and chatted, eating rice with boiled mutton and potatoes in a visually unappealing thin greasy sauce that tasted surprisingly delicious. Halvor and I ate from the communal plate with a spoon and fork, while all the local staff scooped up the stew using naan bread.

Just after lunch, a five-year-old boy was brought in with an acute bone infection from a fractured femur that hadn't healed properly. His thigh was twice its normal size, red hot and deformed, but he had been taught the stoical way of the mujahidin fighter. I remembered seeing mujahidin nurses play with a baby, pinching its leg and then, just as it screwed up its face to cry, making it laugh. I told them they were being cruel, but they just laughed, saying their children needed to be tough and this was a way of getting them used to pain. So there were no screams or shouts from our young patient, just a few murmurs of 'Allah! Allah!' as we transferred him and his mother into the Land Cruiser for our return journey to the ICRC hospital in Kabul.

We set off at speed, none of us wearing seat belts in case we came under fire and needed to be able to move fast. Suddenly, Sher Afzal saw one of the mujahidin at a checkpoint raise a hand. I hung on to a strap, bracing my foot against the dashboard as he screeched to a halt. Someone was wounded. Following directions, I ran to a hollow by the roadside, where I found a wheelbarrow with some filthy bloodsoaked blankets thrown over the contents, flies swarming round it. Two bloodstreaked feet stuck out of the end, propped on a bit of wood resting across the handlebars, with a large pan of hot coals beneath to warm them. Tentatively, I removed a bit of blanket, allowing the flies to go crazy on the bloodsoaked face underneath. The eyes were swollen shut and a bloody bandage circled the injured man's head. He must have been about twenty-five, and he was covered in dust, his long, tangled hair matted with it. As I pulled back the blanket, he moaned quietly, 'Allah! Allah!' At least he was still alive. Halvor ran over to join me. We were told that the man had been wounded in shelling a couple of hours earlier and had been pushed here over three kilometres of rough ground. Using a wheelbarrow was a common way of transporting the injured to safety because it allowed them to be easily pushed along narrow tracks and manoeuvred to circumnavigate minefields. The man's entire body was peppered with shrapnel, which had caused characteristically small entry wounds with minimal external bleeding but potentially extensive internal damage. We had enough dressings to cover only the largest of the wounds.

We found a vein in one hand, the other being too lacerated, and put up a drip to replace the fluid he'd lost in bleeding and to counteract the shock, as well as administering antibiotics and painkillers. We laid him as gently as possible on a stretcher and I sat on the floor of the Land Cruiser beside him, monitoring his condition as we drove off. I was happy to hear him moan occasionally as we went over bumps, which meant he was still alive.

Unbelievably, Sher Afzal drove even faster than usual, daring anyone to get in his way, over- and undertaking whenever he could. When we reached the hospital, we left the boy with the infected leg with his mother in the waiting room before transferring the man to the trauma unit. Everyone there was preoccupied with another badly injured patient, so Halvor and I stayed with him. When the scissors didn't work, we just tore off his clothes, sending clouds of dust flying all over the beautifully clean admissions room, making us sneeze. Halvor put another line into his neck for more fluid and took blood for crossmatching. Meanwhile I gently soaked off the old dressings, which were stuck to him like stamps, and dressed the wounds again. Then the hospital staff came to take over and that's where we had to leave him, our job over. The next day we were told that he had been operated on for a lacerated liver and kidney and a collapsed lung, as well as having various bits of metal removed from the rest of his body. Only twenty-four hours later, we found him sitting on the edge of his bed and he even managed to give me a smile.

It was after this adventure that I decided that there was no way I would risk my life on these daily 'suicide' missions with Sher Afzal at the wheel. So, when we were alone, I told him firmly that I'd be doing the driving in future. He must have seen how determined I was, because he just nodded his head and said, 'Miss Claire. You will drive from now on. I will arrange it.' Women didn't drive outside Kabul, where it was deemed unseemly and unsafe, but he never complained. If anyone commented, he'd always spring to my defence, saying, 'Claire is more experienced in driving than I am,' and dismiss the question with his head held high and a flick of his hand.

Even before the Taliban took control of the country five years later, Afghan women traditionally stayed at home from the age of thirteen, received no schooling and covered their faces and bodies with a heavy burkha before leaving their home or in front of strangers. Only a small square of netting in front of their eyes was allowed so that they could see out. They were not allowed to speak to anyone outside the family and, if ill or injured, they could be looked after only by a woman. This meant that wounded women would come to the first-aid post when I was there. One female patient was left at home for several days with toothpaste rubbed into her blistered and burned legs before her family heard that I was on duty and brought her to me. Another, eight months pregnant, was brought in by her distraught husband and neighbours. She had been making bread beside an underground oven when the ground gave way, plunging her into the fire. She had severe burns all over her body, her face was blistered and raw, and her breathing was laboured from smoke inhalation. She was too badly burned for me to find a vein for a drip, so I gave her an intramuscular sedative and painkiller. I desperately tried to contact the ICRC hospital in Kabul, while her family grew increasingly angry that I wasn't paying enough attention to the patient. In the end, I abandoned the attempt and, covering her with a clean sheet, I loaded her into an ambulance, hoping I would get her to the hospital in time to save the baby. As I drove, the acrid smell of burnt flesh and hair filled my nostrils, while the poor woman fought for breath. I went as quickly as I could, but it was hopeless. Both mother and unborn child died shortly after our arrival.

During the Soviet occupation of Afghanistan from 1979 to 1989, loosely aligned opposition groups of mujahidin – 'holy warriors' or 'freedom fighters' – had fought to force a Soviet retreat. In 1989, the Soviet troops withdrew, leaving the country under the communist government of President

Najibullah. However, internal fighting intensified as the rebel mujahidin forces fought for control of Kabul and other government-controlled cities. These various fighting units, led by regional warlords, also waged war against one another. This was the situation in the country when I arrived in 1990. The ICRC had been admitted into Afghanistan in 1988 and had established bases in three towns, Kabul, Mazar-i-Sharif and Herat. Field missions set out from each of these cities to bring back war-wounded from the front line for treatment. Before that, the mujahidin warlords had had to carry their wounded all the way across the mountains of the Hindu Kush to Peshawar in Pakistan. The journey took days and many lives were needlessly lost.

It had taken ten years to complete the negotiations for a neutral ICRC surgical hospital to be allowed to open in Kabul, the capital, to treat war-wounded from every side of the conflict without interference from the Afghan government. An existing building had been chosen at a reasonable distance from any strategic or military installations, next to the river and with enough space around it to put up extra tents should it become necessary. Although built for sixty to seventy patients each, the wards were overcrowded, with an intake of at least double that per ward. While I was there, there were four surgical teams who worked around the clock. Security was tight. All knives, guns, grenades and knuckledusters were confiscated on entry, put in a storage container and returned to their owners when they left the grounds. As the hospital was designated a 'neutral area', people who had been fighting against each other in the same battle could find themselves in neighbouring beds. Only the women and children were separate. Surprisingly there was never any trouble while I was there. The patients were all protected by the Red Cross – just a little piece of cloth – and, bizarrely, all hatred and aggression was left at the door along with their weapons.

Only fifteen kilometres away, the surrounding countryside was under the control of the mujahidin. As one of the field nurses in the delegation, my responsibility was for the Shakadara area north of the city, where at least eight rival mujahidin warlords controlled an area of twenty square kilometres. As well as fighting against the government troops, they often fought among themselves over their territory. One warlord admitted to me, 'Fighting has now become a habit.' It was too complex a situation to understand fully and, although I was able to sympathize with their different experiences and suffering, I concentrated on maintaining an open mind and getting on with the work I was there to do.

The country around Mir Bacha Kot was flat, with mountains rising on either side. Grapevines were cultivated everywhere, not pruned back like those I remembered in Switzerland but as scrappy bushes. The grapes were for eating fresh or for drying as raisins but not used for wine as in Europe, as this was a Muslim country. On any raised land, there were terraced fields that could be as small as ten square metres, with irrigation channels running through them. Cornfields could be seen as well as pasture with a few grazing sheep, but cattle were a rarity by then. Apple, almond, mulberry and walnut trees grew haphazardly across the valley. You could see that the area had once been fertile and productive but now much of the land was left uncultivated, mainly because of landmines. Buildings everywhere were in ruins. Russian tanks, old lorries, containers and oil tankers – all twisted by shelling, blown out by grenades and riddled with bullet holes – lay abandoned by the roadsides.

In the middle of this bleak landscape, our first-aid post was built in the ruins of a fortress that had stood for over a hundred years. It was like a walled corral, with rooms encircling a central courtyard – wards for the wounded, a casualty room, a communal room for the staff, a teaching room and a storeroom. The latrine was a hole in the top floor of a small turret on the side of the building. All the gun sights in the turret had been filled to stop prying eyes, although the doorway up there remained open to all. The first few times I went to the post, heavy shelling from one of the fighting factions rocked the walls and shook the windows. It wasn't long before the staff added sticky plastic sheeting to stop the glass from shattering over us. All the warring mujahidin commanders in the area had agreed

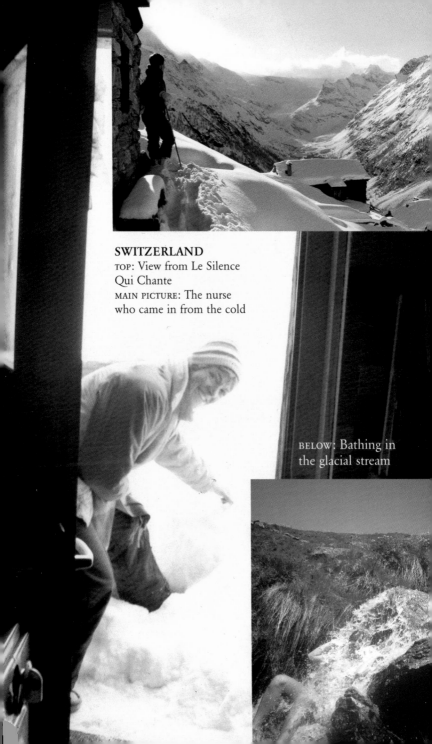

SWITZERLAND

TOP: View from Le Silence
Qui Chante

MAIN PICTURE: The nurse
who came in from the cold

BELOW: Bathing in
the glacial stream

LOKICHOKIO

RIGHT:
SPLA truck bringing
in the wounded
BELOW, LEFT:
Turkana women
BELOW, RIGHT:
Recovering patients

RIGHT:
With Alice
the ostrich

OPPOSITE PAGE:
Turkana man
with lunch

AFGHANISTAN
ABOVE: With the team, wearing
traditional Afghan costume
BELOW: Lunch with the boys

RIGHT: Treating a wounded woman
MAIN PICTURE: Sher Afzal

LEFT: Treating the wounded by the roadside
ABOVE: Hostage negotiation
BELOW: Snowbound: walking
to the ambulance

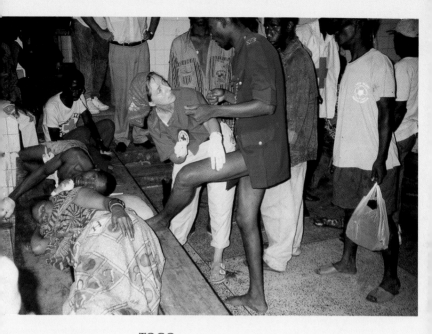

TOGO
ABOVE: Sierra Leone coup d'état
BELOW: Meeting the King of the Land

TOP: Return to Ethiopia with Michael Buerk

ABOVE: Meeting Girmay again with his wife and Brenda the BBC producer

RIGHT: Receiving the Florence Nightingale Medal

BELOW: With Bob Geldof.

that this was a neutral place where any wounded could come for help. The original post had been destroyed a few months earlier by shelling, and Halvor and Aline, my predecessor, had been lucky to escape with their lives. Afterwards, it had taken some time for the commanding warlords to agree who should have the prestige of having the new ICRC post built on their territory.

To maintain neutrality at the post we made sure that we had two or three local workers from each mujahidin command. There were no women, because it was not their place to work outside the home. All the men were typically dark-haired, often wearing their shalwar kameez under a pocketed photographer's jacket or a large blanket as well as the traditional pashtun hat, all with the regulation four-fingers' length of beard. The five nurses in our nineteen-strong staff weren't trained in the way we would recognize in Europe, but they had practical experience from at least ten years of fighting.

It was a while before the nurses, Ali, Abdul, Hassan, Mohammed and Daoud, accepted me as part of their team. In all my travels, I found that it always took time for the local workers to get to know me and my ways – especially in a strict Muslim country as this was – as indeed it did for me to know theirs. I was used to this. My strategy was to keep quiet at first and just watch how they did things. Then I would muck in and they'd become surprised at my willingness to work hard. After that, I would be accepted.

As the workers relaxed, we could begin to be friendly and share jokes. Next they'd try the 'relationship' phase, seeing how far they could go with me. They were unused to having a professional relationship with a woman, and any Western woman seemed fair game. This for me was the most difficult phase. They'd make innuendoes or try to touch me inappropriately, but when they'd learned I was no pushover, they stopped. Once we'd been through all that, I found that the mujahidin working in the first-aid post were kind and generous to a fault, and they supported me 100 per cent. They never panicked; when we came under fire, they would carry on with whatever they were doing, saying, 'No problem. No problem.' Even when our windows were smashed, the whistle and whoosh of shells sounding overhead as they exploded as close as a hundred metres away, sending red-hot slivers of shrapnel into the courtyard, still they remained calm, just muttering a few words – 'Bismillah ar-Rahman ar-Rahim' – after each volley of rockets, and 'Oh Allah.' After a quick look round we'd continue whatever we were doing, unless the lookouts on the roof reported injuries. Occasionally I had to turn my head and bury my face in a friendly arm for comfort.

Meeting any foreign health worker was an opportunity for these men to learn. The nurses were especially thirsty for knowledge. When the post was quiet, I gave them English lessons. They were so receptive that by the time I left, they knew enough to read simple medical textbooks as well as medical information on the packaging of imported drugs bought in the bazaar. They were so eager to read anything in English that I would bring them the English magazines I was sent from home, but first I had to rip out any photos showing bare arms and legs – soap ads with silhouettes in the shower, anything suggestive and any pictures of voluptuous females, dressed or undressed.

On one occasion, I remember, I gave them a copy of *Homes and Gardens*. Within moments Ali and Abdul were roaring with laughter, and the others charged over to take a look. Oh my God, I thought. I've left something in. I'm going to get in such trouble. I dashed over to find, to my relief, that the picture causing the fuss was of a dog on a settee.

'What's so funny?' I couldn't see it at all.

Ali explained that, to them, a dog was a filthy thing and they couldn't get over the sight of one being allowed inside this ritzy house, let alone on the furniture.

They were always asking me to explain things about which I had only the vaguest knowledge: how a satellite worked, for instance, or something about the latest cars or computers. I would begin every explanation with 'I don't know...' which made them laugh. 'That's what you always say, Claire. Come on. Tell us what you do know,' Daoud would say encouragingly. I would always surprise myself by managing to come up with some kind of explanation. They were greedy for knowledge about the modern world, simply because they hadn't had access to books, television or radio from the West for the previous ten years. They soaked up all the information I could give them; and the more I gave, the more they wanted. I remember thinking how odd it was that I, the one who was so hopeless at school, found myself in this position, but they were so grateful for everything I could tell them. Halvor and I also gave them lessons in advanced first aid so that they could put up a drip, regulate fluid balance through monitoring blood pressure, give intravenous drugs and analgesia, and dress wounds correctly.

Halvor, my fellow ICRC nurse for the area, was tall, fair-haired and rugged. He was a highly trained emergency nurse, used to working in the field as a paramedic on emergency rescue helicopters in Norway. He loved to party, and burned the candle at both ends, but was always up on time for work the next morning. One day just as we arrived at Mir Bacha Kot, shells began falling. A couple of hours later, they were raining from the sky, landing as close as a hundred metres away. We gathered that two local warlords were battling over some disaffected men who had swapped their allegiance. We were trapped. Halvor and I discussed the best way to deal with the situation. He was more of a risk-taker than I am and thought we should make a run for it, hoping for the best, but I refused to leave. I didn't want to play Russian roulette. Although we might get hit by a stray shell on the post, to me driving down the road the

warlords were fighting across seemed much more dangerous. Eventually he agreed that I was right. We stayed put
until late afternoon, when there was a let-up in the shooting, and we quickly loaded up and got out of there as fast
as we could. For the next two days, we couldn't get to the
post, and stopped two kilometres away, waiting for the
local helpers to bring out the wounded to us whenever
there was a lull in the fighting.

Halvor and I worked well together, and were always
accompanied by the third member of our team, Sher Afzal.
A distinguished local man in his forties, as well as being our
field officer he was our translator and our eyes and ears in
the field. As a white-bearded mujahidin, he was well
respected in the community and treated accordingly. Like
all Afghan men, he hated taking orders, and taking them
from a woman was unheard of, although he wasn't reticent
about giving them himself. When he said to me, 'You will
do this,' I had to be subtle in my refusal and make it look as
if he was the one making the decisions. Losing face was not
an option. For example, one day he tried to order me to
take his sheep from the market to his house in the
ambulance. I would have humiliated him by simply saying
no. Instead, I asked, 'Do you think the head of the
delegation would agree? I'm not sure.' That was enough
for him to decide for himself that his idea wasn't such a
good one.

I had learned my lesson once while we were at the post,

when he was promising money to the cook for food, even though it wasn't his money to give, and I directly questioned what he was doing. He turned on me furiously, in a way he never had before. I was shocked. Where was all this antagonism coming from?

Later, on our way home, I asked him, 'Sher Afzal, why did you talk to me like that?'

He looked at me and quite matter-of-factly replied, 'But you questioned me. You must never question an Afghan in front of other people. And most especially you mustn't give orders.'

'But why?' I was puzzled.

'Because you are a woman.'

From then on, it was agreed that every morning we'd first discuss what had to be done that day – just him and me in private. That way, when we got to the first-aid post, he could be seen to be in charge, telling people what to do. But I was always one step behind him, and when he tried to diverge from the plan, a great game for him, I only had to clear my throat or gently call his name, and he would revert to the original plan that we'd made earlier.

Once we both understood the ground rules, working with him was a pleasant challenge. He was my greatest ally, arranging anything I asked, as long as I didn't 'show him up' in public. He was utterly invaluable to us and totally dedicated. He was protective too. I remember arguing with him when we'd been radioed to pick up two wounded from the fighting zone. He felt that the mujahidin fighters might not be able to contain themselves if they saw a white woman out there. I was furious. 'I've always felt safe here and the fighters have never shown me any disrespect,' I protested. 'I've worked in four other war zones and I am the most experienced field nurse out here. So what if I'm a woman? I want to share my knowledge with the Afghan people and I just want to help these people help themselves...' He eventually agreed, though I suspect it was more to shut me up than anything. But he saw that, although it was not what he was used to, I was right and from that moment on I had won both his respect and his protection.

Our job involved arranging ceasefires and security guarantees with the different commanders so that we could cross the front lines and pick up the wounded. Eight o'clock each morning would find us checking our two white Toyota Land Cruisers, each fitted out with HF and VHF radios, which acted as our ambulances, displaying large red crosses on their sides and on the flags we flew from the bonnets. They weren't beautiful but they were convenient. They were equipped with a pair of stretchers and a padded mattress, as well as basic intravenous infusions, sedatives, strong analgesia and field dressings. Having only two stretchers didn't mean we could bring in only two wounded at a time. We'd have to squeeze in as many as possible, putting them – badly injured amputees, people with horrendous chest injuries, mothers holding babies, shocked and wounded children – head to tail on the stretchers, and sitting them propping each other up on the floor. There was often no alternative, as we never knew when we'd be able to get back into the fighting area. Once out, the wounded would have a better chance of survival than if they were left a day or two till the fighting died down and we returned.

On an average day, at around nine thirty, we'd get the green light from the government side and with me at the wheel and Sher Afzal beside me, we'd pick up the treated and discharged patients from the hospital and take them back to the field where we had picked them up. Once out of the government-controlled area, although I didn't have to wear a burkha, I had to cover my head and my clothes had to be loose fitting in order to conceal my arms and bottom. Sher Afzal used to tell me, 'Claire, you have to look like a sack of potatoes. Look at the women in their *chadors* [body veils]. You cannot see their shape.' I never stopped wearing my earrings, though. I experimented until I found a head covering that wasn't too hot or too tight and didn't keep slipping off while I was working. Eventually I settled for the Benazir Bhutto look, a long white chiffon scarf that, coupled with my bright pink and blue ski jacket, made me an unmistakable figure. Being so distinctive played a large part in keeping me safe, I'm sure.

One day, as I was leaving the post, I saw a little party of

people carrying something on their shoulders. As they got closer, I made out a bed on which lay a pretty ten-year-old girl with black hair and big black eyes. She had picked up one of the butterfly mines that the Russians had littered over the Afghan countryside. These are among the deadliest anti-personnel mines. Jettisoned from aeroplanes, they plummet to the ground without exploding, primed to go off when they're picked up or trodden on. Often brightly coloured, they exert a fatal attraction for children. This little girl's shattered right hand was hanging from her arm by a couple of sinews, and her left hand was missing a couple of fingers. She had the look of all newly injured patients: she was staring wide-eyed in shock, unable to cry or move, and covered in mud and blood. Halvor had gone ahead to Kabul, accompanying a man suffering severe gun-shot wounds to his abdomen, so I was on my own. Even if I could get her quickly back to the hospital, I knew that we had no facilities for the microsurgery that might be able to re-attach and save her right hand. My only option was to cut through the remaining sinews and leave the hand behind. As I cut through her flesh, I remember thinking about the finality of what I was doing. What made it worse was that she began screaming and crying, though not from the pain. Sher Afzal translated her screams: 'Allah! Why didn't you kill me? Let me die and be buried by my father. I am no good to my husband like this. I must die.' Beside her, her grandmother joined in. This was a catastrophe for their family: the child would no longer be able to fulfil her place in society. She was one of the real casualties of war, an innocent child caught in the crossfire and maimed for life. I could do nothing to make up for the loss of her future. The end of her arm had been cauterized by the explosion, so there wasn't a lot of blood, and I carefully dressed it with a pad and bandage before taking her to the hospital. Two weeks later, when I went to see her, I found that she had become an out-patient, staying with a relative in Kabul, and had been referred to the artificial limb centre.

Of course there were many whose lives we were unable to save at all. I remember young soldiers blown apart with terrible injuries; I remember gunshot wounds that perforated a man's liver and bowel, a ten-year-old boy with shell injuries to his head and all four limbs; a farmer with shrapnel embedded in his skull. However hard we fought for such lives, often we lost them. This was the price of war. And what was it all for? This was a question that was increasingly preoccupying me. Why was it that some people's aim in life was to destroy others and the environment?

As field workers, our own lives were also constantly at risk. Once, with his father's blessing and encouragement, I dragged a distraught young boy whose leg had been shredded by shrapnel from his father's arms so that I could take him to Kabul for treatment. His mother had to stay behind to look after her other six children. The father, who was a mujahidin fighter, gave us contact details for a relative in Kabul who would come and stay with him. But the boy's face twisted in terror and confusion. He was screaming, 'Don't leave me, Daddy. I'll die if you leave me.' We had no choice but to lock him, sobbing and yelling, in the back of the ambulance and step on the accelerator. No amount of consoling by Sher Azal helped to calm him down.

At that moment, the mujahidin across the valley let rip with a Soviet-issue rocket-launcher nicknamed Stalin's Organ. It was so big that it was mounted on the back of a truck and it could fire up to twenty rockets at a time, blanket-bombing a confined area, leaving nothing standing. Driving along in the ambulance, I felt the vibrations of the rockets being fired and heard their deep pulsating roar, one after another. The boy was shocked into silence. I began to count the seconds, knowing that if I got to ten, we were in the clear and the rockets had hit elsewhere. Those were ten terrifying seconds. Even today, I get flashbacks to them. The similar sound of a motorbike accelerating towards me is enough to transport me back to Afghanistan. I freeze, counting, waiting for it to pass or hit me. For a split second, I closed my eyes in fright; then I opened them quickly, thinking, 'Christ, you can't do that.' Gripping the steering wheel for dear life, I whispered to myself, 'Relax, Claire. Stay calm. Relax your grip and drive.' The shells were exploding all around us. I could smell the cordite.

This was far too close for comfort. I didn't want to die like this. I had too much left to do. I had to keep going until we were out of the line of fire. Just as we went over the brow of the hill into Kabul, we were flagged down by the boy's cousin. Somehow the bush telegraph had alerted him and he accompanied his young relative to the hospital and made sure he was looked after.

By now I'd lost the gung-ho recklessness of new field workers that I'd had in Lebanon, and at last I had started to appreciate the real danger we faced in the field. Within the first week of being in Kabul, I asked Halvor why we were driving a petrol engine across the front line.

'What do you mean?' he said.

'Why not diesel?' I said, remembering Yves' advice in Lebanon. 'If you get a bullet in a tank of diesel, all you get is a hole in the tank. If you get a bullet in a tank of petrol, the whole truck goes up.'

'Well, if you're too scared, Claire . . .'

'No. No. You've missed the point. It's not that I'm scared. It's just stupid. If we get blown up, the whole Red Cross mission will have to stop and we won't be able to continue our work here.'

Among the precautions I now regarded as essential was leaving vehicle windows slightly open so that if a shell landed near by, the shock waves could travel through the car and the glass wouldn't get blasted in. It was also a decided advantage to be able to hear what was going on outside the vehicle – for example, someone shouting, 'Stop!' Travelling without seat belts meant we could react quickly if we suddenly came under fire. We always carried jerry cans of water with us, and I'd always have some dried fruit to nibble on. While waiting at the checkpoints it was important never to have the radio on too loud; and to be constantly vigilant, watching for signs from the soldiers. Were they relaxed, smoking and joking? Or were their guns at the ready? If they were, which way were they aimed? Was there smoke anywhere? In Lebanon, I used to think that the picturesque puffs of smoke against the sky came from fires in the mountains until someone pointed out they were shells exploding. Many of these common-sense points became vital to me as I grew increasingly aware of our vulnerability.

Sometimes I had to take people into the field so that they could understand the work we did, and invariably they'd comment on how calm I was and how easy it was to cross a front line. But they had no idea what was going on in my head and how vigilant I was of what was going on around me. I was always alert to anything that might threaten our safety. It was in Afghanistan that I wrote a pamphlet called 'What They Don't Teach You in Geneva – Security Rules' for new recruits to the ICRC. At our briefings, we were all given a thick book of instructions that we had to read and sign, but I found it very technical and not of much practical use. I wrote my booklet so that anyone coming into the field with me would know what the dangers were and how they could be best prevented. I'm pleased that it was incorporated into the ICRC's security guidelines and training days.

This was the most dangerous work I had ever done. The situation was extremely unpredictable. I remember travelling to the first-aid post at Mir Bacha Kot one wonderful crisp sunny December morning. Fresh snow that had fallen the night before covered the countryside with a virgin-white sparkling carpet. We passed a farmer, barefoot and ankle deep in a small stream that he was trying to clear so that it would run freely. At a checkpoint, most of the military were out of sight, keeping warm in their underground shelters, but a dwarf militia man stopped us and asked for a field dressing – not to use, but for his collection. He jumped on to the running board and poked his head through the window. When told we didn't have any, he backed off despondently, shaking his Kalashnikov at us, and then laughed and dared us to come the next day without one. I made a mental note not to bring one for him – bluff with bluff. War is dangerous but one must not give in too easily. We sailed through the rest of the mujahidin checkpoints with a gentle bob of the head, smile and hand on the heart.

About ten kilometres further on, we saw a red smudge on the horizon, contrasting with the stark white landscape. The dramatic peaks of the Hindu Kush made an imposing backdrop. Getting nearer, the red crosses painted on the low white-washed walls of the first-aid post became more distinct. It had been a quiet night with no wounded, so we filed into the familiar communal room, leaving our boots at the door. We lazed around, talking about our Christmas, eating lunch, and afterwards I gave the nurses an English lesson. When it was over, Sher Afzal, Halvor and I dragged ourselves up to return to the chaos of the city before nightfall and the ten o'clock curfew. It was a tranquil day made in heaven.

On the way back, we passed the farmer again, still up to his ankles in freezing water. We crossed the checkpoints into no-man's-land. The sun was a ball of fire, sinking behind the mountains and making the snow sparkle like a bed of jewels. But then I noticed what looked like large ink spots silently splattering across the scene. I watched, fascinated by the patterns they made. Suddenly I realized these were shells landing in the snow. We were right in the line of fire. Driving like hell to get out of there, we over-took a transit van packed with women, children and old men, some of them hanging to the side rails, all screaming for help. But only a madman would stop in the line of fire. Once we'd got safely over the col and through the govern-ment checkpoint, we waited for them. When the van drew up, out tumbled shocked men, women and children, a chicken and a caged canary. They motioned behind them, crying and shouting. I climbed into the back of the truck, where a woman was lying motionless. I lifted her veil. Her chest was blown open. She must have been killed instantly. Beside her an old man was still alive, but half his head had been blown away. None of the bystanders helped Halvor, Sher Afzal or me as we hefted him on to a stretcher; they just stood watching. I sat in the ambulance, holding his head all the way to Kabul and trying to calm him as he thrashed around. He had no idea where he was and at one point I was practically sitting on him to prevent him from sitting up. We all knew he was a goner. I hoped he'd be dead by the time we reached the hospital so that the staff wouldn't moan about my bringing in such a hopeless case. Only a miracle would have saved him. In fact he died about an hour after our arrival and I was berated by the staff for 'wasting' their time. But what choice did I have? I had to bring in people who were still alive, even if they were fatally injured. That was my role.

That night, at the delegation, I hosed the blood out of the Land Cruiser, finding spots that had got trapped in tight corners, before I wandered exhausted into my office. Just then, the head of the delegation called down two flights of stairs, 'Claire, come up here, would you?'

I'm tired, leave me alone, was the only thought in my mind. 'I'll be up in a minute,' I called.

'No, Claire, you must come up now.'

'Let me have a cup of tea, first.' That was what I needed before I could do anything else.

'No. You've won a medal. Come and see.'

Whatever was he talking about? I dragged myself up the stairs, silently cursing. The excited chief showed me a telex saying that I'd won the Florence Nightingale Medal awarded to nurses for exceptional courage and devotion to the wounded, sick or disabled. My only reaction was, Yeah, so what? All I want is a cup of tea and a good wash. I was so exhausted that I honestly didn't take in that I'd been awarded such a prestigious honour.

Later, returning to my lodgings, one of the people I shared the house with looked up as I walked in and grimaced. 'What the hell have you got all over your arms, Claire?' Only then did I realize that I was still covered in blood. Trying to wash my super-de-luxe dry-clean-only ski jacket clean was a nightmare. After four changes of water and plenty of washing-up liquid, the jacket was finally presentable again, but the bathroom was awash with red water. I'll always remember it – it was like a scene from *Psycho*.

16

LOVE, LABOURS, LOSS

MOST THINGS COULD BE FOUND IN KABUL IN THOSE DAYS: evaporated milk, scrawny chickens and fresh vegetables from the countryside, even the luxuries of Russian champagne and caviar. It was all so cheap that we often used to eat caviar spread thickly on toast as if it was sardines. I learned how to open a champagne bottle *à la russe*, decapitating it with one fell swoop of a sword. There were dried wild apricots to be found in the market. After a party, I'd go downstairs in the morning and take the left-over champagne and soak the apricots in it for two or three days before boiling it down. Delicious, especially if we could get tinned cream to go with them. Once I ordered some Russian chocolate especially to make a glorious chocolate mousse for a big party we were having one evening, to which we had invited the head of the delegation. Just as we were serving the pudding, two Red Cross pilots dropped by. For some reason they were teasing me and I threatened to tip the mousse over them if they didn't stop. They didn't. So the dinner party degenerated into a chocolate mousse fight – not, I might add, to the amusement of the guests.

I shared a house with a hard-drinking, life-loving crowd of other ICRC workers. We lived well, with a cook, who prepared a hot meal for everyone at midday, but as I was usually in the field then, he'd leave me something to heat up later. We had a big bar, a communal room and even a swimming pool. The house was used like a club and people would come round after work for a drink. As there were several spare rooms, we often had visiting delegates to stay. To begin with, I shared the house with Yannick, a large and bearded, affable French flight coordinator who loved to party and regularly invited other delegates over as well as friends from the French Embassy. He seemed to have a never-ending supply of whisky. I always preferred a cup of tea and thought it was daft to try to drown the sorrows of a difficult day in alcohol.

My large room looked towards the hills in the centre of town but the view was blurred, thanks to the sticky plastic on the window to stop the glass shattering if a shell dropped near by. We had a large shelter under the stairs in case of emergency. Although there were always lots of people coming to and going from the house, as a field nurse I always felt a little out of the social circle because my hours and my work were so different from those of other workers. Once again it was the regular letters from home that kept my equilibrium, and I read them again and again, reassuring myself that life elsewhere did go on as 'normal'. Of course I still listened religiously to the BBC World Service, my friend, teacher and lifeline to the outside world. My closest friends in Kabul were two nurses who worked in the ICRC hospital, Åke Hayden, a Finnish nurse/midwife who had been in Kenya at the same time as me (I remembered him covering the holes in the floor of his room with shoes so that snakes wouldn't slither in), and Annie Sewell, another nurse from England. She was a dynamic, talkative woman of my age who was extremely organized and active, often networking with visiting journalists, UN diplomats and soldiers. She was very professional, worked hard and knew how to enjoy life; she was full of ideas about who to ask to dinner, what to eat and how we could amuse ourselves. Åke and Annie lived on the other side of town, near the hospital, but they were the ones I went to when I needed support, though it was often hard to see them because of the nightly ten o'clock curfew. I had asked Åke to be sure he was the one who looked after me should anything happen to me in the field. He promised to make sure that I got the right treatment. With staff coming and going every three or six months, I wanted to know that someone with lots of experience would be on my case. Wherever he went, he adopted animals, and his garden was home to various lambs, turkeys and chickens. I was particularly fond of him because, unlike some of the other nurses who would just moan when I brought 'enemy' mujahidin casualties into the hospital at the end of the day, he would easily find a bed for them and always kept me up to date on their progress. Some of the others failed to grasp that the 'other side' were not the enemy as far as we were concerned: we were there to care for all the wounded from whichever side they came.

Early in 1992, many of my friends came to the end of their contracts and were replaced, so it was an unsettling time for me. Because of the Gulf War, there was a shortage of available field nurses, and when Halvor returned to Norway, I was left to work on my own with Sher Afzal, as Halvor's replacement, Julio, a Swiss/Spanish hospital nurse on his first mission, was sent to work south of the city. Another addition to the delegation was André, a bespectacled young Swiss who was to be delegate for our region, a new post. Until his arrival, Halvor and I had done all the negotiating with the mujahidin commanders ourselves, ensuring our safe passage through the combat zones, but it was made clear that this was his responsibility from now on.

Despite the changes, I enjoyed a wonderful birthday that year which neatly summed up the growing contradictions in my existence. In the morning I drove as usual to the first-aid post, where Sher Afzal had organized a 'private' celebration behind closed curtains so that the patients couldn't see us enjoying ourselves. It was rather a formal event, at which each man kissed me on the cheek or gave me a rather timid hug as he came in the room. I felt a bit ridiculous and embarrassed, but I was also touched. When I asked Sher Afzal about the unusual welcome, he replied, 'But that's what Western people do.' He had once worked for an American company in Kabul, seen Western ways and thought that was the custom. 'You are kissed by your brothers and sisters,' he explained. The day before, the carpenter, chaperoned by five other local men, had taken my measurements with his metal tape measure, decorously measuring my front and back without touching me or putting the tape measure around me. I was now presented with a traditional long loose tunic and trousers in lilac nylon silk adorned with frills and bows that came with an enormous white shawl and trousers, pink plastic shoes and blue plastic bracelets. I felt a bit like mutton dressed as lamb but wore it for the day, much to everyone's delight, and rimmed my eyes with the kohl that one of the men gave me. Luckily there weren't many wounded that day, just one young man who'd badly damaged his hand on a mine and was brought in just as we were finishing a celebration spread of pilau, yoghurt, chicken and chips. I saw surprise register in his eyes beside the pain when he saw me in my finery coming towards him to dress his wound.

I'd invited seventeen people for dinner at the house that evening. In the end twenty-three turned up. Our lunchtime cook had agreed to joint and debone some chickens for me so that all I had to do when I got home was cook them. Instead I returned to find no cook, no chicken pieces and the dining table covered in blood. Yannick was gaily chopping up a slaughtered calf that he'd bought and was sharing with the neighbours. Somehow we had the place ready by six thirty (always an early start because of the ten o'clock curfew). Once I'd boned the birds myself, I made chicken satay, rice and veg while Åke made chocolate biscuit cake and Annie made chocolate ice-cream. I arranged the tables in a long line in the middle of the room, covered them with a white sheet and decorated them with candles and a bunch of dead flowers. In Afghanistan, it was normal to keep cut flowers for a whole year. Yannick put on loud rock music which the others begged me to turn down so that we could hear ourselves talk. The meal was accompanied by Russian champagne, which we kept chilled outside the back door, and rounded off with Irish coffee. Happy to bed.

The next afternoon found me high up in the mountains in the Valley of the Flowers, where blankets of yellow crocuses were pushing up through the mud and snow. These were the source of pure saffron, sold for the same price, pound for pound, as gold. Our first-aid post lay in the distance. I was sitting inside a commander's fortress with fifteen mujahidin, discussing humanitarian law and the Geneva Convention, requesting they guarantee our safety in the area, while eating fried eggs and dried meat from the communal plate. Sher Afzal was with me to translate. It was a great honour to be invited to such a *shura*; it was a mark of the respect in which the mujahidin held me and the seriousness with which they took the work of the ICRC. We had left our shoes outside the stuffy room, where we sat on carpets. I was aware of the insistent background drip of the oil travelling through the metal home-made oil burner in the centre of the room. As they discussed strategies for fighting and how they would best achieve peace, one of them turned to me.

'How can you, a gentle woman, make a difference in this situation, Miss Claire?'

I was surprised and delighted to be included in the conversation. For once, I could give my own opinion. I wasn't sure how to word it. 'Fighting is not the only way,' I replied. Then, out of the blue, the words of an Eastern proverb came to me. 'There's nothing sweeter, gentler or softer than water, but water has the power to move mountains.'

Despite their fierce reputation, I found many of these men both philosophical and poetic. They often used metaphors in their own speech, so they understood immediately what I was saying. 'Ah, yes . . .' They nodded thoughtfully. Then, 'But that is not our way.'

Four hours later, having transferred seven wounded from the first-aid post to Kabul, to cap my schizophrenic existence, I was out feasting with friends again, invited to the French Embassy for dinner – crystal glasses, the best silver, St Emilion 1982, pâté de foie gras, fresh oysters, smoked salmon – the works. It was another world again.

In one way I was dying to try all these delicacies. I wasn't the only one there who felt we had to seize every opportunity we were given, since none of us ever knew what would happen the next day. We could be killed. I couldn't help thinking of Shirley MacLaine coming down the steps in *Sweet Charity*. If only my friends and family could have seen me now. I couldn't believe I'd come so far since I'd left home.

But I found the contrasting lifestyles increasingly difficult to balance, and as time went by, I grew to prefer the company of the mujahidin. It was an extraordinary thing to visit a village of mud houses, where there were no women in sight, surrounded by dozens of wild, long-haired, bearded and armed fighters. Ali would sometimes come with me as translator and chaperone instead of Sher Afzal. We might be shown into a little private courtyard with a wounded man lying on a wood and string bed, half in sunshine, half in shadow, whom I treated with the soldiers looking on. I had become a well-known figure in the area.

Once, one of the men said to me, 'It must be difficult for you being a woman in Afghanistan.'

Quick as flash, Ali said, 'But Claire's not a woman.'

I looked at him amazed. Later I took him to one side and asked him what on earth he'd meant.

'But, Claire, you're not a woman,' he protested. 'You don't do women's things. You don't dress like a woman. You're not married with children. You don't behave like a woman. You drive a truck. You give us orders. So therefore, Claire, you cannot be a woman.'

It was true that when we were tending the wounded by a roadside, I'd bark out all the Afghan phrases I'd learned: 'Come here.' 'Stand still.' 'Hold this.' 'Higher.' 'Lower.' 'Where is the pain?' The nurses who knew me would laugh.

'What's wrong?' I'd ask anxiously. 'Aren't I pronouncing it right?'

'Yes. Yes. You are.' They couldn't get used to seeing a woman giving instructions and working with them, but it didn't stop them from doing what I asked. Besides, as Sher Afzal had told me when I first arrived, I was in my late thirties and women of that age were definitely seen as over the hill and no threat of any kind. At first I was a bit disturbed by Ali's words, thinking he'd gone too far, but I quickly realized what a compliment it was to be seen as an honorary man.

That April André and I went to visit a clinic in an area

we'd never visited before. It was pouring with rain and one of the Land Cruisers got stuck in the mud, sinking deeper as it got wetter. André drove off in the other Land Cruiser to get some rope, while the mujahidin from the first-aid post who were travelling with us nobly took off their shoes and socks and tried to dig, push, lever, lift and pull the Land Cruiser free. It was hopeless. There was no sign of André, so we had to abandon the vehicle till the next day and walk the ten kilometres back to the first-aid post. On the way, we found André, whose vehicle had also got stuck in mud, as had the passing truck that had tried to help him. There was no alternative but to stay the night at the first-aid post. This changed the whole situation for me.

It was Ramadan and at 18.30 the mullah called, marking the end of the day's fast. Although wet and covered in mud, we sat in the communal room and ate. The room was scented by a pot of almond blossom and full of laughter. The men were delighted we were staying and wanted to entertain us, so out came the cards. The area commander arrived with his bodyguard, and insisted we stay at the command base, but André had already disappeared to sleep in the *chokidar*'s (guard's) room. Eventually I was given pride of place in the only bed in the teaching room where everyone slept – fully dressed. It took me ages to get to sleep, as I couldn't get comfortable on the sagging bed and was far too excited. To be invited by Ali, Abdul, Hassan, Mohammed and Daoud to share Ramadan with

them and to be allowed to share so closely in their lives –
what a privilege! You couldn't pay to have experiences like
these. At 03.30 we were woken for breakfast. At 05.00 there
was the call for prayers. At 06.00 we were ready for
patients. Despite all efforts, the Land Cruisers were stuck
until late the next day, so we had to stay another night.
Throughout this time the mujahidin were magnificent,
working hard to free the vehicles without a harsh word,
singing and joking. That night I slept soundly, and I awoke
so refreshed that I didn't want to leave Mir Bacha Kot at all.
Returning to Kabul would be such a culture shock,
especially the hectic social scene. I decided that after
Ramadan, I would try to spend two or three nights a week
at the post. It would give me more time for teaching. The
next time I stayed, I was better prepared, and slept on
the floor with the others rather than on the saggy squeaky
bed and, having brought ear-plugs, I wasn't disturbed by
the call to early morning prayer.

I had a good friendship with these men. I trusted them
implicitly, as they did me. I got proof of this when
Mohammed asked me to go with him to a friend's house off
the main road in an area that wasn't familiar to me. I was
ushered into a courtyard and up some back stairs into an
annexe of the house. An old woman greeted me and
showed me into a large, light-filled room. There stood a
young and very handsome mujahidin with his demure
young bride, who was pretty with wild black hair and

dressed in bright turquoise silk with a white veil and the gold necklaces she'd received as wedding presents. Speaking English the young man explained that they had got married the week before. As was traditional, they had met for the first time on the wedding day, when the bride was brought to his home. For one week, they had to stay in their room with his mother posted outside. Nobody was allowed in or out. During that time, they had to show proof that they had consummated the marriage: according to their tradition, the bloodstained sheets had to be handed to the groom's mother. He shyly explained that although he and his wife had tried to make love, there wasn't any blood to show for it. He had somehow got word to the first-aid post that they wanted me to visit them.

I was aware that male and female anatomy and sex were taboo subjects in the Afghan culture. During one of my first teaching sessions with the nurses at the first-aid post, I had given them a book called *Where There is No Doctor*. Within hours I saw that the page showing a diagram of a woman giving birth had been torn out. I angrily asked Sher Afzal how they could tear up a book I'd just given them. He explained that in their culture the picture was blasphemous. I also remembered Daoud confiding to me the advice his uncle had given to him when he got married. 'You know there are two openings? You have to go in the front one.' And that was the extent of his sex education.

The groom anxiously asked my professional advice. I'm

sure Mohammed can have had no idea of what he'd brought me here for! I suggested a lubricant. 'We tried that. Look.' He picked up a bottle of shampoo and thrust it at me. I explained that perhaps it wasn't the best solution. After a careful discussion on the art of love-making to make sure that they really understood what was involved, I said that I'd return the next day with something to help them.

The next day, I went to the ramshackle dispensaries in town, looking for vaseline. In one, I found an enormous pot of the stuff. A big dollop was scooped out by hand, slapped into a twist of a torn grubby plastic bag, wrapped in old newspaper and handed over. I discreetly took it back to the newly weds, together with a syringe and needle from the stores that I hid in my money belt. My advice was simple: 'If you have any more problems, just take some blood from her arm like this.' I carefully showed him how. 'Hide the needle and syringe and put the blood on the cloth.' Problem solved. I never saw the happy couple again and, to my knowledge, no one ever learned the real reason for my home visit.

I was more than touched when one of the nurses, Abdul, wrote to my mother:

To My Dear and Honourable Mother!
[Claire] is not only a doctor for our wounds, but she is relief for our soul – a friend to make us laugh and

cheerful. A sweet sound bird to sing us the melody of humanity and love. And a kind teacher too.

She is laughing with us loudly when we are happy and is sorrowful when we have disaster.

Sometimes I think she is actually a flower but in the shape of a human . . . Our people call her Koko Gul – it means a flower as big as a mountain.

They were uncomplicated people with simple pleasures. I once caught them playing with a bird, stuffing it up their jumpers and into their pockets, and throwing it around like a ball. When at last I managed to dodge between them and catch it, I rushed outside and let it free. They thought it hilarious that I was so worried about the welfare of a bird.

But things at the first-aid post were becoming much more complicated than I had intended. I had fallen in love with Omar, one of the mujahidin in the area. Tall and thin, he had big dark eyes, a bushy black beard and a warm smile. His breath was faintly scented from the cardamom seeds he chewed. Only twenty-seven, he spoke good English and told me that he worked in the first-aid post because he didn't like fighting. Occasionally he would come to help me in the field. He had been one of the few who didn't try it on with me at the beginning and perhaps that's why I was initially drawn to him. All I do know is that we just clicked. He was respectful and kind, and it was wonderful to find someone who cared for me while I was living in such a hazardous situation. Perhaps it was the aphrodisiac of war at work again, but gradually our friendship developed into something more, although I battled hard against it. I knew it was dangerous to get too close to any of the local people and, until now, on all my missions had been careful to avoid that. But Omar and I were on the same wavelength, always laughing and joking together. It just seemed a very natural thing, despite the dangers.

I wrote home, 'One man has fallen for me hook line and sinker and I have for him – yes, I could get stoned to death if it continues but it's worth the risk.'

I was more cautious in my diary, confiding to it on 11 May, 'Close encounters with "X" this morning – great but dangerous maybe if caught. What to do? What to do? Leave is only real solution and I can't/won't do that.'

Nobody must know of or even suspect our relationship. In Afghan culture, relationships were arranged and chaperoned until couples were married. Until marriage, men and women never socialized together. Even within families they kept a women's room and a men's room. The only one who might have had an inkling of what was going on between us was Sher Afzal, but he said nothing. I have a feeling that he thought it was more prudent to keep me happy.

Omar and I were always incredibly circumspect, conducting our affair in snatched moments when we found ourselves alone together. The first time we made love was a natural occurrence in the sequence of events. We hadn't planned it at all. It was late one night, when we'd been sitting quietly talking together. Afterwards, I was petrified because we hadn't used any protection. The last thing on earth I wanted was to return home pregnant. There weren't any proper pharmacies in Kabul, so I had to resort to my copy of *British Medical Formula*, desperately flicking through the pages to find the correct formula for the morning-after pill. I noted down how many milligrams of oestrogen it required and headed out to find some in town. The ramshackle pharmacies hadn't been resupplied for months, if not years, and contraception was hardly the norm there. I hunted among dusty bottles at the back of shelves, and finally found some contraceptive pills with which to make up my own cocktail. I was so panicked that I'm sure I overdosed myself, but so long as it worked I didn't care.

After that I was more careful. The Red Cross thoughtfully supplied condoms in all our first-aid kits, but when I presented them to Omar he was mystified. He was totally inexperienced sexually and had no idea what they were or how to put them on. So I showed him, but he thought they were awful and remained resolutely unimpressed by this 'Western' invention.

One of the reasons no one suspected our relationship, either in Mir Bacha Kot or in Kabul, was that as an ICRC nurse I had always been extremely prudent. Nobody expected me to have a boyfriend because they knew my work always came first. It was totally out of character for me, although it was not uncommon for ICRC expat personnel to go out with local people. It happened, although never to me. The secrecy, plus the fact that we were often under fire, added to the tension but certainly didn't deter us. This was something stronger than me and the more of a challenge it became, the more I wanted it.

Of course our affair was doomed. We both knew it had to be. Marriage was out of the question. It couldn't have worked for us because of the difference in our cultures. I wouldn't have been happy to stay and lead the life of an Afghan wife and, even if Omar had wanted to come back to England with me, I'd seen too many people who had brought back partners from other countries only to discover that they couldn't integrate successfully. Besides, I fully intended to carry on working in the field, so I had no space in my life for a full-time relationship.

The end came when Omar's family decided that it was time he got married and began arranging a bride for him. He was excited by the prospect and I encouraged him, knowing that our relationship would never come to anything. He knew only what he was told about his bride, having met her just once or twice before the wedding. Of course she always wore a burkha, so he saw her for the first time on their wedding night. Until then he was teased mercilessly by the other nurses that she would turn out to be fat and ugly with sticking-out teeth. I honestly hoped she'd be tantalizingly beautiful and would make him very happy. Nevertheless even though I'd known from the beginning this was the way it had to be, when we couldn't be together any more I was heartbroken.

In the spring, the fields and vineyards around Mir Bacha Kot were spotted with wild red tulips. Recovered patients brought me bunches of them as thank-yous, and it wasn't unusual to see a member of the militia with a tulip poking out of his rifle butt. The mountainsides were covered with wild flowers, and the trees were full of blossom. The sides of the valley were cut with gushing glacial streams and the narrow-streeted villages gleamed in the sunshine. All was overshadowed by the snow-capped Hindu Kush. I found it unbelievably beautiful.

In the meantime, the fighting raged on. In dangerous situations I often found André, our young Swiss delegate, more of a hindrance than a help, despite his impressive command of Arabic. Once when we were at the first-aid post, shells started exploding close by. I was tending to a lorryload of wounded soldiers injured by landmines. The nurses, my 'boys', were working steadily, although we knew that the shelling was getting closer and closer. I was so proud of them. When I came outside, André was standing on the roof, just watching the shells landing a few yards away, shrapnel flying.

'Aren't you going to do something?' I yelled. It was his job, after all.

'Well, what can I do, Claire? I'm watching to see if they come any closer.'

'How close do you want them? We'll all be blown up if you don't do something now. They're coming from a government area. You must contact Kabul and arrange a ceasefire.'

'Oh?' He looked lost. 'What can Kabul do?'

'They'll contact the government commanders and tell them we're in the line of fire and they'll stop the shelling.'

At that moment, a shell landed on the road, blowing an old man and his donkey to pieces – yet another ghastly reminder of the fragility of life. André looked stunned and continued to stand there, despite being urged by Sher Afzal and the nurses to take action. I couldn't wait any longer. I dashed inside and called Kabul myself on the emergency radio frequency. After a nerve-racking couple of hours, as at first the government denied firing in our direction, the shelling finally stopped. I loaded my ambulance with ten badly wounded men, packing them next to one another with blankets and pillows as gently as we could, and got out of there before the fighting resumed.

The danger didn't always come from the fighting. One night I'd been woken by one of my housemates coming in late with her date, one of the doctors. A couple of hours later, I was woken again, this time by the walls shaking and the cupboards flying open. My first thought was, 'Wow! That doctor must be quite a stallion!' Then I realized that the whole house was moving. It was an earthquake. I grabbed my sarong, shouted to the others, and ran downstairs, past the rattling cups and plates in the kitchen, snatched my coat and boots, and went outside. The first wave was over in minutes and the second shock was milder. But my heart was pounding. We had been spared serious damage, but later we heard reports of damage and deaths suffered elsewhere. The hand-dug well at Mir Bacha Kot collapsed and had to be dug out again. One woman was brought in the next day, having been trapped under a beam of her house. She was in great pain and had horrific internal injuries, so we rushed her to Kabul for surgery. From then on I went to bed with my trousers, jacket, jumper, coat, boots and house key at the ready, although I was told that instead of rushing madly outdoors where you could be hit by falling masonry or glass, the thing to do was stay indoors and hide under a table or bed until the quake was over.

As 1992 progressed and the Gulf War worsened, Afghanistan became more volatile and there was an increasing danger of being taken hostage. Richard, another ICRC field nurse in the south, and his translator were 'taken for tea' by the mujahidin. Fortunately they were released after a few hours as they were transporting a seriously ill tetraplegic to Kabul. But one of their Land Cruisers was stolen and they were told to pass on the warning that those who went north to work in Mir Bacha

Kot must stop working there or else there'd be trouble. However, after urgent discussions with the warlords in our area, we continued to go to Mir Bacha Kot, although I travelled with a toothbrush and spare set of underclothes just in case. Then it was our turn.

They came out of the bushes by the side of the road, their faces masked with turbans, only their eyes showing. As they flagged us down they were clearly agitated. 'You must come with us. We have a person who's badly injured.'

'Wait while I get my medical bag,' I said.

'No, no. Not necessary. Come quickly.'

Sher Afzal guessed what was going on and insisted they should let me go back alone to the first-aid post to fetch the local doctor. We bundled all the patients we were transporting into my Land Cruiser. We hardly had time to talk it through, as the bandits were keen to get off the road, taking André and Sher Afzal with them and abandoning the other Land Cruiser. I raced back to the post, and called Kabul on the emergency radio frequency. The operator said she was busy and could I wait? I screamed at her to get the head of the delegation immediately, but I had to repeat myself several times before she understood the urgency. Ali and Abdul motorbiked from the first-aid post back to the spot where we'd been stopped to assess the situation. They walked round the fields for several hours before André and Sher Afzal were returned to the Land Cruiser unharmed, the wounded man having mysteriously 'disappeared' – as had the bag containing the monthly salaries. All they brought back was a message from one of the kidnappers that no women should ever be allowed in the area again.

We were immediately put on standby while requests were sent out for a guarantee of free and safe passage for all ICRC vehicles and personnel. Within a week I was back at work with the full support of the local warlords, who had written saying that they not only wanted but needed a female nurse in the field so that their women could be treated. But not for long.

André decided to take some discharged patients home, against the advice of Sher Afzal, whose instinct was warning him against going north of the first-aid post that day. That was enough for me: you have to trust your field officers and know the right time to ask questions and when to keep them for later. However André would have none of it, and insisted he and Sher Afzal went anyway. Normally I would have gone along with him but Sher Afzal said, 'No. It's not a good day to go to that area, Claire.'

In the meantime, I followed up a request from a neighbouring commander nearer Kabul to take a look at his eye infection, with Ali as my translator. We drove down the dirt track, across the dried-up river bed, over the rutted fields, escorted by the commander's enormous lorry. We were greeted by armed guards and taken across a little stream to the hut where the commander was waiting. The entrance was covered by an old blanket, the shoes outside the door telling us many men were with him. I had brought my extra-big white shawl, which always went with me on official visits even though it was way too cumbersome to wear when working. It covered my hair as well as my scarf, and went over my shoulders and across my chest, down to my waist. When I sat down I pulled one end round to cover my legs. I was ushered inside and sat down on a long, narrow mattress that ran round the walls with a big bolster to lean against. The room, in need of a lick of paint by our standards, was dry and airy. The windows were covered with a piece of cloth to keep out the summer heat. On the walls hung banners with Islamic slogans as well as a picture of the commander as a young mujahidin.

After a few minutes of greetings, we discussed the problem the commander was having with his eyes, and although I was not allowed to touch him I gave him appropriate advice on treatment. Then it was time for lunch. The youngest of the fighters, a boy of about thirteen, brought in a long roll of plastic, which he rolled across the floor. First we were presented with an ornate spouted metal jug of water and a bowl in which to wash our hands, with a sieve in it hiding the dirty water below. Ali told me that they wouldn't do this every day but it was a gesture of respect for me. When we had washed our hands, a grubby towel to dry them was passed along the row. Each person was served with a huge piece of unleavened bread to be torn into pieces and dipped into communal bowls of delicious aromatic broth. With spoons we helped ourselves from a bowl of fresh creamy yoghurt. There I sat, a lone woman among these fighting men, their Kalashnikovs slung on hooks on the wall or propped beside them within easy reach. Tea, a choice of green or black, was served in glasses after the meal.

I recognized several of the men. One had been in the first-aid post two days earlier accompanying his niece, who'd fallen from her roof, scared by a rocket. I remembered him sitting stroking her hand as I tended her wounds and bandaged her leg. I thought the leg might be broken, but the uncle was adamant that they didn't want her sent to Kabul, so I put a plaster cast on her there and then. She had stayed at the post for twenty-four hours before going home to recover. I was glad to hear that she was comfortable and would be brought back to the post in a couple of weeks to have the plaster removed by the nurses. Another of the men was an envoy from one of the other commanders, who I was told had vehemently supported me when the question of females in the field was debated at the *shura* of all the local commanders.

Our mission over, we left the room. I emerged from the darkness into the dazzling light of day, to discover the Land Cruiser smothered with brilliant red tulip petals as a thank-you, soldiers standing round sheepishly as if they had nothing to do with it. I was stunned. After the tense, official atmosphere inside, this was such a contrast. These men were the epitome of machismo yet this seemed such a 'feminine' thing to do. As I drove away, the petals all blew off into the wind, like tears of blood raining down around me. This was the other face of war.

I'd been back at the first-aid post for only ten minutes when Sher Afzal radioed in. 'Claire, André has been taken. I'm on my way back now.' They'd been stopped by armed men and told to fetch some wounded. When André had resisted their demands for the car key, he and Sher Afzal had each got a gun barrel in their ribs. The two patients they were carrying were dumped by the roadside in the midday sun while they had been forced to drive the mujahidin to a deserted village. After an hour, Sher Afzal had been released.

I got on to Kabul on the radio and told them the situation, and sent various first-aid post personnel back to their respective commanders to find out if they knew what was happening and to arrange negotiations to get André released. After we left to return to Kabul, the commanders held a *shura* at the post with hundreds of armed body-guards on duty outside. Contact was finally made with the commander of the group holding André, and negotiations for his release began.

All ICRC operations in the area had to stop until two weeks later, when he was finally released with no explanation. I remember him telling people, 'I showed them who was in control by refusing to wash or eat.' I didn't like to remind him that all the guidelines on what to do if you were taken hostage said you should retain your captors' respect. That's the baseline, I thought. Not washing would make it easier for your captors to treat you like a dog, kicking you around before shooting you. He had been lucky. André was evacuated home immediately afterwards.

My time was cut short too. During my time working there, over six hundred war-wounded patients had been evacuated to Kabul and returned safely to the area. I didn't feel that my work in Afghanistan was finished. I wanted to stay on. But the ICRC was increasingly nervous about the dangers threatening the field staff and trips into the field were being kept to a minimum. I protested that I felt that I was safer than anyone in the field. I knew what was happening and what to look for. The mujahidin north of Kabul knew me. I was angry that the ICRC seemed to take no notice of what I was saying. I felt as if I wasn't being taken seriously because I was only a nurse.

With my future as a field nurse looking pretty bleak, I volunteered for casualty work in the ICRC hospital in Kabul. Early one evening, after my shift, I went to see Annie, who was working late. We sat outside on a stone ledge, swatting the flies and talking about the programme for the Christmas Ball she was helping to organize for the expat community in the Baghe Bala Palace. We had both been invited on to the committee. 'How many bottles of champagne do we need for a hundred people?' we mused.

'Did you know you can get it for four thousand afghanis [£2] a bottle at the big boys' shop in Chicken Street?' Suddenly there was the reverberation of flying shells, and everything shook as they landed nearby.

'Incoming,' we shouted together.

'Come on, Claire. Let's get some infusions run through.' I grabbed a white (well, paler shade of grey) coat and ran after her. We'd only got as far as preparing two infusions when the first casualty was brought in: a woman whose teenage son was cradling her head, her legs grotesquely twisted and broken. They brought in so much dust with them that it was hard to breathe. She was closely followed by dozens of others, all in various stages of shock and injury. Like the rest of the staff, I went on to automatic pilot.

Two hours later all the patients had been stabilized, their bleeding stopped, their wounds covered (they would be cleaned in theatre) and X-rays taken. Thirty-nine were admitted in all and six died. We were told that thirty or forty more had died at the scene. The rockets had been fired from Mayden Valley and aimed at the Ministry of Defence, but they had missed, landing in a busy market area. Our courtyard was a mass of bodies ranked out on the ground, a rope stretched across the courtyard acting as a drip stand for all the infusions. Miraculously by midnight everyone had been operated on and we were ready for the next lot.

This was the kind of incident the hospital staff were having to deal with constantly. But although there was always work to be done there, I was desperate to return to the field, where I was more experienced and where I believed I still had more to contribute. But the ICRC were adamant: it had become too dangerous. Instead they offered me a posting in Papua New Guinea, where the Bougainville Revolutionary Army clashed with the Papua New Guinea military forces in what was to be a ten-year civil war. I reluctantly accepted. It was a good job, but I didn't want to leave Afghanistan. I tried to persuade them to allow me to stay at least until after the Christmas Ball so that I could see through the entertainment I was preparing. I had organized the music and choreographed the steps of a snatch of *Swan Lake* that were to be fetchingly danced by one female swan and a chorus line of men in boots and tutus. Not a smile was to cross their faces as they jeté'd across the stage. But the situation in Papua New Guinea was escalating and I was told I had to leave before the performance.

Too soon I was back in Switzerland. But after all the rush, I didn't get to Papua New Guinea. Instead, I found myself laid up in hospital. Driving on those bumpy Afghan dirt tracks had given me backache that was exacerbated in a minor collision when I was travelling in the field. The routine medical in Geneva at the end of my posting decreed an urgent operation on my spine. From my hospital bed, I kept in touch with my 'boys' at the first-aid post, hoping that perhaps there would be a way that I could return one day. But within months, the male field nurse who had succeeded me was shot at point-blank range while collecting the wounded south of Kabul. Would the same thing have happened to me? I have no way of knowing. As far as I was concerned, I hadn't lived the experience through to the end and I felt short-changed. But now there was no going back.

17

IS THAT IT?

REMOVED FROM AFGHANISTAN AND PREVENTED BY MY convalescence after the operation on my back from taking up the post in Papua New Guinea, I was eventually asked by the ICRC to go to Togo instead. I didn't bother looking it up on a map. I thought the South Pacific would be a welcome change, so I went to my briefing feeling positive. It was only then that I found I'd confused it with Tonga, and that, far from being sent to a South Sea island, I was being posted back to Africa, this time to the newly created position of regional training officer for West Africa. My brief was to organize and run training courses to prepare Red Cross/Crescent volunteers for work in conflict and disaster situations. I was to cover sixteen countries, in all of which civil unrest was endemic. In Togo itself, there had been an interim government in place since the previous year's attempted coup d'état, which had resulted in many dead and hundreds wounded. With local elections due in April, the country was predicted to erupt into violence again, and the local Togo Red Cross needed support if they were to cope. This was at a time when the world's richest countries were cutting back their overseas aid budgets and levels of overseas aid were decreasing yearly. Until this point, the national Red Cross/Crescent societies had been amply supported by their richer European cousins, but this support was not going to last and I was the one who had to explain that to the local members. In particular, what was needed was the training of local volunteers as first-aiders who would know how to cope by themselves in an emergency situation. In the event, the elections were postponed until 1993, but putting provisions in place couldn't come too soon.

I arrived in Lomé, Togo's capital city, in March 1992 and was put up in the luxurious Palm Beach Hotel, where my room looked east along the coast to the port. Tropical yellow sands and palm trees stretched into the distance and rolling waves crashed on to the shoreline. I never saw anybody swim there because the undertow was so strong. But on Sundays, the promenade above the beach came alive with people walking up and down, passing the time of day and buying from the local women home-made lentil rolls, grilled fish heads and other unrecognizable delicacies to be eaten with fingers.

It was a lonely existence for me. Because I had just arrived and stayed only a few nights at a time in Lomé in between travelling to other West African countries, it was hard to make friends. I was told that it was too dangerous for me to go out alone. Because my role was a new one, I didn't immediately slot in at the ICRC delegation, and my colleagues, while kind enough, didn't altogether know where I fitted either. To begin with, as I was only using Lomé as an administrative base, there was no desk for me at the delegation office, so I did my work in my hotel bedroom, writing reports and drawing up disaster plans with my new best friend – my laptop. I couldn't have lived without it. When I wasn't working, I felt as if I was imprisoned in this ivory tower of luxury while the real world that I wanted to be part of lay outside.

While I was at the Togo Red Cross headquarters, I spotted on the wall a photo of a white man. I asked who it was. The local priest? Doctor? Rich American? No. It was a picture of the ICRC delegate who had worked there two years earlier and who had died of malaria because he had delayed getting treatment. The staff also told me that the year after that, there had been seventeen repatriations from West Africa of overseas aid workers who had contracted malaria. Seventeen! Perhaps I should have seen this photo as an omen. The following week I was on the Ivory Coast in Abidjan and when I took Marguerite, the ICRC delegate there, to the doctor to have her malaria diagnosed, I had the opportunity to ask for advice for myself. The doctor was extremely sympathetic and put me on a new regime of malaria prophylaxis, which seemed to be made for the region and was adaptable to the seasons. But as I knew, nothing could be 100 per cent effective against malaria.

In April and May, I visited about half a dozen countries to see what was needed – Ivory Coast, Sierra Leone, Liberia, Cameroon, Ghana, Nigeria, Mali. What struck me most forcibly was that not one of the national Red Cross societies offered any follow-up to the initial first-aid courses that they ran. Not all the problems I encountered during those months were 'on the ground', however. The airlines were notoriously unreliable and however conscientiously you booked and confirmed your seat, it was never guaranteed that you would get on. Once, when I was flying from Abuja to Lagos, Nigerian Airways decided to leave twenty passengers behind on the tarmac because the plane didn't have enough fuel to carry them. The passengers stampeded for the plane, brandishing their boarding cards and swarming up the steps until they were pushed away. Some were injured in the rush, their shoes lost and bags broken. Luckily I was at the front of the queue and had managed to get a seat. Once the plane had taken off, the passengers and crew were taken aback to see four people pile out of the toilets where they'd been hiding.

Then I discovered that most of the seats on my connecting flight from Lagos to Lomé had been requisitioned by the government for a football team, and I had no alternative but to take a five-hour taxi ride home. Cancelled flights were as common as re-routing and overbooking, and getting around was a hit-and-miss affair that became increasingly stressful the longer I was there.

On the inside of my suitcase lid I had stuck cards and quotes from letters from my family so that wherever I was when I opened it, I was always at home. I always took some emergency rations – oats that I'd mix with sterilized water to keep the wolf from the door – and something to keep me occupied when alone at night or at the weekends – a book, my diary and, of course, my radio.

I flew back to Geneva for a regional meeting to tell them my findings, and to propose we reinforce training courses and that the courses should be adapted for the local conditions. By then, I had discovered that the first-aiders were currently learning from an inappropriate programme that included a couple of days on cardiopulmonary resuscitation. I wondered what on earth was the point of using valuable training time teaching that, or indeed mouth-to-mouth resuscitation, if the local medical infra-structure couldn't provide the essential back-up of oxygen or defibrillators. I believe that good first-aiders don't need to be able to distinguish between a vein and an artery: they just need to know how to stop bleeding, any bleeding.

They don't have to be able to diagnose a fracture, dislocation or sprain, but they do need to know how to make the patient reasonably comfortable and safe while getting them to a medical facility. The first-aiders I met in West Africa were concerned to know what to do when there was no equipment available; how to improvise with a sarong, a belt for a sling; how to transport the patient; how to comfort and care for the victims. It was no good knowing how to put a neat figure-of-eight bandage round a knee if you'd run out of bandages. When it came to first aid, the most important thing was to train people to be imaginative and resourceful.

It was decided that I would train the trainers, running regional courses around West Africa, teaching them how to cope if a crisis occurred. The courses usually lasted a day. We'd spend the morning running through basic first aid – stopping bleeding, splinting, putting a patient into a safe position for evacuation to the nearest medical facility. I'd discuss drawing up an emergency action plan, which included how to alert local first-aiders. The afternoon was spent putting the principles into practice. Local school-children or Red Cross personnel acted out a disaster, each of them wearing a tag saying what injury they'd suffered. They'd be sprawled on the ground, under trucks, in holes and some even up trees. In the midst of the mayhem we'd always have a belligerent soldier (often played by me), bursting on to the scene, getting in the way, warning the first-aiders to step away from the enemy injured and generally trying to cause trouble. My students would be somewhat confused at first but would then get into the swing of trying to calm me down. Several weeks later, I'd return and follow up by going over the action plan they had drawn up for the area in the meantime. Disaster plan maps had to be made in all the regions, with the position of the hospitals clearly marked. It should not have been difficult but it always took longer than I expected.

As I travelled around, I found that most of the national Red Cross/Crescent societies I visited had always been well supported by the European societies, who regularly sent financial support, training staff and equipment. I now had to explain that aid from Europe was being cut back. In Lomé, I tried to find out what had happened to all the equipment that had been provided. After hours of side-stepping the question, the local Red Cross workers admitted that it was all safely locked away in a warehouse. As they had recently had several nasty skirmishes in town, I was interested to know why they hadn't used it. Eventually they managed to find the key to the warehouse, where I found dozens and dozens of unused, brand-new first-aid bags full of equipment and with little pockets for pens, books, lotions and potions. Elsewhere, I found ambulances that had broken down and been left un-repaired. The only things sent from Europe that were used were the Red Cross uniforms. Unlike the bags, they were thought so 'smart' that they were used as ordinary day wear.

I explained that they would have to start supplying their own equipment.

'But we have to have medical bags from Europe,' they'd protest.

'But there are good bags in the market here.'

'No, no. They're not right.'

So I'd have to show them what local materials could be used, even if the bags didn't have a red cross on them. I showed them how to make bandages from calico, as we used to do when I was with the St John Ambulance Brigade as a teenager. It was all part of the disaster relief preparations. Wherever I went, I had meetings with the general secretaries of the national societies, ICRC delegates, local chiefs and doctors. I would dash around, getting lists of medical suppliers, finding where I could get stretchers made and organizing training programmes.

At least that was the theory. The reception I got varied tremendously from place to place. In Monrovia in Liberia, I was helped by an energetic first-aid coordinator who made an action plan for the city as per my instructions and then went on to make one for each outlying area of the country. I was encouraged to see it working so well. Yet, in Freetown in Sierra Leone, the first-aid coordinator couldn't see the point of an action plan. I was even told by one of the local Red Cross trustees, 'You know, in our country, women are made for having babies not for telling us how to run our country.'

One day I travelled up-country in Togo to Touhoun for the official opening of a regional first-aid course. We branched off the road on to a dirt track that led to a remote little village with no electricity or running water. There we found over a hundred people eagerly sitting in the 'school room', an open shelter with desks and benches. The *préfet* of the region was there, along with the local chief or 'King of the Land', the president of the Red Cross, the ICRC representative from Geneva, the chief of police, the local gendarme on his scooter and me. We were welcomed with singing and clapping before the business of the speeches began. The night before, I had prepared a speech in French with the help of Florence, the vivacious local press officer, but my problem was trying to work out the order in which I should address the local dignitaries. Being third in line, I hurriedly scribbled on the back of my hand the order the previous speakers used, but each one seemed to do it differently and I ended up none the wiser, with a hand that looked as if I'd dunked it in an inkpot. But my speech itself seemed to go down well and afterwards I had the great honour of being presented to the King of the Land. He was a venerable old man who commanded everyone's respect. He wore a bright green, black and red robe and carried a fly swat made from a lion's tail decorated with beads, which I was allowed to touch as a mark of respect.

In the months that followed, I put my experience to use to write a second booklet for the ICRC called 'Preparation of First Aid Activities for Conflict Situations'. It explained how to organize an action plan, gave guidelines for ensuring personal security, laid down essential first-aid procedures and provided a list of basic first-aid material that is normally easily accessible for looking after the injured. This was an important part of my work in supporting the national societies and gave me something to do in the lonely hotel evenings when I wasn't writing up reports or trying to pick up a signal on my trusty radio. Remembering the booklet I'd written in Afghanistan, I could hardly believe that I had come such a long way from my darkest days of struggling with dyslexia to be able to provide this kind of written communication. Funnily enough, I think it was precisely because of my dyslexia that I could do it, writing to create pictures instead of just using words.

In April 1992, I was in my hotel on the outskirts of Freetown, Sierra Leone, with an ICRC delegate, Peter Mikula, when we heard the sound of shooting in town. At first we thought it must be a bank raid, but then word reached us that it was a coup d'état. Captain Valentine Strasser was leading the disaffected military in a coup to oust President Momoh and establish himself as leader of the new National Provisional Ruling Council. Strasser had spoken on the radio earlier that day, saying, 'Our people are suffering, our children cannot go to school, our roads are in a deplorable condition,' but nobody had any idea that he was planning to take matters into his own hands like this.

Despite warnings not to leave the hotel, we naturally had to see for ourselves what was happening and if it was safe for us to provide help for any wounded. That, after all, was exactly what the ICRC is for and why I'd been sent to West Africa: to give support to the national Red Cross societies. We put on our tabards and raised the Red Cross flag on the Land Cruiser before driving it carefully into town. The streets were alive with uncontrolled soldiers swarming through the town and shooting at anything suspicious. We somehow arrived at the Red Cross first-aid centre in one piece and were soon putting all I'd been teaching into practice. The first-aiders were organized into two teams. One was dispatched to the hospital and the other worked out of the society's headquarters, collecting the wounded and trying to create some order out of the surrounding chaos.

The next few days were anarchy. Soldiers, many of them drunk as skunks on looted alcohol or high on drugs, were hijacking cars until the petrol ran out, then dumping them and taking the next best one they laid eyes on. They would pile into them, sitting on the bonnets and roofs, hanging out of the windows or swinging from the open rear doors, shouting and cheering about their success. They shot at anything that moved and pillaged the shops. For us, getting through the streets was a risky business, as we dodged bullets from joyriding soldiers in stolen cars, fire engines and trucks.

Although it was dangerous to be out there, we were urged on by the local people, most of whom had friends or relatives in the affected areas of town and realized that we had free passage to help those who needed it. We went to pick up the wounded wherever we found them. The hospital was a blood bath, with civilians and soldiers lying side by side bleeding, groaning and crying, waiting for help. The electricity and water had gone down, so my first job was to get them running again. A Red Cross worker and I had to go out and find a plumber and an electrician to fix things. Many of the hospital staff had been too scared to come in so we went to their homes and convinced them to come back with us, protected by the red cross on our truck. We also supplied the hospital with dressing sets and infusions.

On a foray to find one of the surgeons, I was threatened at gunpoint by a wild-eyed soldier who wanted to pull me out of the van and shoot this 'white American'. My driver, the senior local training officer, remained icily calm and reasoned with him. 'She's not American. She's Swiss. We're trying to pick up a surgeon and take him to the hospital to care for the wounded.' Although I was shaking with fear, I knew we had to show him respect and sympathy for his anger. Eventually he was persuaded to change tack, whereupon he asked us for a lift. We refused to take him with his gun, so he left it at the roadside with a friend and climbed aboard. He came with us to pick up the surgeon, and then, when we got to the hospital, he went to visit a wounded friend.

Each evening, Peter, the ICRC delegate for the area, and I would sit up on his roof with a couple of secretaries from the delegation, going over everything we'd done that day while looking down on the looters smashing up the houses around us. We could see men carrying tables, chairs, beds, linen and even toilets on their heads. Although we were frightened that they might raid us, Peter was great at calming us down. The house was distinguished by lots of Red Cross flags hanging from the windows and in the garden. We made sure that they were well lit at night by starting up the generator as soon as it began to get dark. I was exhausted and fell into bed every night with my mind racing, reliving what I had seen that day and the decisions I'd made, unable to get rid of the tension from a day of trying not to make any false move, a day spent trying to stay alive.

One image that I could not shake off was that of a young man I was called to about thirty seconds after he'd been shot. Everyone else seemed to be scared to go near him. As I got closer, I could see why. His abdomen had been blown apart, leaving his guts to spill out. I forced myself to stay calm, reassuring him that he would be all right even though I knew he would not. I kept asking for dressings, trying to get something that was big enough to cover the wound. The shock meant that he wasn't experiencing any pain, so I could help him on to the stretcher, trying to hold his guts in at the same time. We got him to the hospital, where there were many other seriously wounded people lying unattended. I can still see him, lying in his own blood, looking imploringly up at me. 'Will I be all right?' he kept repeating. 'Yes, of course,' I'd reply. He didn't survive for long.

We had no fresh food in the house and of course all the shops were closed, so we lived off dried lentils and chick peas in the evenings and during the day on the bananas and Coca-Cola given to us as we went around town. There was a lot of joking from the first-aiders about how I must have arranged the coup especially so as to see their action plan work. We were cooped up in the house for a week. By the end of the week, things had quietened down and I was no longer needed. Despite the intensity of the fighting, reports of deaths were few. All I knew was that when I visited the mortuary, most of the bodies had been removed by relatives so we couldn't arrive at an accurate number. What the episode proved to me was how, within three dreadful days' experience, the Sierra Leone Red Cross society had become the best of all the national groups I worked with. The coup resulted in Captain Strasser being appointed chairman of the National Provisional Ruling Council, but four years later, President Strasser would in turn be ousted in a military coup led by his defence minister, Brigadier Bio.

Towards the end of May, I travelled to Nigeria, where I was to be driven from Lagos to Abuja and Kaduna, so that I could survey the area after reports of a massacre there. In southern Kaduna state, violence had erupted between Hausa-speaking settlers and the local Katafs over an attempt to move the main market away from the Hausa quarters to a predominantly Kataf area. Hundreds of people died in fighting that lasted several days. When news of the killings reached Kaduna city, riots broke out, resulting in many more deaths. The official death toll was three hundred but unofficial estimates were as high as several thousand. Over sixty thousand people fled their homes. Whole families were living in the military barracks for safety. The local delegate couldn't come with me, so I left in a Land Cruiser with a driver, Isiaka, following an ambulance from the Nigerian Red Cross, complete with driver and a training officer called Taiwo. Part of my brief from the ICRC was to act as a 'silent witness', visiting the scene and reporting back to recommend whether or not the ICRC's help was needed.

After six hours on the road, the ambulance swerved dramatically, skidded into a double turn and landed on its side. We got out in the pouring rain and eventually righted it. No one was hurt so, spurred on by Taiwo, we pressed on, soaked to the skin. A few hours later, the Land Cruiser coughed and stopped dead in a ramshackle village in the middle of nowhere. With not a mechanic to be found, we had no option but to pile into the ambulance and tow the Land Cruiser the remaining sixty kilometres to Abuja. The tow rope was ridiculously short, a dangerous six feet long because it had snapped when we had used it to right the ambulance, so we could only drive very slowly. At last we arrived in Abuja, exhausted and with fraying tempers, ready for a good night's sleep. The next day, we left the Land Cruiser with mechanics and travelled the rest of the way to Kaduna in the ambulance.

Just outside the town was a sign: 'WELCOME TO KADUNA NORTH LOCAL GOVERNMENT. WISHING YOU A HAPPY STAY!' The irony was not lost on us as we crossed the first armed military checkpoint into the city. The soldiers were nervous but efficient, stopping and searching us, asking us questions. There were similar checkpoints almost every five hundred metres into town. At one of them, Taiwo nearly got himself shot as he got out to speak to the armed civilians/soldiers manning it. From then on, he refused to get out of the vehicle and left me to do the negotiating. With hindsight, I can see that that wasn't much safer. As dusk fell, the soldiers got more touchy. Every time I asked a question, I could hear the guns being cocked. Nobody was taking any risks. We were misdirected to our hotel several times as it got later and later and we grew more and more nervous. Eventually we abandoned the search and settled for a small but beautifully clean lodging house before the curfew came down.

The next morning we drove around. The large sprawling town was quiet, the shops shut, the marketplace silent. Burnt-out cars and others damaged beyond repair lined the streets, where dead and rotting human bodies had been left in the open. We visited the Ministry of Health, the hospitals and then the Nigerian Red Cross headquarters. I was surprised to find it guarded by a tank and ten soldiers. I tactfully tried to explain to the local Red Cross chairman that the ICRC didn't encourage armed persons on Red Cross property, but he told me firmly that the place would have been burned down without them. The hospital mortuaries were overstretched, with corpses piled up outside the doors under black clouds of flies. It was a horrendous sight.

Taiwo took responsibility for registering the displaced persons who had been forced to leave their homes, while Isiaka and I returned to Abuja, leaving everything in the hands of the local Nigerian Red Cross. I reported back to the head of the delegation in Lagos, saying that giving financial support to reinforce the local Red Cross infrastructure was the best way we could help the situation. At the hotel, I was astonished to see on Sky television that while there were regular reports from Thailand about the military opening fire on student rioters there, there wasn't a word about what had happened in Kaduna, where it was estimated that thousands of people had been massacred. When was the world going to sit up and take notice of what was happening in Africa?

After a regional meeting in Geneva, I returned to West Africa in early August. This time I was based in Abidjan in Ivory Coast. This made my travelling round much easier, as most of the flights to other parts of the continent were routed through there. At last, I had a base and could unpack my suitcase. I was given a ground-floor annexe room in the delegation's house. It had large windows that I could leave open at night with the security gate drawn across. Reynard, the administrator, asked the gardener to plant some flowers round the patio outside so that I had an English garden when I looked out. I really appreciated that.

Looking at my letters home, I can see quite a change in tone as the year began to draw to a close. 'For the first time, when I arrived in Timbuktu [Mali], I realized my heart was not in it. I no longer want to live like that – another corner turned.' I had dreamed of travelling round a continent's troublespots but the reality was that it wasn't as exciting or fulfilling as it had once seemed. It was extremely tiring and lonely, with little time even to do my washing at weekends in readiness for the next trip.

Days later I was in Burkina Faso, travelling from

Ouahigouya to Ouagadougou on a local minibus – twenty people packed inside a twelve-seater with chickens, crying kids and, on the roof, three motorbikes, eight gallons of paint and indescribable bundles of clothes, food, and plastic pots. Several times we were stopped by the police, and some people were forced off the bus as they had no identity papers, but they were always replaced by more. Halfway there, the bus stopped and I was told that this was the end of the line. I was turfed off in the back of beyond, where I stood by a roadside stall surrounded by flat featureless desert with no idea how I was going to get any further.

Eventually another vehicle turned up. Yes, it was going to Ouagadougou. I was squashed into the front with three others who chatted away, quite unconcerned by the tight squeeze. Luckily the window was open so I could hang out of it as well as joining in the conversation as best I could. What should have been a two-and-a-half-hour journey lasted five hours, ending at a hotel with no electricity, no hot water and plenty of big hungry mosquitoes. 'There was a time when I enjoyed the adventure of a trip like this,' I wrote, 'but no longer. I've had enough of the hassle and find no fun in writing about it for you any more.'

Despite feeling jaded, when my year's contract was up, I asked to stay on for another six months to consolidate what I had begun. At the same time, I was offered a post in Geneva in the medical division, training, briefing and debriefing the medical personnel who went into the field, and helping to organize and run nursing courses for would-be field nurses. But before I had a chance to think about either option seriously, something I hadn't accounted for rode into the picture. Malaria.

I had just returned from the Central African Republic, having fought my way on to the weekly flight back to Abidjan. It had been a stressful three-day visit that had been extended by another four days as I waited for a flight. With nothing to do and no vehicle, I was virtually incarcerated in a hotel with a scant water supply, one in ten light bulbs working and a group of businessmen for company. The only other women there were hookers. At night I'd lie listening to them in the corridors, knocking on doors to see if the male guests wanted company. I was desperate to get home.

The evening I returned to Abidjan, I didn't feel hungry and went to bed feeling shivery. The others in the house agreed that I must have a touch of malaria. The following morning, I saw the French doctor we were registered with. He agreed with our diagnosis and gave me some anti-malarial medication: three treatments to be taken over twenty-four hours, another three to be taken a week later. I spent the day at home, feeling worse and worse. That night I tossed and turned, one minute ice-cold, the next burning hot, and troubled by bad dreams. In the morning, after the others had left for work, I got up to make myself a cup of tea. The next thing I knew was that I was coming to on the floor of the living room. I had never fainted before and decided not to tell anyone. I didn't want them to see that I couldn't cope. So I made my tea and went back to bed. After a couple of days in bed, I went back to work, but I was still feeling nauseous and generally lousy. By the time I took my last dose of the course of medication, I was fainting regularly. Eventually it happened when I was alone in the office. When I came to I dragged myself to the desk, pulled the telephone on to the floor and managed to call Finn, a delegate from Denmark who had become my friend and who was working on another floor, before I passed out again. I came round to see him kneeling anxiously beside me. 'I think we should get you to the doctor, Claire.' But I was adamant. 'No. No. Just help me get home to bed,' I begged him.

When I'd complained of feeling bad earlier in the week, the doctor had told me I must be rundown and should try to drink more fluid and eat something, so Finn tried to tempt me with Coca-Cola, toast and honey. It was hopeless: I had no appetite for anything and I couldn't keep anything down. I was still nauseous and felt terrible.

That evening things came to a head. I felt a by-now familiar feeling of heat whooshing up my body from my toes to my head, followed by a sensation of disappearing down a tunnel. Then I lost consciousness again. When I woke up, I couldn't even lift my head from the pillow, my hair was clotted with vomit and I was covered in sweat. I had no idea how much time had passed or what was happening. Finn told me later that he hadn't been able to find a doctor to come to the house or an ambulance to get me to hospital. The poor man had spent several terrifying hours keeping me breathing while the house guard tried to raise some other foreign nationals to bring help. Apparently I was going blue as my vomiting had compromised my airway. He finally managed to contact a nurse and somehow they got me to the local hospital.

The next thing I knew I was coming round in the intensive care unit of a very chaotic and dirty hospital. Apparently I had been fitting for six hours. My arms were like black-and-blue pincushions where the nurses had tried to put up a drip. They treated me with intravenous fluids to wash the toxins from my body. I lay there beside a premature baby in an incubator and opposite an old man on a respirator, with no curtains between us, no privacy and one nurse who flitted in and out. They gave me heavy anti-convulsants and sedated me. When I told them I'd had a fit in the night, in spite of the medication, nobody believed me. 'Well, you're all right now,' was their answer.

I couldn't get out of there quickly enough and after three days the hospital judged me well enough to be discharged. But the ICRC were anxious to fly me out to be treated in Europe as soon as a flight was available.

After about a week, just after Christmas 1992, I was invalided out of Africa. I could never risk living in another malaria zone again. A known side-effect of the treatment I had been prescribed to cure the malaria was convulsions and unconsciousness. Unfortunately, I was one of the rare few who reacted badly to it. I was told that I had come close to dying. I couldn't risk the same thing happening again. My dream was over.

18

A LIGHT-FILLED WORLD

IN THE MONTHS THAT FOLLOWED, MY LIFE FELL AWAY. From one day to the next, it seemed that all the pieces had been thrown up in the air and nothing would ever be the same again.

I flew into Geneva from Abidjan for my routine ICRC debriefing and medical check. All I can remember of the flight is being upgraded and sitting in business class with tears rolling down my cheeks, unable to take even a bite of the food offered to me or to sleep, despite feeling terribly tired. I was a wreck. When the occupational health nurse from the ICRC saw me, she was horrified. I was pale, exhausted and miserable. I had lost so much weight that my clothes hung off me and she didn't recognize me. She made the snap decision to get me on to a plane home to England the next day.

Nobody could tell me what was wrong with me. A routine medical at the Hospital for Tropical Diseases in London revealed that I was clear of malaria and any other infections. The hospital referred me to a neurologist, who gave me numerous brain scans to check whether I had a brain tumour or tropical cyst. Again I got the all-clear. In the absence of any other explanation for my collapse, my GP concluded it was the continued side effects of the anti-malarial treatment that were giving me the symptoms of depression.

I couldn't concentrate on anything, from driving to watching television or listening to the radio. I had no appetite. Even my much-loved first cup of tea of the day made me feel nauseous. For the first time in my life, going out into the garden did nothing to lift my spirits. I remember my father suggesting I help plant out the tubs with primulas, something we always did together in January when I was at home. But this time I felt it was pointless. What was wrong with me? Where was the usual joy I felt in the garden? I just felt numb. My parents worried about me but hoped that time would be my healer, along with fresh air and exercise. I certainly didn't want anyone's sympathy; I just wanted to shake myself out of it and get on with my life. But I was often tearful and I couldn't sleep. Usually so motivated, I found that all my drive had vanished. There seemed little reason for me to do anything at all.

In the end, I decided to take myself in hand. I methodically set myself a daily routine, forcing myself every few hours to eat and drink something, however small. I made myself go out and work in the garden, trying to keep myself occupied by doing something constructive. But all the things that had once given me my greatest pleasure were now just empty chores.

I found it hard to accept that I might need help to pull myself out of this state. Eventually my GP referred me to a clinical psychologist, much to my disgust. However, I agreed to go. I had reached a stage when I was beginning to feel that anything would be better than the numbness I felt. The psychologist, Tony Bedford, was like a breath of fresh air. After I'd briefly described my life and family background to him, he looked at me in amazement and said, 'I'm not in the least surprised you're feeling as bad as you do, after all you've been through.'

'What do you mean by "all you've been through"? As far as I'm concerned, what I've been through has been normal,' I protested. 'It's the only life I've known.'

'Mmm. But none of us is invulnerable. Everyone has their breaking point. There comes a time when one has to think of oneself and put oneself first. I think that's what you must do for a bit now.'

Having nothing to lose, I agreed to try. I began to see him regularly. Once he asked me what I would wish for if I could have anything in the world, regardless of expense.

My reply was, 'Happiness. Because if I'm happy I can make others happy, and that's the most important thing in the world to me.'

'You're not asking for much, then,' Tony snorted.

I owe much of what has happened to me since then to Tony. He picked up the pieces and made me whole again. He persuaded me to take the course of anti-depressants prescribed by my GP to help tide me over until my depression lifted. Whenever I saw him he boosted my depleted morale and helped me to see the positive side of my situation. He gradually rebuilt my confidence and self-esteem, convincing me that I was allowed to feel low about what had happened to me in Abidjan and elsewhere, and that I shouldn't expect myself to be perfect. I went over and over my life with him, beating myself up about every-thing that I felt I had done badly, whether it was the selection of the starving children in Ethiopia or my inability to stop my hands shaking when I had had to put up a drip with shells exploding nearby in Lebanon or Afghanistan. Over the months, he taught me to see things differently, to understand what I had done had been no worse than any-one else would have done in the same situation. He taught me that I could forgive myself for not being perfect, and that it was all right to sometimes put myself first.

After three months off sick, I had recovered enough to return to Geneva, where the ICRC needed an experienced field worker to brief medical staff going into the field. It seemed an ideal opportunity to work in a calm environment while I was still not 100 per cent, yet I found it terribly hard. The work itself was interesting enough, organizing and running training courses for HELP (Health Emergencies for Large Populations, run by the ICRC, the University of Geneva and the World Health Organization), briefing and debriefing staff on their way to field positions. But I was lonely and, more importantly, I couldn't see the point any more. I was always asking myself what had I got to live for? I'd look at people in the streets and wonder what we were all contributing to the world as a whole as we went about our apparently pointless everyday business. I got up every day and went to work. One day the same as the next. My sense of purpose had gone. The sparkle had left me.

I derived the most pleasure from the weekends, when I'd cycle to visit relatives who ran a farm just outside Geneva. I was welcomed into their extended family and I'd help in the kitchen and in the vegetable garden. The best thing was helping with the cows. In the summer, they were taken up to the summer pastures on the Salève, a mountain just over the French border. The family drove up every day to collect the milk and I'd go with them whenever I could. It was wonderful being back in the midst of nature, picking huge bunches of yellow globe flowers, wild pinks, alpine poppies, aquilegia, marguerites and vivid anemones, enjoying the fresh air and the beauty of the mountains again.

I returned to London regularly for sessions with Tony. My life had always been about relieving other people's suffering and about stopping wars. These were more important to me than getting married and having children. Those things hadn't ever been a priority in my life and the opportunities had just never arisen. I didn't regret that at all, but I realized that I needed to find something else to create value in my life. As I began to recover, Tony suggested I might look for a philosophy that would help guide me through life. We discussed religion, Christianity as well as utilitarianism and humanism. But I felt that none of them offered me the guidelines I needed. I was looking for a path that I could believe offered real hope for peace in the world.

After about six months, Tony mentioned Buddhism as another possibility. I rejected it immediately. I had the cock-eyed idea that Buddhists went about in scruffy orange robes, never enjoying life. I thought Buddhism meant that you had to chant, wait to be reborn as a man and patiently let countless lifetimes go by before reaching nirvana. Waiting wasn't for me: I wanted to change things now, in this life. Then Tony surprised me by admitting that he was interested in Buddhism himself and had even started chanting with a friend, the singer Sandie Shaw, who was a practising Buddhist of many years. He told me that he recited part of the *Lotus Sutra* with the words Nam-myoho-renge-kyo. I was astonished. I couldn't believe it and couldn't imagine Tony, this Savile-Row-suited English gentleman, chanting out loud. It seemed so ridiculous. Besides, how could it possibly make a difference? He then explained that his wife had died recently so he, like me, was suffering grief and looking for support. 'Let me give you this book to read,' he offered, giving me a copy of Richard Causton's *The Buddha in Daily Life*.

'No way.' I was adamant that I didn't want anything to do with it. 'I'm not reading that.'

For the first time he showed his impatience with me. 'Oh, for goodness sake, just go away and read it,' he said firmly.

I began reading the book on the plane back to Geneva and, despite its heavy theoretical slant, I couldn't put it down. It was like a door opening into a light-filled world. Here was a religious theory and philosophy that exactly echoed what I had just assumed was another of my unattainable dreams. They offered me a framework for exactly what I had believed all my life.

I decided that as I had been prepared to take the antidepressants that I had initially felt so negative about, the least I could do was give Buddhism a try for a few months. I was encouraged by the knowledge that research had shown that regular meditation and chanting can improve one's state of mind. I visited a number of different Buddhist groups in Geneva to see how they differed. The practice that appealed most to me was Nichiren Daishonin's Buddhism as practised by the Soka Gakkai International – the same path that Tony had taken. It not only answered the question 'Why?' but also gave me the answer to how we can create peace and happiness for ourselves and others, in this lifetime, not just in the next. I found a small group practising this form of Buddhism and went to my first meeting and immediately I felt at home. The atmosphere, far from being solemn and religious as I'd expected, was warm, bubbly and joking. And, just like Tony, I have been chanting every day ever since.

After a couple of years in Geneva, I decided to go back to college to do a Master's degree in medical anthropology. I hoped that it would give me more authority, so people would listen to me, and that it would back up my experiences. I took a sabbatical from the ICRC and rented digs so that I could attend the course at Brunel University in west London. The advent of computers had revolutionized my life. They made my dyslexia so much less of a day-to-day problem, so I knew I could rise to a new challenge. I couldn't get a grant and my money was running out, but I was encouraged by another student to take up tutoring young children at home. I advertised in the local post office, slightly inflating my qualifications, and sure enough, people began phoning up asking if I would help their children with homework. In this way I paid my way through university, as well as by occasionally lecturing at the London School of Hygiene and Tropical Medicine on disaster relief, the care of war-wounded and security in the field. I bought a camper van and made a few trips to Switzerland with my sister and occasionally went to do some climbing on my own. I still had my old wanderlust and wanted to go on being able to experience the majesty and challenge of the mountains. But for the first time in my life, I felt very alone.

At one point, I had to move out of my Uxbridge lodgings. A Buddhist friend, who was moving from a house in Maidenhead, suggested I take her room there. It was only two doors away from the vice-general-director of my Buddhist association, Kazuo Fujii, and his then wife Carolyn. I worried about being too close to them and that things might become tricky for me if they tried to get me more involved in the association than I wanted to be – I remembered how excessively evangelical the missionaries in Africa could be. In the end, however, the location – it was close to the River Thames – and the lightness and airiness of the room overcame my hesitation. In any event, I needn't have worried. Carolyn and I became firm friends. She was an inspiration to me as she looked after their three kids, her disabled mother and a thriving business with a husband who was dedicated to his religion and constantly travelling the world. Like me, she was dyslexic. I remember us attempting a magazine quiz that would reveal the extent of our dyslexia, but however hard we tried, we couldn't even begin to understand the questions. We ended up rolling off the sofa with laughter. Her warm welcome made me feel part of their extended family, and I soon found myself spending more time in their house than mine. I enjoyed this wonderfully busy and generous household, where people were coming and going all the time. In Carolyn I had found a true and lasting friend. It was she who encouraged me to get a dog, something I never thought I'd do. I soon found myself the proud owner of a bundle of white fluff I called Chou Chou, a Bichon Frisé who was always happy to see me and showed me what it meant to receive love unconditionally.

At the beginning of 2003, I was contacted out of the blue by a BBC researcher who wanted to talk to me about my experiences in Ethiopia. Did I remember Michael Buerk? We sat by the fire and chatted before she told me that Michael was proposing to revisit the country twenty years after his original news broadcast, to see how things had changed. Would I be interested in going back with him? My immediate reaction was: why should I? But the more I thought about it, the more I realized that really I was scared of what I would find. How would the people I met remember me? How would they remember our shared experience? Would I find I was a hate-figure to them? Why risk finding out?

Yet I realized I was being offered a unique opportunity to confront my ghosts and deal with questions that had

haunted me for twenty years. And if, by going back with a
television crew, I could give the world a positive message
for peace, I had to do it. I had no idea how, but I was certain
that with sufficient determination, something good would
come of this opportunity.

I hadn't gone back to the ICRC after my sabbatical was
over but was working as a nurse in the genito-urinary unit
of a local hospital. They were short-staffed at the time and
were unable to let me have time off on the dates I'd
requested. 'Couldn't they get someone else?' they asked,
even after I had explained what the trip to Ethiopia was
and how important it was to me. So I handed in my notice.

Of course I remembered Michael Buerk. I could
remember our original interview in 1984 so clearly,
especially his unbearable question about the task of
choosing the children to save: 'Making that decision day
after day, does that do anything to you?' And my outraged
answer: 'Yes, of course it does. What do you expect? It
breaks my heart.'

We flew together to Addis Ababa on 5 August 2003. We
stayed at the Hilton, my old stamping ground, and I spent
the first day with a driver, looking round the town, the
market and a few old haunts, while Michael and the film
crew interviewed the current president, Lieutenant Girma
Wolde-Giorgis. The city was as dusty but much more built
up, and much noisier than I remembered. There were
people jostling past each other in the streets, car horns

beeping, the sounds of shouting and bartering. Everywhere we went I smelled the familiar scents of coffee, eucalyptus and frankincense mixed with diesel fumes, which transported me back twenty years. But my excitement at being there again was mingled with apprehension. That night I went out for a meal with Michael and the crew. He asked me what I had thought about their visit to Mekele all those years ago. I was my usual honest self and confessed, albeit rather shamefacedly, that at the time I had thought him an arrogant prat. It had seemed to me that he had breezed into the feeding centre with his crew, asked a few questions about me and not about the practicalities of running the station or about the kids, and then left. I didn't know how the eye of a camera worked. I stupidly mistook their professionalism for lack of interest. He practically choked on his food, appalled that I could have so misread his intentions.

The crew took me to see Asmara, our field worker in Mekele, who had always been such a source of strength. She was now living in a little house with her son in Addis. When I saw her, I knew at once that she was very ill. She coughed continually and seemed a little confused. But she recognized me, and was surprised and happy to see me. She welcomed me and soon we were both in tears. After the crew had filmed our meeting, they left us together for a few hours, during which we reminisced about Mekele and our work there, and I caught up with news of her family. It was then she told me that she was dying of AIDS, as her husband had the year before. She hadn't gone to get a formal diagnosis, even though she knew that there were anti-retrovirals available at one of the clinics in town. The stigma of having the disease meant that she was too proud to be seen there. I gave her some money to buy food and went out to buy her some anti-biotics, painkillers and vitamins. But there was little I could do. It was too late. She died just a few weeks later.

The next day we flew to Mekele. What sort of reception would we find there? I was excited to be on the way at last. I realized that I hoped to show people the truth about what had happened there and to put that part of my past to rest. I was ready to move on.

Although it had been bombed several times after my time there, Mekele had become visibly more prosperous over the intervening years, boasting many more brick buildings with tiled roofs, tarmacked roads busy with vehicles and shops that buzzed with activity. Many of the people I saw had abandoned traditional for Western dress. It had been transformed into a busy little town. Finding the site of the old feeding centre was difficult, but eventually we identified it, tucked behind the regional school of nursing. The corrugated iron walls were still there but the entrance was barred by large gates locked with a padlock. Undeterred, Michael and I climbed a tree and jumped in over the wall to find a dump, full of old motorbikes, car parts and tyres. The years disappeared as I recognized where the kitchen, the latrines, the medical centre and storeroom had been. I was overwhelmed by the memory of all those starving people, the ones who had stared helplessly in at us from outside the compound as well as the ones we did manage to help.

Although I had given the local Red Cross worker some photos of people I'd worked with in the camp, disappointingly he'd been unable to contact any of them. However, the producer found a young man called Girmay, who had been a child in the Maichew feeding centre and remembered me looking after him. His story was typical of so many. His mother had sent him to get water but when he returned, she was dead and his baby sister had disappeared. He was told that a white woman had taken her. Searching in vain for his sister, he was found by a helper and taken to the feeding centre, where he was given to a smiling happy woman in a pretty dress – me. He was a grown man now, whom I met in the grounds of his old school in Mekele. He seemed very shy, and hardly spoke to me, although he smiled and looked pleased to see me. However, I doubted I was the woman he thought he remembered. He had been only four or five at the time and it seemed to me that one white nurse would have been the same as another to him.

The next day we visited the Castle Hotel, standing in splendour overlooking the town. It had been modestly refurbished since my time there. We went up to my old room, looking out to where the displaced people had struggled for survival. I remember the horns sounding a death and the hyenas howling in the night. Michael asked me how I felt, and suddenly it all came pouring out. For the first time I confessed to someone else that I felt I'd done a dreadful job here; how I'd felt like a Nazi sending innocent people to certain death; how everyone else had praised the marvellous work I had done and called me an angel when I hadn't felt like that at all. It had been such a dreadful time. I read a little from one of my letters home:

I can't think of anything amusing to write in this letter. What is amusing about a starving father running into the road and kneeling down with a bundle of skin and bones that was his baby son and begging me to help them? Or the others just lying there in the road, too weak to walk. All they ask for is a bit of food and water, just enough to survive. Not chocolate mousse or colour television or even shoes for their feet – just a bit of food.

I went on to describe what it had been like when the first RAF plane arrived bringing food. I looked up to see tears in Michael's eyes. When I described counting the rows of starving children, I could see how moved he was again. Seeing his tears, I felt for the first time that someone else really understood what it had been like. When we finished talking I was completely drained.

That evening we ate with the television crew in an Italian restaurant. During a break in the general conversation, Michael leaned over and, laughing, teased me for being vain because, earlier in the afternoon, I hadn't wanted to be filmed with sweat marks under my arms. I was hurt. Vain? Me? I couldn't understand how he could accuse me of that. Me, of all people. How could he?

Later, walking back to the hotel, I confronted him, asking him what he'd meant. He teased me some more, not just about the sweat marks but also about my painted toenails and the fact that I was happy to bare my soul on national television. I couldn't see the funny side.

'How dare you?' I exploded. 'I haven't talked as openly as I did in the interview this morning to anyone for twenty years. That's not vain. How dare you say I am? I'm telling my story now because I want people to know the truth.' I burst into sobs.

Poor Michael. He was so apologetic for upsetting me and insisted on staying with me when we reached the hotel and going on talking. I went over and over the nightmare we had both witnessed all those years before, still worried that he might really think I had agreed to return with him out of some sort of vanity. We confessed emotionally to one another how our experiences of the famine twenty years earlier had affected us ever since, and I saw how very wrong my first impression of him had been. This was a man who really cared deeply. Eventually, once I had calmed down a bit, he left. I couldn't sleep. Vivid flash-backs to 1984, the feelings, smells and memories haunted me. I lay in bed worrying about my motives for returning to Ethiopia. Would the world see me as arrogant or would it realize that I just wanted the truth to be told? In the end I decided that I would have to trust the production team to show the truth. Rightly, as it turned out.

I had been going to stay for only a week in Ethiopia, but once there, I was anxious to return to Maichew as well, so I stayed on for a few days longer. Michael and the television crew came with me and filmed the entire journey. When we arrived, we tried, with the help of my old photos, to find familiar places and people who had worked in the feeding centre. We stopped a group of youths who, in one of the photos, recognized Astair, one of the local Red Cross workers from the centre who had been trained to use a microscope to diagnose such things as anaemia and malaria. 'She's the pharmacist now and lives over here,' they told us, excitedly. I jumped out of the car and went with them to find her.

She was in church, praying, but they fetched her out so that we could embrace and catch up. It was great to see her so healthy and happy, still smiling as I remembered her. She invited me to her home for coffee, where she told me about her family and how she'd qualified as a pharmacist and set up a shop just outside her front door. She described the training college that had been built on the site of the feeding centre. I asked her if she knew how any of the other workers were. She still knew one of the guards and his son, who was tall and handsome, and spoke beautiful English. The guard was so pleased to see me and we laughed when I told him that I remembered seeing him trying to pull out a friend's tooth with a piece of string. Astair told me that Raya had escaped to Sudan and then emigrated to Australia long before.

She sent one of her sons to find Almaz, the cook who fell into the boiling water. She turned up while I was looking at our hotel and my old room, having heard that I was there. We were overjoyed to see one another and hugged tightly. We sat down, holding hands, in my old room, the rain falling outside. She reminded me of the time I'd been sick and all the workers had come to see me when all I wanted was to be left alone. Since then she'd had a son but hadn't got married, largely because she felt that the risk of HIV/AIDS had become too great. She spoke very good English but worked as a cleaner at the college. I felt it was such a waste of an intelligent woman who deserved more. All too soon the crew dragged me away so that we could film where the feeding centre used to be.

Girmay, the young man I had met in Mekele, had come with us to Maichew. This time we had longer to talk and he was more relaxed. We stood in the grounds of the training college where the feeding centre had been and oriented ourselves by getting out my photos. By looking at the position of the mountains we worked out where the prefab buildings of our feeding centre and the displaced persons' camp had been. It was drizzling with rain but we were so engrossed that we were oblivious to it.

Then Girmay spoke about his memories of the centre. 'I had terrible sores all over my hands and body,' he remembered. 'You put me and some other children into a big oil barrel of cold water. You had added some special medicine to the water and then you washed my sores with soap. You didn't wear gloves. Everyone else did but not you.' At that moment I knew he really did recognize me. It was true that I had not bothered with gloves. I wasn't proud to tell people that we had washed the children in potassium permanganate, because it was a rough and unconventional way of dealing with scabies; but it was such an infectious condition that we had to treat it somehow and at the time, it was the only option. Because I hadn't worn gloves, I had caught scabies myself, but that didn't matter to me then.

Girmay and I went on to reminisce about what had happened in the feeding centre and how unrecognizable the area had become. I took him off to walk in the grounds. At the end of our reunion, with tears in his eyes, he thanked me for saving his life. He told me that because he had lost his parents, he had always remembered me. 'My mother could not give me milk from her breast but you gave me milk instead. Because of this, I think of you as my mother.'

I was profoundly touched. I told him that if he was my

son, I'd be very proud of all he'd achieved. We gave each other a big hug.

Returning to Maichew was very special. I found a thriving small community, still very poor but with an abundance of vegetables and goods for sale in the market. Its main road was still a dirt track that, while we were there, was churned into mud by the rain. So it seemed not to have moved on that far. Most importantly for me, the warm reception I'd received made me realize that I wasn't hated by the people there – far from it. We had all lived through a dreadful experience together and I was greeted as 'Mamma Claire' and welcomed with open arms.

When I returned to England, I felt transformed. Revisiting Ethiopia proved to be the catalyst for me to change my view of myself and to see my past in perspective. Over the years, my memories of my time there had become distorted and had obliterated the affection and gratitude the people had had for me. Instead I had focused on the terrible choices I'd had to make. In questioning my motives for the trip and for making the television programme, I began to understand how my feelings of guilt had affected me over the years. As the weeks passed, I saw that through facing what had happened twenty years earlier, I was also finally confronting the fear and guilt that I'd created and held inside myself ever since. I had always been afraid that someone would find me out and reveal me as the monster I'd come to believe I'd been at that time. But, with a new perspective, free from fear, I could enjoy the memory of the love that I gave and received in the midst of such a disaster. With this came the knowledge that it was time to create something of value from the experience. This had not been possible until now, because I had been dominated by my negative feelings about myself. As long as I had these, in spite of all my efforts and hard work in remote places, my desire to help mankind and bring about change could never feel fulfilled. Returning to Ethiopia had made the difference. Finally I felt that I could talk about my past and even write a book about it without shame.

When I saw the documentary for the first time, I saw how moved Bob Geldof had been when he was filmed for it, talking about his memories of the feeding centre at Mekele and his response to the terrible choices he had seen me having to make.

'In her was vested the power of life and death,' he said. 'She had become God-like, which is unbearable to put on anyone, but certainly on one so young and in such devastating circumstances.' I saw him compassionately remembering. 'There was immense dignity both in those chosen for death and those chosen for life, and the aware-ness of what was happening was in the adults' – the parents' – eyes.'

When I saw him break down on film, unable to go on speaking because of the sheer power of the terrible memory I shared with him, something inside me shifted. It was another turning point. It made me understand that each of us has a part to play in the drama of life, and that it's how we respond to the drama that makes the difference. Bob Geldof had used his life experience as a musician and a celebrity to try to bring about a change in the world by pushing people in the West, especially young people, into taking some responsibility for the poor of the developing world and encouraging them to act. Michael had had the same impulse and had used his power as a news journalist. And now I realized that I, as an unknown nurse in the back of beyond without any electricity or means of communication – or so I'd thought – had had my own essential role to play. It helped me realize that we can all make a tremendous difference, in our own way and in our own environment, not only to our families and the people in our own lives but also to the world in which we live. It all starts at home. Simply the act of challenging the fears, anger and stupidity in one's own life has the power to change the world.

When Michael's film was shown by the BBC in early 2004, I was running the diploma in tropical nursing course at the London School of Hygiene and Tropical Medicine. There and elsewhere, until then I had never wanted people to know about my background. I just couldn't face the questions that I knew they would ask about what it had been like. The short answer was, 'Hell,' but that wasn't what anyone wanted to hear. At last I could comfortably refer to my experiences in my lectures and conversations.

For the first time, I felt ready to tell my story and share my experiences of the truth of human conflict as I saw it, drawing on all my letters and diaries, which my father had meticulously kept. The fighters I met in Lebanon, Afghanistan and Kenya were individually just friendly ordinary people, like the people you know who live next door. But because of their experiences in the midst of armed conflict they'd become consumed with tremendous hatred for the 'other side', which distorted their humanity and made them capable of carrying out terrible deeds. Many had witnessed family members being raped and murdered. But I knew that they too had blood on their hands. This is the nature of war. It can change ordinary people. We all have anger inside us. The anger we exhibit towards an annoying colleague in the workplace or a noisy neighbour is exactly the same in nature as the anger that is expressed in war.

I believe that you can prevent war only by starting within your own self. The power to change the world is there in us all, in our own lives. You can take away nuclear weapons, but if mankind still holds on to greed, anger and stupidity we will only find another way to destroy each other. If we are to have any hope of achieving world peace, what we must all teach ourselves to do is to find the compassion and wisdom that are inside ourselves.

People ask me how I feel, given all that has happened, about knowing that there are twice as many starving people in Ethiopia today as there were twenty years ago. In reality, I can only repeat what I said to Michael then: 'It breaks my heart.' Africa continues to face some of the world's greatest challenges: poverty, famine, war, and HIV/AIDS. I believe that people can be helped to re-build and take responsibility for their own lives, but not until we see peace brought back to these countries. Our global society has hardly changed at all in terms of understanding the effects of our own greed and anger on the world. It is not just the politicians who are responsible for this. Every one of us should take responsibility for it too. Daisaku Ikeda, the international leader of the Buddhist movement, once wrote, 'A great revolution of character in just a single man will help achieve a change in the destiny of a nation and further, will enable a change in the destiny of all Mankind.'

Power to change the world and stop wars and human suffering, then, lies with ordinary people like you and me. If we care about changing the world, we must also look at changing our own lives: challenging our greed and anger and nurturing our wisdom and compassion; using our desire to change the world as a reason to challenge ourselves; getting rid of isolationism and becoming global citizens; viewing each encounter in our daily life as an opportunity to make things better for others.

Chaos theorists say that the flapping of a butterfly's

wings can cause a tornado in another remote part of the world. We are the butterflies. By thinking globally, yet acting locally, each of us can and will make a difference. We all have the power to move mountains and change the world.

FOREVER TODAY
A memoir of never-ending love
By Deborah Wearing

'A REMARKABLE, RESILIENT AND RESOURCEFUL
WOMAN...YOU CAN'T READ THIS BOOK
WITHOUT CRYING'
Sunday Times

Forever Today is Deborah Wearing's astonishing account of her
husband Clive's devastating amnesia, which struck almost overnight
and wiped out Clive's entire past. Trapped in a frozen moment of the
present, he was left with only his talent as a musician intact, and his
profound love for Deborah. She fought single-mindedly for years – for
Clive, and for pioneering treatment, until a desperate need to save
herself made her flee to America, leaving Clive behind. But their bond
was too strong to be ignored and Deborah was drawn back to England
and to Clive, in a most moving demonstration of enduring love.

'OVERWHELMINGLY MOVING . . . A DESCRIPTION OF
UTTERLY UNSELFISH LOVE'
Daily Mail

'A HARROWING, HAUNTING AND HEARTENING BOOK –
A LOSS-STORY WHICH IS ALSO A LOVE STORY'
Andrew Motion

'AN EXTRAORDINARY STORY OF CONSTANCY IN LOVE,
AND DEBORAH WEARING TELLS IT BRILLIANTLY'
Evening Standard

'DELIVERS A MESSAGE OF HOPE ABOUT
HUMAN IDENTITY'
Mail on Sunday

'LOVING, TERRIFYING AND OFTEN EXTREMELY
FUNNY . . . ASTONISHING'
Deborah Moggach

0 552 77169 4

BANTAM BOOKS

A SELECTION OF NON-FICTION TITLES
AVAILABLE FROM TRANSWORLD

40664 7	CHE GUEVARA	*Jon Lee Anderson*	£14.99
81711 6	UNDER THE WIRE	*William Ash*	£6.99
81600 4	WE'LL ALWAYS HAVE PARIS	*John Baxter*	£8.99
99469 3	THE ROAD AHEAD	*Christabel Bielenberg*	£7.99
81672 1	GWEILO: MEMORIES OF A HONG KONG CHILDHOOD	*Martin Booth*	£7.99
77079 5	LAFF	*John Boyle*	£6.99
15437 7	MY WAR	*Colby Buzzell*	£6.99
14869 5	OUT OF THE DARK	*Linda Caine and Robin Royston*	£6.99
99981 4	A PROFOUND SECRET	*Josceline Dimbleby*	£7.99
14239 5	MY FEUDAL LORD	*Tehmina Durrani*	£6.99
13928 9	DAUGHTER OF PERSIA	*Sattareh Farman Farmaian*	£6.99
12833 3	THE HOUSE BY THE DVINA	*Eugenie Fraser*	£8.99
81596 2	NORTH OF ITHAKA	*Eleni Gage*	£7.99
50636 6	MEMOIRS	*Mikhail Gorbachev*	£12.99
99983 0	OVER THE HILLS AND FAR AWAY	*Candida Lycett Green*	£7.99
13953 X	SOME OTHER RAINBOW	*John McCarthy & Jill Morrell*	£8.99
14127 5	BRAVO TWO ZERO	*Andy McNab*	£7.99
14288 3	BRIDGE ACROSS MY SORROWS	*Christina Noble*	£7.99
14607 2	THE INFORMER	*Sean O'Callaghan*	£6.99
81302 1	LA PRISONNIERE	*Malika Oufkir*	£7.99
81657 8	ONE FOURTEENTH OF AN ELEPHANT	*Ian Denys Peek*	£9.99
81554 7	DAD'S WAR	*Howard Reid*	£6.99
81717 5	FROM MY SISTERS' LIPS	*Na'ima B Robert*	£7.99
81640 3	MAYADA	*Jean Sasson*	£6.99
81528 8	NOBODY IN PARTICULAR	*Cherry Simmonds*	£6.99
99988 1	BEFORE THE KNIFE: MEMORIES OF AN AFRICAN CHILDHOOD	*Carolyn Slaughter*	£6.99
81630 6	BURNED ALIVE	*Souad*	£6.99
81360 9	IN HARM'S WAY	*Doug Stanton*	£6.99
81444 3	WHERE THEY LAY	*Earl Swift*	£7.99
77169 4	FOREVER TODAY	*Deborah Wearing*	£6.99
99891 5	IN THE SHADOW OF A SAINT	*Ken Wiwa*	£7.99
77314 X	GERMS	*Richard Wollheim*	£7.99